PUTTING VOIP TO WORK

Softswitch Network Design and Testing

Bill Douskalis

Prentice Hall PTR
Upper Saddle River, NJ 07458
www.phptr.com

ISBN 0-13-040959-6

90000

9 780130 409591

Library of Congress Cataloging-in-Publication Data

Douskalis, Bill.
    Putting VoIP to work: Softswitch network design and testing / Bill Douskalis.
        p. cm.
    Includes bibliographical references and index.
    ISBN 0-13-040959-6
    1. Internet telephony.   2. Computer networks.   3. Switching theory.   I. Title.

    TK5105.8865 .D69 2001
    621.382'12--dc21   2001036428

Editorial/production supervision: *Patti Guerrieri*
Acquisitions editor: *Jill Harry*
Marketing manager: *Dan DePasquale*
Manufacturing manager: *Maura Zaldivar*
Editorial assistant: *Justin Somma*
Cover design director: *Jerry Votta*
Cover designer: *Design Source*

© 2002 by Prentice Hall PTR
Prentice-Hall, Inc.
Upper Saddle River, NJ 07458

Prentice Hall books are widely used by corporations and government agencies
for training, marketing, and resale.

The publisher offers discounts on this book when ordered in bulk quantities.
For more information, contact: Corporate Sales Department, Phone: 800-382-3419;
Fax: 201-236-7141; E-mail: corpsales@prenhall.com; or write: Prentice Hall PTR,
Corp. Sales Dept., One Lake Street, Upper Saddle River, NJ 07458.

Printed in the United States of America

10 9 8 7 6 5 4 3 2

ISBN   0-13-040959-6

Pearson Education LTD.
Pearson Education Australia PTY, Limited
Pearson Education Singapore, Pte. Ltd.
Pearson Education North Asia Ltd.
Pearson Education Canada, Ltd.
Pearson Educación de Mexico, S.A. de C.V.
Pearson Education — Japan
Pearson Education Malaysia, Pte. Ltd.
Pearson Education, Upper Saddle River, New Jersey

To Penny

Contents

Foreword

The term VoIP was coined several years ago when hobbyists utilized a PC to transmit voice packets over the public internet. This initial phase of VoIP, although exciting, has proven to be a somewhat insignificant event in terms of actually enabling the transition of PSTN toll quality voice services to VoIP. The second phase of VoIP included a handful a carriers who attempted to utilize immature VoIP technologies as an arbitrage play on paying local access charges. Although the business plan seemed viable, the scalability and maturity of the technology combined with a clumsy user interface and competing pricing pressures resulted in failed business plans and reduced focus in this area.

The third phase of VoIP, coined the infrastructure phase, is paving the way for the future of IP-based voice services. The infrastructure phase was enabled by significant investments in the research and development of new VoIP technologies, such as media gateways and softswitches, with an evolving new set of standards for interconnecting the equipment. This new "carrier grade" technology is fueling the business cases for next generation carriers to build these networks based on optimized capital and operational costs. Further, this equipment enables networks to be interconnected to the legacy PSTN network and provides toll quality voice services in a way that is indistinguishable to the user. When someone picks up their phone, whether attached to a local class 5 switch of a business PBX, they get dial tone, make their call, and there are no noticeable differences with the service. The biggest challenge of the infrastructure phase is to get the new technologies from the equipment vendors to work. There is significant new software and hardware being created at record speed that is replacing feature sets that took decades to build. Thus, as you can expect there are many challenges. This book will provide you insight on many of the key areas, including engineering and standards, that should be understood in designing carrier grade VoIP networks.

This infrastructure phase, which we are in the midst of as this book is being published, paves the way for the future of VoIP services by their extension to end users environments. Endpoints are all becoming IP enabled. Further advancements of technologies and standards are enabling the delivery of real time services to these endpoints. Successful infrastructure networks will enable these services to follow the industry standards, such as H323 and SIP for endpoint control. Further, these networks will be built to scale in the core, and control services from intelligent network centric software. This will enable the advancement of a new class of services and the convergence of voice, data, and video, as these services will be built as part of virtual private data networks. The progression from the infrastructure phase to the advanced services phases is under way. However, to be successful in this phase the service provider must have solved the infrastructure challenges and then evolve into this phase.

As various VoIP networks are built out, there will be compelling business reasons to interconnect them. This concept is called peering, which is based on the peering concept from the public internet, where various ISP interconnect their IP networks at peering points. This configuration enables ISP to utilize each others connectivity to end users and content. This same concept will drive VoIP carriers. They will look to interconnect their voice networks in a way to save interconnection costs and deliver value-added services to endusers. The interconnection of these networks will require many challenges to be addressed, including security and the handling of deterministic services such as voice through the peering point.

I hope this Foreword provided an overview based on experience, of what is important to the advancement of VoIP networks. With or without my words this formidable book will speak for itself.

Brian Fink
Global Crossing

Preface

It has been a little over a year since we looked at the evolution of the new public telephone network, and things have moved quickly enough for us to take another look at our progress and current direction. Indeed, the move towards adoption of IP-based integrated services by the service providers has accelerated over the last several months, from the perspective of creating an IP-based infrastructure for consumer and business applications. At the same time, a lot has been learned, and is continuing to be learned from the technical issues and testing challenges we have had to overcome in the design of VoIP networks and services.

Some say there are signs the business drivers for the new technology may not be materializing as quickly as industry analysts had hoped and expected. The so-called "killer application" that will capture the fancy of the consumer and will generate wonderful revenue streams for the service providers is not staring us in the eyes. Maybe the reason is because the enabling technology itself has not been ubiquitously deployed yet. Instead we seem to be operating in a space of multiple business opportunities, which require careful assessment of provider capabilities versus customer needs to identify the few business opportunities that will turn a profit. The promise of integrated services technology remains as exciting as ever, but it is also becoming more and more complex as we learn in detail about what we really need to deploy in order to offer viable—both technically and economically—services to the consumer. We are in the process of moving from network architecture and feasibility studies to bringing real solutions to the wall socket in the customer premise, and any conclusions about the success of the new and converged public network are still premature.

We have learned over the past year that network security, privacy, and traffic engineering are of paramount importance and not as easy to implement as had been originally expected. We always had the feeling this was the case, but we have now experienced glaring examples of security breaches in well-managed corporate networks, security attacks in the form of denial of service, and perpetual hacking attempts, and we have struggled with the subject of offering quality of service to the consumer in a manner that can be guaranteed in a contract.

The theory behind each piece of technology of the new networks is good and getting better, but putting it all together in a working product is a daunting task. Fortunately, the standards organizations have continued to formalize protocol specifications, thus bringing some predictability and stability in the transition between network architecture and implementation. However, we have also seen a continuing stream of new draft proposals to address follow-on issues arising from the adoption of those brand new standards. Again, this has always been the case to some degree for every new technology, but the magnitude of the redesign of the PSTN highlights the level of effort that continues to go into settling the specifications upon which equipment and the network topologies that employ them are being built. Furthermore, there are major areas of the new technology that have not even been addressed to the point where services can be reliably deployed. Starting from simple telephone conferencing between parties using solely VoIP technology across heterogeneous autonomous system boundaries (i.e., different service providers), and ending with the all-promising video teleconferencing service and multimedia collaboration, there is a significant amount of work waiting to be tackled.

One thing is certain—the new packet-based telephone network does not have a clear winning protocol for setting up a simple telephone call. We have seen the resilience of H.323, with all its incarnations, implementations, complications, and alleged flaws, and the proliferation of SIP in call signaling and in support areas deep inside softswitch platforms. On the other hand, MGCP is now both a formal standard and a major protocol of choice between the softswitch and the Media Gateway/Integrated Access Devices (MG/IAD) on the customer premise. The Megaco protocol is very elegant and seems to be addressing some interesting problems, but its timing is late and its rate of adoption will depend on whether business drivers are strong enough to dislodge what has been designed into the deployed equipment already.

Looking towards the core of the PSTN, we are now attempting to replace the SS7 signaling network with IP-based methods used to transport upper layers of the SS7 protocol (i.e., SCCP/ISUP/TCAP and above) over packet infrastructures. For those who are skeptical about the security ramifications of such an undertaking, we can all rest assured this issue looms large in the minds of the service providers and, by extension, the equipment manufacturers. A lot of work is going into addressing security problems in every aspect of VoIP telephony. The good news is that we seem to have accepted the use of the upper layers of the SS7 protocol (e.g., ISUP, SCCP) and the focus is on the technical effort to integrate those upper layers with the packet infrastructure of the network layer. What does this mean in simple terms? As an example, if you did global title translation in your old PSTN network, you will most likely still be doing global title translations in the new model, using most of the same TCAP messages, but this time transported over an IP infrastructure. From the viewpoint of robustness and reliability, this is a much less risky approach than defining an entirely new public signaling protocol from scratch, and if you are familiar with SS7, you are almost halfway there. Finally, equipment using the GR-303 and V5.2 protocols is also breathing new life to the TDM access network.

This year has brought us important technical breakthroughs that have demonstrated the commercial viability of optical switching in replacing traditional packet routing methods and optical-to-electrical conversions in the core network. Among the promises of λ (*lambda*) switching are much higher bandwidth and migration to mesh optical topologies that could revolutionize core network design. Of course, let's not rush to exuberance too quickly, because SONET rings are not quite obsolete yet, and a lot of money is still being spent in mainstream traditional optical network installations using SONET/SDH. But pressure will be mounting in the next few years to develop reliable backbones with designed-in scalability, high bandwidth, and invariant performance characteristics of the transported applications, while offering protection switching from link and equipment failures. One nice and obvious benefit of optical switching in the core is the ability to use some form of label switching from the edge of the network, where signals are still in electrical form, through the high-speed backbone and out the other end, by somehow associating labels to lambdas, thus maintaining the utmost end-to-end performance for critical customer applications. When we consider the impact on VPN construction using optical means, the list becomes long and very exciting, with many technical and business benefits all around.

We are all aware of the quest for "five nines" reliability. We must keep in mind that this is an end-to-end figure, and not simply the reliability of a box in the network, and it is hard to predict the network reliability by just looking at the specifications of a box. There is much more to achieving the "five nines" than designing a fault tolerant switch, gateway, or router. Reliability is inseparable from the subject of network testing methodology and predicting network behavior in the presence of failure scenarios. I recall spending many hours on these two topics during the specification phase of a large VoIP design. The first temptation to conquer is the tendency to assume reliability and failure account-ability is something that can be inserted in the network at a later date and thus should not be used as a reason to delay deployment. This notion could not be further from the truth. The rule of thumb is, the more complex the technology, the more diligent we have to be in the accounting of failure scenarios. The word "accounting" here is meant literally—the process of enumeration of failure scenarios is an accounting process. Those failures that have been accounted for in the design phase will have a higher probability of graceful and predictable handling, but the rest of them will cause trouble.

In this text the approach is to place the current state of the art in signaling and media transport on top of a reference topology that would require a multitude of specifications to be correctly implemented in order to function properly. Many of the protocols will need to interwork simultaneously, even for the simplest transactions. In this context we will discuss the infrastructure simple calls, conferencing, requirements and interoperability, interfacing with the PSTN, replication of existing Intelligent Network features and services, new telephony services, as well as issues associated with the underlying infrastructure. The reader must be familiar with TCP/UDP/IPs, as we will also cover the progress that has been made in devising a more streamlined, connection-oriented, reliable transport protocol. This new protocol, Stream Control Transport Protocol, or SCTP, will be discussed in the last chapter.

It is impossible to cover the entire technological breadth of an IP-based integrated services network in a single text, but the hope is that this effort will shed some light on the major issues facing key areas of this still very new technology. The intent is to provide a good reference for architectural decisions made by designers of networks and services. I hope you enjoy the book!

Bill Douskalis
April 2001

Acknowledgments

My many thanks to Dr. Tushar Bhattacharjee for editing the text. I also wish to thank Shannon Silvus and Maureen Foley of Global Crossing for their support and stimulating technical discussions in this young and evolving field. My appreciation also goes to Brian Fink, Allan Van Buhler, and Ted Dimmer of Global Crossing, along with my admiration for their pioneering pursuit of the new frontier in voice telephony. My thanks also to Jill Harry, executive editor of Prentice Hall, for her support and patience throughout the manuscript development process.

A great many thanks to Agilent Technologies for sponsoring the speaking tours in the U.S., Canada, Japan, and Europe when my first book was introduced last year, which gave me valuable perspective on many outstanding technical issues in VoIP test and measurement.

Editor

Dr. Bhattacharjee teaches Graduate level courses in Data Communications at the Polytechnic University of New York. He is also in high-speed network infrastructure and design at AT&T Labs. He holds a Ph.D. in Electrical Engineering and is a senior member of the IEEE.

PART 1

Technology and Infrastructure

1

Protocols and Topologies of the New PSTN

1.1 THE CONTINUING EVOLUTION OF THE VOIP PROTOCOL STACK

Things are getting pretty complex in the world of the new IP-based protocols, and we are not quite done replacing the public switched telephone network (PSTN) yet. The good news is that the protocols for call signaling and device control are stabilizing, and we are getting closer to achieving media interoperability. Media Gateway Control Protocol (MGCP) and H.248/Megaco are now official standards (RFCs 2705 and 3015/H.248, respectively), whereas the improvements of the recently approved version 4 of H.323 facilitates its use with other protocols to produce complete telephony system solutions and peering connectivity for packet networks. Session Initiation Protocol (SIP) is evolving as a primary signaling protocol in softswitch platforms for call control within an administrative domain and across domain boundaries. Of course, the aim of each Voice over Internet Protocol (VoIP) signaling protocol is to offer the maximum flexibility, coverage, and scalability in the areas where it offers solutions. Not surprisingly, with flexibility sometimes comes considerable complexity, which is further aggravated by the need for interworking and interoperability among the various flexible protocols, all of which need to be tested in realistic environments prior to being enabled for live user traffic. The costs for system integration and testing are proportional to the number and complexity of the interworking protocols supported in the architecture and the complexity of the switch platform itself.

As we gain more confidence in the ability of the device and call control protocols, as well as in the media transport mechanisms to do the job right, attention is shifting towards other needs of the applications that will be hosted or facilitated by the new telephone switches. Unified Messaging and wireless Web browsing are two such applications that will need to coexist with basic voice call control. Accounting, performance, configuration, security, and statistics gathering have always been important to network operators, and the list continues with many applications and requirements that have been identified as we move from design to implementation. The ultimate goal is for the consumer—business or residential customer—to embrace packet-based services as a reliable, robust, and economical integration of basic voice telephony, video, and data on a single physical transport medium. Still, little technical progress has been made in the delivery of more complex services, such as packet broadcast video, or in achieving a high-quality, efficient, interoperable, reliable, and economic solution to videoconferencing. The hope in the industry is that once we lay down an end-to-end IP-based broadband infrastructure, we will have acquired enough technical knowledge and prowess to integrate whatever packet-based service exists in the new network, without redesign or major overhaul of topologies and equipment. In other words, *it should work*! But judging by the time and effort it has taken to replace ye olde DS-0 with an IP-based voice service, things will probably remain exciting and challenging for a long time.

The IP protocol stack is getting some new additions, while other aspects of existing stacks, for example H.323, are getting more attention and revisions, primarily for internetworking and performance reasons. The protocol stack shown in Figure 1.1 is a good starting point for a tour of the new protocol landscape.

1.2 H.323: MORE EFFICIENT WAYS TO SIGNAL, WITH A COMMON DENOMINATOR

Persistent news of the demise of H.323 in the last couple of years was greatly exaggerated. The H.323 protocol is expected to remain strong in the enterprise and to complement media gateway control protocols like MGCP and H.248/Megaco in providing signaling for call establishment and control. The H.323 stack has been drawn differently in this text in order to underscore that H.245, the media and logical channel control protocol, and H.225.0, the call control protocol, can be operated in more than one way, when we account for the possible methods to route signaling in a call and transport of the signaling protocols themselves. The various options of running H.323 are summarized

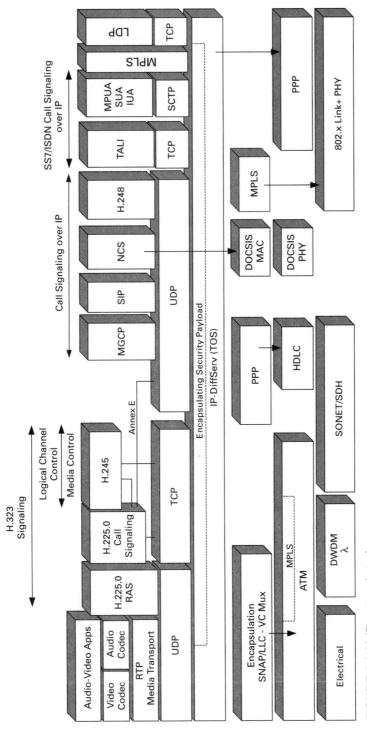

FIGURE 1.1 VoIP protocol stack.

5

in Figure 1.2. All the options shown default to H.323v1, native protocol transport over Transmission Control Protocol (TCP), when an attempt to invoke one of the other options is unsuccessful.

The basic H.323 operation, which utilizes different TCP connections to transport H.225.0 and H.245 signaling, has been covered extensively in the literature, and we will concentrate here on the other modes of operation. These are finding technical drivers based on performance and efficiency of the implementation, when gatekeeper (GK) functionality is designed into a softswitch. In our nomenclature, a softswitch is a device that combines all the required signaling capabilities for a complete multivendor telephony solution, such as an H.323 GK, a proxy server, a redirect server, a media gateway controller (MGC), as well as a signaling gateway (SG). Access and trunking gateways are managed by the softswitch via signaling. Distribution of signaling functionality within a softswitch platform is a matter of implementation, the pluses and minuses of which are examined in the context of system performance and scalability versus cost. General-purpose, complete telephony systems will invariably operate in multiprotocol, nonhomogeneous signaling environments, into which they are expected to integrate seamlessly and transparently from the user's perspective. This is indeed the case when a peer relationship exists between autonomous systems (AS) or between domains within an AS. A view of two GK domains[1] connected via gateways is shown in Figure 1.3. The terminology we use is intentionally generic, as this will allow us to view networks employing multiple signaling mechanisms and review them in broader terms, while focusing on the requirements of each call flow as it becomes necessary.

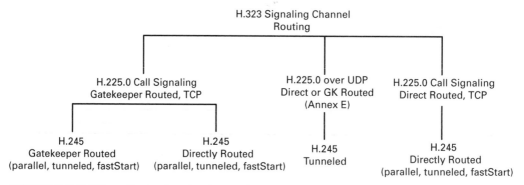

FIGURE 1.2 H.323 routing and protocol operation.

---

1.   The term *domain*, rather than zone, is preferred in this context because it is consistent with a heterogeneous signaling topology, which includes the H.323 protocol, among others. An administrative domain can include one or more zones.

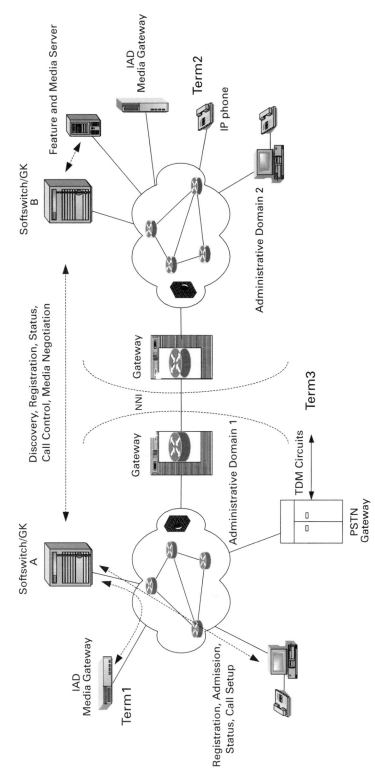

FIGURE 1.3 Multi-signaling domain connectivity.

7

The H.323 component protocols for VoIP signaling are RAS (Registration, Admission, and Status) and a subset of the *Q.931* signaling specification for calls establishment and termination, both of which are described in recommendation H.225.0. The H.245 protocol is also an integral part of H.323 and performs logical channel control as well as terminal and media format negotiation. H.245 messages can be exchanged using dynamically established reliable transport connections—currently over TCP—or included as part of Q.931 messages in the **FastConnect** or **Tunneling** methods of call control.

The RAS messages and a brief description of their use are shown in Table 1.1, and the H.225.0 call-signaling messages are shown in Table 1.2. (O-Optional, M-mandatory.)

Key H.245 messages and their use will be examined in the context of composite call flows.

H.323 Tunneling is a simple concept and enables H.245 control messages to be transported inside H.225.0 call-signaling messages. If there are no H.225.0 messages waiting to be sent when the need arises for an endpoint to send a logical channel control signal, the H.225.0 FACILITY message is used to *backhaul* H.245 signaling. Alternatively, either endpoint can invoke H.323v1 procedures at any time during a call by establishing a TCP connection and running H.245 in its native form. Tunneling of the H.245 protocol saves TCP resources in the GK platform (sockets, memory, and processing power), and results in faster call setup times and higher active call capacity. However, once the common denominator has been sought and reached in a call for any reason (i.e., endpoints revert to H.323v1 procedures), the system will stay in that mode for that call until the call is terminated. This results in an interesting problem.

The uncertainty of whether H.323v1 operation will be defaulted during a call creates an interesting dilemma in specifying system capacity for active calls and signaling speed for call completion in mixed capability signaling domains.

Which system resource allocation do we use for specifying performance: those for v1 procedures or those for the other procedures, which use fewer TCP connections and signaling steps to establish a call? When GK signaling routing is used as a default, it is usually easier to predict the answer, since all signaling for all endpoints is proxied by a single entity.

The H.323 FastConnect approach also saves time and resources (TCP sockets), and results in fast call setup. FastConnect and Tunneling can be indicated simultaneously by the calling endpoint when sending the first SETUP message, but Tunneling will override FastConnect.

The H.323 Annex E operation is over a "reliable" form of the User Datagram Protocol (UDP) and thus requires no TCP connections and assorted system resources for call control and media channel signaling. In addition, it allows for the multiplexing of Protocol Data Units (PDUs) within the same message, thus further minimizing overhead and round-trip delay times in the

TABLE 1.1 H.323 RAS Messages

MESSAGE	MEANING	ENDPOINT	GK	USAGE COMMENTS
GRQ GCF GRJ	Gatekeeper Request Gatekeeper Confirm Gatekeeper Reject	Optional, both ways. If GRQ is generated by the endpoint, GCF/GRJ must be supported.	M	GRQ is sent by an endpoint trying to discover its GK.
RRQ RCF RRJ	Registration Request Registration Confirm Registration Reject	Optional, both ways. If RRQ is generated by the endpoint, RCF/RRJ must be supported.	M	With version 4, endpoints can do additive registration of their addresses and properties, with additional RRQ messages containing parameters, such as the call signaling and RAS address, terminal type and alias, endpoint and GK identifier, etc. The RRQ carries the list of H.248 packages supported by the endpoint (see Megaco/H.248 discussion). The RCF may offer pregranted ARQ to the endpoint and a list of events for which the GK is giving the green light to the endpoint in advance.
URQ UCF URJ	Unregistration Request Unregistration Confirm Unregistration Reject	URQ is optionally generated by GKs and endpoints. If received by an entity, it must be processed, and UCF must be sent. The GK must support sending URJ, whereas an endpoint may optionally send it, although it is unlikely.	URQ = O UCF = M (send) URJ = M (send)	These are bidirectional commands and responses. The association between an endpoint and the GK can be terminated by either entity.

9

TABLE 1.1 H.323 RAS Messages *(continued)*

MESSAGE	MEANING	ENDPOINT	GK	USAGE COMMENTS
ARQ ACF ARJ	Admission Request Admission Confirm Admission Reject	Mandatory	M	ARQ is issued by an endpoint to request the GK's permission to place a call or answer an incoming call. Initial bandwidth requirements and the call model routing are also stated in the ARQ. The GK may accept, reject, or modify the parameters and the call model of the request.
BRQ BCF BRJ	Bandwidth Request Bandwidth Confirm Bandwidth Reject	Mandatory	BRQ = O BCF = M BRJ = M	An endpoint may request additional bandwidth from the GK. The GK may request an endpoint reduce or increase its used bandwidth. Either entity may accept or deny the requested bandwidth adjustment.
IRQ IRR IACK INAK	Information Request Information Response Information Resp ACK Information Resp NACK	IRQ = M (receive) IRR = M (transmit) IACK or INAK are Optional.	IRQ = M (transmit) IRR = M (receive) IACK or INAK must be sent by the GK if acknowledgment of the IRR had been requested by the endpoint in the IRR message.	The IRQ is sent by the GK to obtain capacity and usage information in an IRR response. Unsolicited IRRs may also be sent periodically by endpoints to their GK, if so indicated in the GK's RCF response to an RRQ (in version 4 unsolicited IRRs must be flagged as such in the IRR message). IRRs carry per-call information, such as the type of a/v and data channels in use, the bandwidth of the call, and possible circuit information, if the call involves circuits on the PSTN.

TABLE 1.1 H.323 RAS Messages *(continued)*

MESSAGE	MEANING	ENDPOINT	GK	USAGE COMMENTS
DRQ DCF DRJ	Disengage Request Disengage Confirm Disengage Reject	Can be sent by the GK to an endpoint or the endpoint to its GK. If DRQ is received by the endpoint, it must be accepted with DCF.	The GK sends DRQ optionally, but must process all Disengage RQ/CF/RJ messages it receives from its endpoints.	If the call model is direct-routed, the GK will not see the normal termination of the call, so this message informs the GK the call has ended. Endpoints do not exchange this message directly between them. The current call capacity of the endpoint can be sent in the DRQ message.
LRQ LCF LRJ	Location Request Location Confirm Location Reject	Optional support for endpoints, but if an LRQ is issued, the response from the GK must be processed. Sent by an endpoint in order to receive the transport address of a remote endpoint from its GK.	The LRQ is optionally sent by the GK, but is always processed when received. For peering arrangements using H.323 as the NNI protocol, support for LRQ by the GK is necessary.	The LRQ may contain the maximum number of GKs that the message can propagate through, before address translation is performed. If the number of GKs has been exceeded, the LRQ is dropped by the last GK in the chain.
NSM	Nonstandard Message	Optional	Optional	This message can contain information not covered by the H.323 specification and is understood only by the source and destination endpoints.

TABLE 1.1 H.323 RAS Messages *(continued)*

MESSAGE	MEANING	ENDPOINT	GK	USAGE COMMENTS
XRS	Message Not Understood	Mandatory	Mandatory	Sent when an endpoint cannot decode the RAS message it received. Only one XRS message per second can be generated by an endpoint.
RIP	Request in Progress	Receivers will process this message and will generate it conditionally (see comment).	GK will process this message and will generate conditionally.	Will be generated by a receiving entity if an RAS command will take longer to execute than indicated by the typical timeout value settings.
RAI RAC	Resource Indicate Request Resource Indicate Confirm	Optional	Mandatory	Gateway will send RAI to indicate its current capacity in calls and bandwidth for each H-series protocol it supports. The GK will respond with RAC to acknowledge.
SCI SCR	Service Control Indication Service Control Confirm	Optional (version 4)	Optional (version 4)	Sent by the GK to indicate the start of a session relating to service control. Endpoints may also send this message to the GK. SCR indicates acknowledgment of the SCI, but not necessarily initiation of the service session.

TABLE 1.2 Q.931 Messages in H.225.0

Q.931 MESSAGE USE IN H.323 (MESSAGES NOT SHOWN ARE NOT ALLOWED)	USAGE	NOTES
Alerting	Mandatory	When sent, it indicates the phone is ringing. The H.245 transport address may be included in the message. FastStart may be included, if the originating endpoint had requested it and the called endpoint supports it. If FastStart was requested but is not supported by the called endpoint, this may also be indicated in this message.
Call Proceeding	Optional	Call establishment has been initiated and no more information will be accepted by the sending entity until the call has been established. FastStart may be accepted or refused if it was requested (see ALERTING comments).
Connect	Mandatory	The called party indicates the call has been accepted. It carries H.245 transport address information, a call ID, and security capabilities. FastStart may be accepted or refused if it was requested—this is the last signaling message in the call establishment sequence that can be used to signal the use or not of FastStart.
Progress	Optional	Keeps the calling endpoint informed of the status of the call. May contain H.245 transport address info, security mode, and capabilities. FastStart may be accepted or refused if it was requested by the calling endpoint.
Setup	Mandatory	The sending endpoint establishes the call by sending SETUP. It contains, among other parameters, the caller's H.245 transport address, call type, request to use FastStart if supported and desired, connection parameters, capacity of the sender, and parallel H.245 control in the form of terminal capability messages. The TCP port for the call signaling channel is **1720**. The secure TCP port for the call signaling channel is **1300** (see ITU-T recommendation H.235).
Setup Acknowledge	Optional	If the sender of SETUP supports overlap sending, it must process this message when it receives it.

TABLE 1.2 Q.931 Messages in H.225.0 *(continued)*

Q.931 MESSAGE USE IN H.323 (MESSAGES NOT SHOWN ARE NOT ALLOWED)	USAGE	NOTES
Release Complete	Mandatory	Indicates the termination of the call and the availability of the signaling channel to establish another call.
User Information	Optional	Sent by an endpoint towards the network to carry information to the remote endpoint carried in user-user Information Elements (IEs).
Information	Optional	May be used to support overlap sending and receiving, keypad facility, and information that can be presented to the user (display).
Notify	Optional	Carried information pertinent to the call, such as suspension in effect, removal of suspension, or bearer info changes.
Status	Mandatory	Sent to reply to an unrecognized signaling message, or to a status inquiry from a sending endpoint.
Status Inquiry	Optional	Sent by the GK and endpoint to request the current call state.
Facility (Q.932)	Mandatory	Used for call redirection, support for supplementary services, and for tunneling H.245 messages when FastStart is in use. An endpoint can use to indicate an incoming call must be routed through a GK. It is also used to terminate FastStart and request the remote endpoint establish formal H.245 signaling procedures.

communication exchanges between the GK and the endpoints in its zone. The reliable form of UDP is accomplished by adding simple stateful operations for keeping the "connection" alive (similar to the TCP "keep-alive" exchange) and a mechanism for requesting previously sent PDUs (packets) which may have been lost in the transmission. The resulting efficiency in signaling improves performance as it reduces the number of messages that must be sent during signaling. A drawback may be the additional operations that must be added to make UDP "pseudo-connection oriented" and more reliable, with access at the application level. Such functionality is normally the responsibility of the network and transport layer protocols.

H.245 can be tunneled inside H.225.0 messages, or the FastConnect option can be invoked when call signaling begins. A major consideration for large scale implementations, especially for those in the wide area, is the requirement to establish media continuity between the endpoints *before* the call is established. In SS7 signaling this is a routine and simple operation, but in H.323 (and the other IP-based signaling protocols) explicit steps must be taken to ascertain the presence of the media path before the call is delivered to the far end and the phone rings. Furthermore, if we contemplate allowing for dynamic rerouting of media flows in mid-call as part of transparent error recovery, the resulting requirements for media path integrity may be impossible. When we include the Quality of Service (QoS) guarantees that must be met for the duration of the call, we can easily see the danger of possible impractical requirements to support transparent failure recovery via path rerouting.

H.323 offers some basic telephony features to the user, such as *call forwarding, call hold,* and *call waiting,* in the form of supplementary services. These are governed by the H.450.n series of ITU specifications, and we will see some examples of their usage in the call flows later. We will also examine the ability of a softswitch to survive failures in the platform *scale-down* by preserving all active calls, maintaining accounting integrity, and achieving orderly degradation of performance without affecting the quality or number of offered features. The orderly *scaling down* is often as difficult to achieve as the upwards scaling of capacity and performance.

In the course of switch system development, it will invariably come up as a question whether the H.323 basic call flow can be mapped to the Advance Intelligent Network (AIN)[2] call model. It is easy to see that the protocol does not offer sufficient resolution in the establishment of a call to tap into all the points in call (PIC) as defined by the AIN model, and from our examination it is a nontrivial exercise to interwork with high granularity protocols, such as MGCP and Megaco (H.248).

---

2. Or simply Intelligent Network (IN), versions 0.1 and 0.2.

1.3 MGCP AND NCS

MGCP has become a standard not only by achieving RFC status (RFC2705), but also via market acceptance in the cable modem industry as the Network-based Call Signaling (NCS) protocol, which is mostly MGCP, and customer-premise-based access devices. Integrated access devices (IADs)[3] have recently appeared in the market and offer a mix of capabilities, depending on the application. Applications range from support of pure voice telephony with 24×7 access to the Internet to more sophisticated virtual LANs and virtual private networks. The protocol itself offers designed-in granularity of high-resolution operations for telephony services over the wide area, including management of remote endpoints and trunking gateways connected to the PSTN and other dissimilar networks. The messages, commands, and responses of MGCP are summarized in Table 1.3.

Every command sent by either signaling entity (MGC or GW) requires a successful or unsuccessful acknowledgment in a return code. The term ACK is used to indicate command acknowledgment; the response itself contains only the acknowledgment code. Responses are sent to the MGC that sent the commands, or to the transport address identified in the Notified Entity parameter, if it was included in the command that is being acknowledged.

An additional command is being proposed in the RFC itself, MOVE connection, which is intended to facilitate telephony features such as call forwarding. The Megaco protocol in fact specifies a MOVE command, and we will examine its use in a call flow.

Infrastructure support and resource management is a significant part of every signaling protocol, to a degree. There are differences and similarities between MGCP and the other protocols with respect to the ease with which a call processor "learns" of its topology and the endpoints "learn" of the call processor serving them. With MGCP, the softswitch too can discover its endpoint topology and guide the endpoints through configuration and high-resolution call signaling, but an assumption is made that media gateways will be initially preprogrammed with the address of an MGC signaling entity. The protocol makes no attempt to facilitate the automatic and dynamic discovery of the softswitch by the endpoints. Although this may not be a significant issue when a protocol is examined in the context of its own application and specification, it gives rise to some implementation issues when a softswitch must control endpoints of multiple signaling protocols for the purpose of

---

3. An IAD is usually situated in the customer premise.

TABLE 1.3 MGCP Command Summary

MGCP COMMAND	CODING	USAGE NOTES
CreateConnection	CRCX	Sent by MGC[*] to create a connection between two endpoints. Parameters of the connection are specified in a mix of native protocol constructs and syntax from the Session Description Protocol (SDP) protocol.
ModifyConnection	MDCX	Connections can be modified to be receive-only, transmit-only, or bidirectional. Other parameters and attributes of the connection may be modified as well through a mix of native constructs and syntax from the SDP protocol.
DeleteConnection	DLCX	A connection can be deleted by the MGC or the endpoint itself. The acknowledgment of this command, if sent by the MGC, carries statistics of the connection that was just terminated. If sent by the endpoint, the command itself includes the statistics of the call and the reason for the termination. This command can be used by the MGC to terminate all the connections associated with an endpoint, using the hierarchical naming conventions of the protocol.
NotificationRequest	RQNT	The MGC sends RQNT to request notification from the gateway when certain events occur. Those can range from detecting off-hook to detecting modem and fax tones. Notification requests can be embedded in other commands to reduce signaling overhead.
Notify	NTFY	This command is sent by the gateway to notify the MGC of the presence of an event. The notification for the event must have been requested by the MGC via an earlier RQNT command. The handling of events is one of the more complex aspects of MGCP and will be examined in the context of call flows.
AuditEndpoint	AUEP	The MGC can obtain detailed current status of the endpoint.
AuditConnection	AUCX	The parameters of a connection can be obtained with AUCX. A useful attribute of this message is that the inquiring MGC in a distributed platform can obtain the identity of the signaling entity that is handling the call.
RestartInProgress	RSIP	Sent by the MG/IAD to indicate some or all of its endpoints are in the process of being taken out of service, or it is being rebooted.
EndpointConfiguration	EPCF	Sent by the MGC and specifies signal encoding.

*   MGC here indicates the media gateway controller functionality inside the softswitch, which performs MGCP signaling with the gateways.

delivering telephony with a seamless integration of dissimilar endpoint devices.

MGCP accounts for failure scenarios that can be identified and reported, which is a subject I dealt with at length in the specification phase of a VoIP network of substantial complexity. Indeed, we cannot overstate the problems that can be caused by infrastructure failures, especially when the infrastructure provides communications between consumers in distributed geographical areas. We will take an in-depth look at survivability aspects with MGCP and at the impact on platform design when multiple signaling protocols are interworking simultaneously.

MGCP is finding acceptance as a signaling protocol in IP phones, initially in the enterprise. IP phones serve as standalone, single endpoints not requiring the presence of an IAD in order to connect to the call processor (softswitch) of a VoIP topology. The types of endpoints supported by MGCP are shown in Figure 1.4.

MGCP runs over the typical UDP/IP stack and uses SDP syntax in conjunction with native protocol constructs for media format negotiation and transport of session-related data.

The signaling resolution of MGCP—that is, the message structure of the protocol that paces a call from the instant a user picks up the phone—makes it easy to map the MGCP basic originating and terminating call model to the respective part of the AIN call model.

MGCP is discussed in detail in Chapter 6.

1.4 SIP (RFC2543)

SIP continues to make inroads in softswitch design, not only as a call signaling protocol, but also as a transport mechanism for other protocols and softswitch signaling to application servers and interactive voice response (IVR) systems. A new SIP method, which was introduced to carry signaling during a stable phase of call—the INFO method—has made feasible the transport of signaling, such as DTMF tones, in mid-call within the same domain or across administrative domains. SIP Telephony (SIP-T) extensions can be used to transport SS7 signaling embedded in the payload and encoded in MIME form between signaling entities. In general, the use of SIP as a signaling backhaul mechanism enhances the native capabilities of the protocol and facilitates switch development, in the sense that existing protocol stacks, such as SS7, can be reused. This reduces development time and improves the reliability of the first generation products. Pure IP signaling procedures can be introduced incrementally in the design, following thorough validation in lab environments.

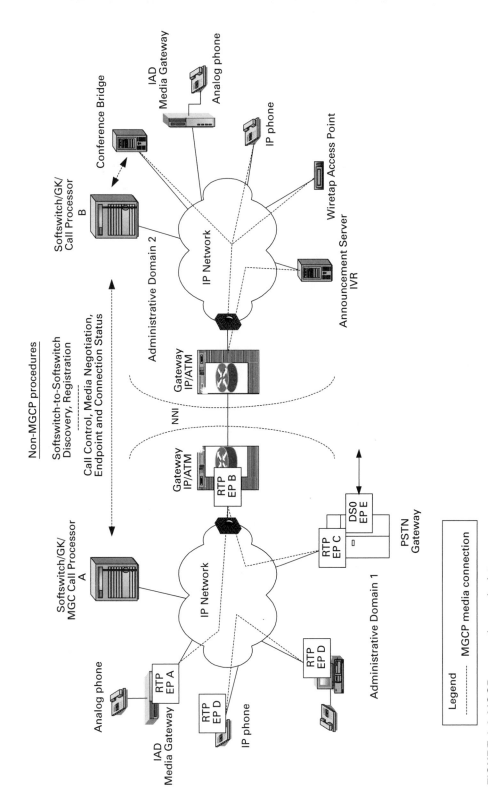

FIGURE 1.4 MGCP connection endpoints.

19

SIP offers redirection, proxy, and network-to-network signaling capabilities to the softswitch, all of which are critical for implementing a peer relationship between enterprises through a third-party network or between an enterprise and an exchange carrier.

As of this writing, SIP has approximately the same granularity in pacing a basic call as H.323: SIP does not worry about digit maps, collecting digits, detecting off-hook, and so on. Those operations are viewed as operations at the media gateway control level, and as a consequence, a call flow using SIP is roughly equivalent, in terms of the AIN model, to a basic call flow using H.323.

Like MGCP, SIP also uses SDP syntax in addition to native protocol constructs in the payload to set the parameters of a call and fully describe the session. The extended protocol specification has grown to support 10 methods (i.e., commands), which are summarized as follows:

1. *INVITE*, sent to initiate call setup.
2. *ACK*, sent after an OK response to complete an invitation.
3. *OPTIONS*, to query the capabilities of a call agent and supply the sender's capabilities.
4. *BYE*, sent to release a call.
5. *CANCEL*, sent to cancel a request in progress.
6. *REGISTER*, for client registration with a sever.
7. *PRACK*, used for providing acknowledgment to provisional responses.
8. *INFO*, to send encapsulated signaling for support of common telephony features.
9. *REFER*, used to implement call transfer.
10. *COMET*, used to determine whether preconditions set in the SDP are met before call processing can continue.

SIP is discussed in detail in Chapter 8.

1.5 THE SDP PROTOCOL: RFC 2327 WITH EXTENSIONS IN RFC 2848 (PINT)

Although almost never used as an independent protocol, SDP syntax is used by SIP, MGCP, and the text version of H.248/Megaco protocols to describe multimedia sessions in text format. The parameter usage and command syntax will be examined later in the context of call flows. SDP is used to convey such information as the session name, the transport address(es) for the media flows, media format encoding, bandwidth use, the media transport protocol, and the person responsible for the session. A summary of key parameters used in SDP descriptions is given in Table 1.4. See Chapter 6 for a discussion of the syntax.

TABLE 1.4 Key SDP Descriptors

SDP DESCRIPTOR	USAGE NOTES
v - version o - owner s - session name b - bandwidth c - connection info t - time of session m - media a - attributes	Optional SDP parameters may be included in protocol messages. The **c** parameter specifies the network type, which is **IN** for *Internet* or **TN** for *Telephone Network*, the address type, which is IP4 for an IP network or RFC2543 when the TN network type is specified. RFC2543 is the *SIP* specification. SDP allows descriptors that are specific to a particular media format to be to be exchanged in a manner transparent to the protocol with the **a=fmtp** syntax.

1.6 CODECS, TONES, FAXES

The avalanche of codec formats has finally subsided, and most designs have settled on preferred support of the all-mandatory G.711—pulse-code modulation (PCM) µLaw and Alaw—and one or two compressed formats, such as G.729a-b, G.723.1, or G.726. Media negotiation during a call, however, is not as trivial as one might imagine, because of the possibility of unknown formats supported by endpoints across domain boundaries, conflicting service level agreements (SLAs) that might be in place between calling and called parties, bandwidth allocation status at the time of the call, fallback mechanisms in case the primary codec of each party cannot be selected for any reason, the QoS guarantees that must be maintained in a transparent failover situation in the core network, and other issues. Only when both endpoints of a call are under direct control of the same softswitch is it possible to enforce codec selection in one pass, without negotiation. If the endpoints are free to present a list of preferred media formats, and the call spans a network-to-network interface (NNI) boundary across administrative domains, care must be exercised in controlling the number of negotiation attempts before the call is completed.

The transport of dual-tone multifrequency (DTMF) tones across administrative domains is quite a task as well. All VoIP protocols have agreed to use Real-Time Transport Protocol (RTP) as the transport protocol for media, but tones offer a different kind of challenge. If the selected codec format in a call is G.711, tones can be transported in-band with the media stream, just as is the case in the telephone network today. When compressed voice is used, however, we know we cannot pass tones through codecs, because codecs implement perceptual encoding principles, which do not guarantee the integrity of the frequency spectrum once the analog waveform is reconstructed at the far end. Therefore, a reliable out-of-band tone transport mechanism is both desired and mandatory in any VoIP implementation. But, we are not so lucky as to have only one method to transport tones out-of-band, and this complicates matters at the interface connections of networks using nonhomogeneous signaling protocols and procedures.

H.323 uses ASCII representation of tones in H.245 protocol constructs. On the other hand, a couple of methods to encode DTMF and other tones have been adopted by the standards groups, using out-of-band RTP packets. This means gateways and softswitches must interoperate at NNI connection points to ensure safe out-of-band tone passage in a timely manner, including accurate representation of the duration of the tones.

On the positive side, when tones are transported out-of-band, they "exist" in analog form only at the endpoints of a call, where they are digitized locally instead of at the central office (CO), which is the case with plain old telephone service (POTS). This results in better quality tones with negligible waveform distortion due to transmission effects.

High on the priority of tone transport is fax service. Fax has been characterized as a service whose time may be past due to the advent of extensive use of electronic mail, and some have even suggested an aggressive campaign to replace fax with electronic attachments to standard email. This is not going to happen, at least in the short term, and fax will continue to grow as a viable and relatively secure means of exchanging documents in the business and consumer market. Up until now, POTS has supported fax in a ubiquitous manner over the same wires that bring us voice telephony, and voiceband signals between the fax machines have been transported using standard G.711 PCM encoding. Since there are no codecs to negotiate in the PSTN, this is an easy process, with no signaling differences between a voice and a fax call.

When a call is initiated, the local telephone switch does not know that it is establishing a fax call at the time the digits are dialed by the calling party. This is true for both POTS service on the PSTN and voice telephony over a packet network. In the presence of voice compression and multiple choices of voice-data encoding in the packet network, codec negotiation will take place between the endpoints assuming it is a voice call, and it is possible that some form of voice compression will be selected as the media format, if such a common format is supported by the endpoints. This is a problem if the call that is being established turns out to be a fax call and other than PCM media encoding has been selected. Tones do not survive codec processing, and a couple of things could happen so that the call can be completed successfully.

1. Once the fax answer tone has been detected by the IAD serving the endpoint, the endpoints can *upspeed* to G.711 format and send the voiceband data, including tones, in-band in the RTP stream. This requires

attention to timing and the speed of switching the media format, but is not difficult to implement and can be made to work reliably if delays and echo control devices are managed properly. Also, timing constraints of the T.30 fax specification must be met, as the presence of the packet network is transparent to the two analog endpoints in the fax transmission.

2. The local switch can intervene and use an intermediate gateway to support the fax call via T.38 (for real-time) or T.37 (for non-real-time) service. This may sound like an easy and obvious solution, since T.38 has been proven to work in controlled conditions, but under general network configurations, including the possibility of peering connections, it requires considerable testing to ensure robustness and reliability.

One thing is for sure: Telephony service comparable to POTS will require unqualified support for Group 3 fax. Possibilities for fax support consistent with the requirements of the AIN call model, the IP signaling protocols, and traffic engineering at the access network will be discussed in the context of a call flow example.

1.7 H.248: THE MEGACO PROTOCOL

H.248 follows the model of MGCP as a **Me**dia **Ga**teway **Co**ntrol protocol, while at the same time, it improves on its capabilities. It was the result of a combined effort of the Internet Engineering Task Force (IETF) and the International Telecommunication Union (ITU) to define a single media gateway control protocol to be the successor of MGCP and features both text and binary syntax. Gateways can support either protocol format, but MGCs (softswitches) are requested to support both syntax types.

The H.248 call model is very similar in signaling granularity and resolution to the basic call model of MGCP. H.248 builds its foundation upon two abstractions: the *termination* and the *context*, both of which broaden the notions of *endpoint* and *connection,* respectively, of MGCP. A softswitch that implements H.248 to control media gateways also implements call signaling and control mechanisms of other protocols, such as H.323 and SIP, for call signaling between platforms and domain boundaries. A termination can source and/or sink media flows and can be physical or logical. Logical terminations can be created dynamically and may last only for the duration of the call. Terminations can be added to a context, moved to another context, deleted, modified, or audited. Terminations can be added to the *null* context, which contains all the nonassociated (dangling) terminations.

A typical connection model of the Megaco protocol is shown in Figure 1.5.

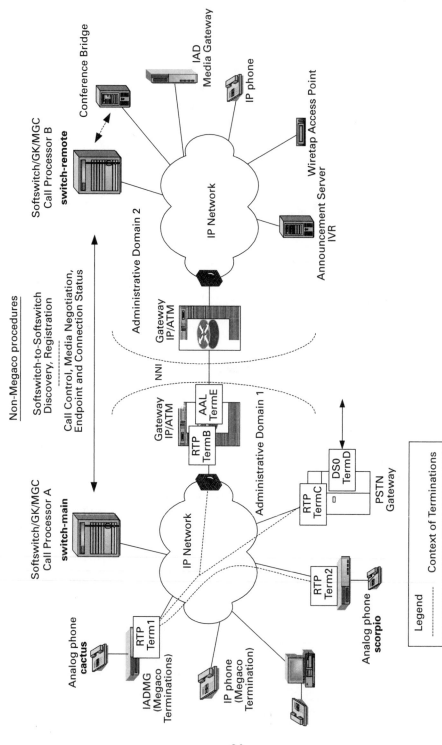

FIGURE 1.5 Megaco connection model.

TABLE 1.5 Megaco/H.248 Protocol Command Summary

COMMAND	CODING	USAGE NOTES
Add Termination	Add	Adds a termination to a context. If there is no existing context, a new one is automatically created by the receiving endpoint.
Modify Termination	Modify	Terminations can be modified through descriptors carried in the message, such as media, signal, digit maps, etc.
Subtract Termination	Subtract	Terminations can be *subtracted* from their current context, i.e., *removed*. If this was the last termination removed from the context, the context is deleted. Statistics of the context gathered at the termination are returned to the MGC. This is analogous to the MGCP DLCX command.
Move Termination	Move	Moves a termination from one context to another in a *single*, *indivisible* operation. Attributes of the termination being moved can be also modified as part of this command.
Notify	Notify	The gateway notifies the MGC of detected events, in the order in which they were detected.
Audit Value	AuditValue	The MGC can obtain the current value assignments of the termination.
Audit Capabilities	AuditCapabilities	The entire range of possible values of properties and attributes supported by the termination are returned.
Service Change	ServiceChange	Sent by the gateway when a termination or group of terminations is taken out of service or is being returned to service. Similar to the RSIP command of MGCP.

The H.248 commands are summarized in Table 1.5 and the protocol is discussed in detail in Chapter 7.

1.8 SCTP: STREAM CONTROL TRANSPORT PROTOCOL (RFC2960)

TCP has served us well as a reliable transport protocol, but its origins were for the transport of data. A telephony application using TCP and only a few hundred active calls at a time may be adequate, but as numbers scale to supporting thousands of active calls, TCP can become a *resource* and *perfor-mance* bottleneck. A more efficient, but as reliable, protocol is necessary for time-critical applications with scalability requirements.

SCTP is a reliable protocol, which is message-oriented and, as such, more efficient than the byte (stream)-oriented TCP. It offers fault tolerance through multihoming support and message-multiplexing capability. SCTP is used for transporting PSTN call-signaling protocols over an IP network, such as M3UA (MTP3 User Adaptation), M2UA (MTP2 User Adaptation), SUA (SCCP User Adaptation) for SS7 message transport, and IUA (ISDN User Adaptation) for Q.921 message transport. It is expected that other signaling applications will be supported over SCTP as it matures in VoIP networks.

The SCTP protocol and the M2UA/M3UA signaling adaptation methods are covered in Chapter 9.

1.9 TRANSPORT ADAPTER LAYER INTERFACE (TALI)

TALI is an alternative signaling adaptation method used for transporting SS7 messages to and from the PSTN of a network, over an IP-based signaling infrastructure. It provides full SS7 signaling interworking between the PSTN and VoIP. TALI replaces the MTP2 and MTP1 layers of the basic SS7 proto-col stack, and it uses TCP as its reliable transport. The basic TALI protocol stack is shown in Figure 1.6.

1.10 SIGNALING TRANSPORT USER ADAPTATION LAYER PROTOCOLS: M3UA, M2UA, SUA, AND IUA

The IETF is also expected to standardize a method for passing SS7 and ISDN signaling over an IP network; these methods are referenced under the common name of *user adaptation layer* specific to the signaling protocol they transport. All user adaptation layers use SCTP as their reliable transport protocol. The basic protocol relationships of M2UA and M3UA are shown in Figure 1.7.

1.11 FIREWALLS

The purpose of firewalls is to protect the consumer and service provider from malicious intrusion of many manifestations and service denial attacks. Once a firewall is inserted in a network, things change for the more complex. Here are some reasons firewalls complicate call flows, network design, and traffic engineering.

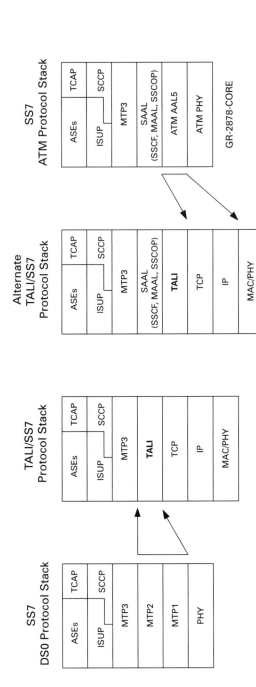

SAAL: Signaling ATM Adaptation Layer

Components

SSCF: Service Specific Coordination Function
MAAL: Management Adaptation ATM Layer
SSCOP: Service Specific Connection Oriented Protocol

Note: SCTP can be used instead of TCP as the transport protocol

FIGURE 1.6 SS7/TALI signaling stacks.

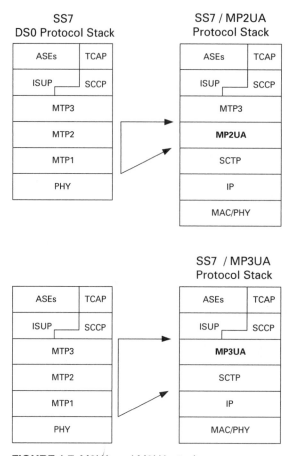

FIGURE 1.7 M2UA and M3UA stacks.

1. Firewalls complicate call flows because "holes," allowing for controlled entry of signaling and media into the domain, must be opened and closed diligently and explicitly. This often spells stateful firewall designs, which run the protocol stacks for which they support passage. It also means the signaling overhead and functionality must be accounted for in the real call flows and performance assessment between arbitrary endpoints.

2. Firewalls must be very "speedy" in authorizing the passage of time-critical flows on a packet basis, as is the case with voice. There are enough issues associated with keeping packet delay to a minimum in the wide area, so it is imperative for firewalls to examine packets in as close to real time as possible. A good target is to keep packet scrutiny down to

one packet's transmission time, thus creating a full pipeline with minimal delay and impact on voice quality.

3. The delay and jitter impact of firewalls is cumulative and proportional to the number of firewalls in the path of the connection.

4. Firewalls can be distributed and involve different physical devices for signaling and media flows. This causes a further complication of call flows in that signaling synchronization between firewall devices needs to be maintained by a softswitch or other stateful signaling management entity.

5. Firewalls must be capable of performing Network Address Translation (NAT).

6. Firewalls in general cannot be QoS agnostic, in the sense of QoS mechanisms that have been devised to assist IP networks in transporting real-time flows. A QoS-agnostic firewall may defeat the purpose of network QoS for time critical applications, such as voice telephony.

The impact of firewalls in VoIP networks serving the wide area will be known in more detail as networks proliferate and more becomes known about their contribution to performance parameters. In this text we will look at the complications involved in setting up and terminating a call across domains in the presence of firewalls on either side, or on both sides, of the call.

1.12 OTHER PROTOCOLS

The following protocols and their procedures have functional and performance impact on delivering high-quality integrated telephony services to subscribers across administrative boundaries. Some of these protocols will enter into the discussion of the call flows in this text.

1. ITU-T Recommendation H.235 Security and encryption for the H-Series (H.323 and other H.245-based) multimedia terminals.

2. The ITU-T H-series of supplementary services: H.450.1 through H.450.9.

3. QoS across domains using Multiprotocol Label Switching (MPLS).

4. TOS-DiffServ.

5. RSVP-TE.

6. Transport Layer Security (TLS)/IPsec.

7. Other related protocols in the context of actual call flows.

References

1. RFC 2453 – *The Session Initiation Protocol.*
2. RFC 2705 – *The MGCP Protocol, version 1.0.*
3. RFC 2960 – *The Stream Control Transmission Protocol (SCTP).*

4. RFC 2976 – *The SIP INFO method.*
5. RFC 3015 – *The MEGACO Protocol.*
6. ITU-T Recommendation H.323 (2000), *Packet-based multimedia communications systems.*
7. ITU-T Recommendation H.225.0 (2000), *Call signaling protocols and media stream packetization for packet-based multimedia communication systems.*
8. ITU-T Recommendation H.245 (2000), *Control protocol for multimedia communication.*
9. ITU-T Recommendation H.235 (2000), *Security and encryption for H-series (H.323 and other H.245-based) multimedia terminals.*
10. ITU-T Recommendation H.450.1 (1998), *Generic functional protocol for the support of supplementary services in H.323.*
11. ITU-T Recommendation H.450.2 (1998), *Call transfer supplementary service for H.323.*
12. ITU-T Recommendation H.450.3 (1998), *Call diversion supplementary service for H.323.*
13. ITU-T Recommendation H.450.4 (1999), *Call hold supplementary service for H.323.*
14. ITU-T Recommendation H.450.5 (1999), *Call park and call pickup supplementary services for H.323.*
15. ITU-T Recommendation H.450.6 (1999), *Call waiting supplementary service for H.323.*
16. ITU-T Recommendation H.450.7 (1999), *Message waiting indication supplementary service for H.323.*
17. ITU-T Recommendation H.450.8 (2000), *Name identification supplementary service for H.323.*
18. ITU-T Recommendation H.450.9 (2000), *Call completion supplementary services for H.323.*
19. *Transport Adapter Layer Interface 2.0,* Tekelec Technical Reference, IP7.
20. *IETF working drafts on M3UA, M2UA, SUA, and IUA.*

2

Topologies, Equipment, and Communications

In order for the reader to appreciate the level of complexity involved with the definition of a *robust* and *telephony feature-capable* signaling protocol, a detour into the equipment and topologies employed in typical networks is necessary. After all, signaling traverses equipment located across distances and dissimilar networks, so it is wise to have a good understanding of what is being "touched" and how information is transformed during transport in order to establish even a simple telephone call. The figures in this chapter do not depict specific networks, but are generic and inclusive enough to paint an accurate picture regarding the points of concern in engineering a high-availability, feature-rich infrastructure that is also capable of interfacing with the PSTN. Later in this chapter we will present a high-level checklist of items that service providers and network planners typically include in the big pot of optimized parameters during the design of services and network topologies. When this part is understood, we will then move to cover signaling communications, service delivery, and real-time testability of the resulting infrastructures.

2.1 WIRELINE, POINT-TO-POINT ACCESS NETWORK

Figure 2.1 shows an example of an IP-based Local Exchange Carrier (LEC), point-to-point, wireline access network, which we look at with respect to call establishment, session control, and testing considerations. There are differences between point-to-point wireline access and the common medium

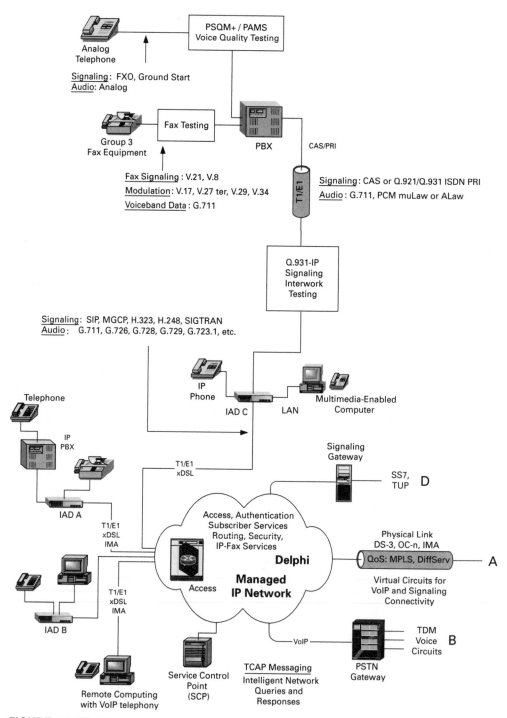

FIGURE 2.1 Wireline access network.

access of the cable television (CATV) distribution system from the CATV operator to the home or enterprise. The latter has many similarities with the point-to-point access network with respect to call signaling and platform composition, and will be reviewed later in this chapter.

There are three pieces to this type of access network. The first deals with support for legacy customer equipment (analog telephone, PBX, modem, fax, LAN, etc). The second deals with support of next generation, IP-based equipment such as IP phones, IP PBXs, multimedia terminals, and other IP-based, intelligent future "appliances." The third piece is the type of physical link or links used to connect the customer premise equipment to the service provider's network.

A device central to the new access network is the IAD Media Gateway (MG), which we have already mentioned briefly. Our reference topology shows three distributed IADs (IAD A, IAD B, and IAD C) connected to the service provider's network and serving a variety of customer devices. A generic IAD is a customer premises equipment (CPE) gateway that supports multiple types of physical interfaces. Its functions are optimized to *collect*, *format*, and *transport* traffic streams between the customer devices plugged into its physical interfaces and the service provider's packet network. IADs exchange signaling with a Media Gateway Controller (MGC), which enables them to *establish calls*, *allocate resources*, *transfer data*, and *collect statistics* necessary for the service provider to know whether guaranteed QoS is reaching the customer. In this text the MGC is considered functionality included in a multiprotocol, multiservice platform, rather than in a separate dedicated box. A *softswitch* is such a multiprotocol, multiservice switching platform which delivers voice telephony and integrated services over the wide area. Among other names used in protocol-specific contexts for MGC functionality are Gatekeeper (H.323) and User Agent Server (UAS, for SIP). In the topology of Figure 2.1, the softswitch is internal to domain Delphi and manages the IADs and signaling "visible" endpoints.

For purposes of using uniform nomenclature throughout this text, we will refer to the logical termination of a packet stream inside an IAD as an *endpoint*, regardless of the protocol used for signaling and call establishment. Endpoints are logical entities and are characterized by a transport address (TA), which is the combination of an IP address and a higher layer port number (TCP or UDP).[1] There are *signaling* endpoints, which terminate the signaling protocol for an endpoint, and *media* endpoints, which terminate the packet streams. In some cases a media endpoint maps to a single physical

---

1.   Sometimes a packet *transport address* is only an IP address, such as for protocols directly over IP on the stack.

interface, such as an RJ11 telephone jack. In other cases an endpoint may map to a timeslot on a multiplexed interface, such as a DS0 on a trunk between the IAD and a conventional PBX (IAD C). For LAN data flows, the notion of an endpoint is rather meaningless and the packet traffic is routed internally between the local LAN physical interfaces and the uplink, or between local interfaces on the same IAD without accessing the uplink. In other words, IADs offer varying degrees of routing capabilities to steer packet streams to the correct endpoint or interface, depending on their complexity. Some packet streams may also traverse an IAD and terminate at an endpoint located in an attached multimedia-capable appliance, such as a PC. Such endpoints are not considered part of the IAD, and for those streams, the IAD acts as a conduit and router of packetized data.

In our reference topology in Figure 2.1, the MGC is centrally located inside the service provider's domain (*Delphi*) and, for all intents and purposes, it is a softswitch. Some MGCs may be located in the enterprise as well, for small networks attached to a larger packet network through peering connections. The signaling protocols we will examine for the purposes of gateway control and call establishment are MGCP, SIP, H.323, and H.248/ Megaco; the physical links connecting the IAD to Delphi can be some form of xDSL, non-channelized T1/E1, or Inverse Multiplexing over ATM (IMA) over T1/E1. Higher bandwidth physical links, such as DS-3 and OC-n, do not affect the general discussion on signaling protocols and media transport, and are less frequent except in larger enterprise networks.

One of the primary functions of the IAD is media encoding for voice and video (if the latter is supported) and, for more sophisticated IADs, the ability to conference and transcode media; that is, convert from one media format to another. IADs support dialing plans for E.164 numbers, emergency numbers (e.g., 911), and customized dialing plan options for the enterprise and home. Voice formats range from the mandatory, PSTN-compatible G.711[2] (64 Kbps ALaw or μLaw) to a plethora of compressed voice formats, some prominent ones of which are shown in Table 2.1. Additionally, the IAD is providing echo cancellation for the voice streams it terminates. We will discuss voice formats and their impact on voice quality and access network traffic engineering in the context of call flows later on.

There are several points in the access network where special types of testing are explicitly indicated. For example, on the analog connection between the "black phone" and the RJ11 jack on IAD C (see Figure 2.1), we may need to perform objective speech quality measurement to assess the impact of the various voice coding schemes that may be present in an end-to-end conversation. The

---

2.   This is one of the ITU-T G-series of digital voice encoding.

TABLE 2.1 Example Voice Encoding Formats (Codecs)

SPECIFICATION	TECHNOLOGY	COMPRESSION	PACKETIZATION RATES
G.711 muLaw / ALaw	Waveform PCM	64 Kbps (logarithmic)	10, 20, 30 ms
G.723.1	10th Order LPC	5.3 and 6.3 Kbps	30 ms
G.726	Waveform ADPCM	16, 24, 32, 40 Kbps	10, 20, 30 ms
G.728	LD-CELP	16 Kbps	10, 20, 30 ms
G.729A	CS-ACELP	8 Kbps	10, 20, 30 ms/10 ms FR
G.729E	CS-ACELP	11.8 Kbps	10, 20, 30 ms/10 ms FR
GSM	RPE/LTP	13.2 Kbps	20 ms

Perceptual Speech Quality Measurement (PSQM) and Perceptual Analysis Measurement System (PAMS) are two such objective speech quality measurement techniques, whose results can be mapped to the more subjective Mean Opinion Scores (MOS). There is also a new specification in the works for the Perceptual Evaluation of Speech Quality (PESQ), ITU-T P.862. For legacy analog fax testing through an IAD, the ITU T.30 specification must be met, and mixed load testing—both across multiple applications and for a single application—is usually the method employed to ensure the quality of fax transmission and the access network's ability to handle simultaneous voice, voiceband, and data traffic from a number of concentrated customer premises. You should keep in mind that a legacy end-to-end fax call may involve packetized hops across one or more carrier domains, such as the method described in ITU-T Recommendation T.38. Unfortunately, fax and modem tones do not survive the perceptual coding of voiceband data by codecs, and it is not certain that such tones would be recognized by the receiving fax equipment if allowed to be processed by a codec. If the network performance parameters allow a translation of fax signaling and transport protocols across a hop without violation of the T.30 specification parameters at the endpoints, the end result would be transparent support for legacy fax across a packet network. However, other schemes are also possible to circumvent the problem of tone transport for fax calls, as we will discuss later.

PBX access into the IAD is either via legacy *Channel Associated Signaling* (CAS), which uses robbed-bit signaling on each of the 24 DS0s carrying the voiceband data for T1 or on the 32 DS0s for E1; or via ISDN Primary Rate Interface (PRI), the Q.931 signaling protocol, which is a *Common Channel Signaling* method over a dedicated DS0 on the trunk. ISDN PRI over T1 uses 23 bearer (B) channels and a signaling channel (D). The E1 version of PRI uses 30 B channels and one D channel for signaling.

In the case of an ISDN PBX trunk, the IAD will either "wrap"[3] all of the signaling messages and backhaul them to and from the softswitch, where the Q.931 protocol stack will be executed, or they will be mapped to VoIP signaling messages of the protocol used to support the PBX. For example, we may have a PRI-to-MGCP message mapping, a CAS-to-MGCP, and so on. Some signaling protocols allow for this nontrivial mapping better than others do. We will cover the protocols later in the text and provide some guidance as to the message-mapping mechanisms that are necessary for proper support of legacy PBX.

Analog phones offer no further challenge in the IP access network other than to support the hardware signaling mechanism's to "make believe" they are still plugged into the RJ11 wall socket. Of note, however, is the survivability aspect of the PSTN, which powers the black phones from the local loop. This means that when we lose power on our premise (home, business), the phones still work, which is a very desirable feature to carry over into the new network, since the digital local loop is not self-powered. There have been many proposals to address this point, but it seems inevitable that if we want to continue to have basic telephone service over the digital local loop when there is a power outage, the IAD will have to supply power to the analog phone for some period of time.

IP phones can be the most challenging of all devices attached in the access network. An IAD runs one or more instances of a particular signaling protocol for all "same" endpoints it supports. For example, it may run MGCP or H.323 for analog phone endpoints, regardless of how many phones are attached to the IAD's RJ11 jacks. This means when there is a need for a protocol upgrade, it is made once inside the IAD and it is easy to track changes and maintain revision levels. On the other hand, IP phones will need to (a) adhere to the particular signaling version of the signaling protocol used by the MGC (when it sees the IP phone itself as the endpoint), or (b) run the same version of the signaling protocol as the IAD (if the IAD is the endpoint and signaling to the IP phone is either proxied by the IAD or simply replicated). IP phones can offer some powerful features to the consumer, especially for business applications, and as such, any potential inconvenience or maintenance risk may be overlooked in favor of the realized benefits.

---

3.   This means to encapsulate and transmit the message units of the original protocol in packets of another protocol without processing or otherwise interpreting the original protocol information.

2.2 SERVICE PROVIDER END OFFICE

The data to and from the customer's devices is placed on IAD uplinks to the service provider's network, where it traverses network equipment that can analyze and route the packet traffic to its proper destinations. For integrated services involving telephony and data, the two types of flows—voice and data—have to be separated and routed over a choice of either separate logical subnetworks or virtual trunks utilizing the same physical links for at least a portion of the service provider's edge devices before they are injected into the core network. Figure 2.2 and Figure 2.3 will serve as our reference drawings for this discussion.

Domain Delphi contains a softswitch that can offer key services to the subscribers in the access network. Effectively, it acts as an End Office (EO) in our reference topology. In this context, a softswitch represents a next-generation integrated voice switch, which takes the place of a traditional Class 5 switch. Later in the overview we will see softswitches in the role of a Class 4 tandem switch and softswitches serving a local area with integrated voice and data distribution through cable modems. Some of the more important services provided by Delphi are

1. Basic telephony service with PSTN-style reachability, plus emergency dialing.
2. Enhanced telephony features, such as call waiting, three-way calling, and caller ID.
3. Network access with authentication for virtual private networking and telecommuting.
4. Subscriber services.
5. Operator services (directory assistance, busy line verification, barge-in).
6. Routing of voice calls and data.
7. Voice and data virtual private networks (VPNs), such as custom dialing plans and secure VPNs.
8. Optionally, real-time and non-real-time fax services for business applications.
9. 24×7 "always on" access to the Internet.
10. Mobility services.
11. Optional remote dial-in Internet access.
12. Pre-negotiated QoS for voice, VPN, and basic data service.
13. Security through the use of firewall technology.

In order for the softswitch platform to deliver these features, it must meet certain performance criteria regarding voice and voiceband call completions per second (cps), active voice and voiceband call capacity, data shaping and policing, and failover recovery from link and equipment malfunctions. Speedy

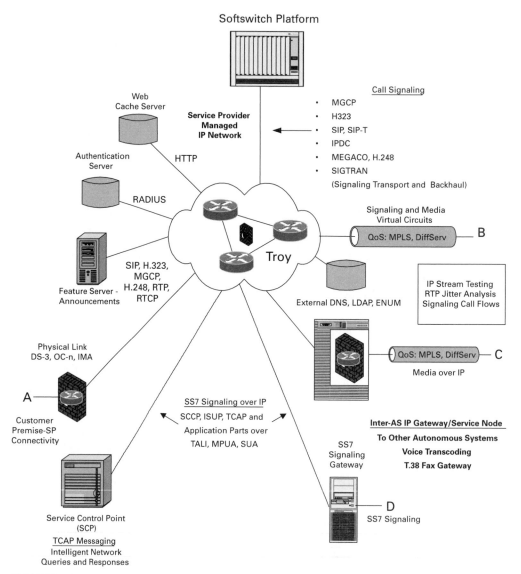

Softswitch Platform

Web
Cache Server

**Service Provider
Managed
IP Network**

Call Signaling

• MGCP
• H323
• SIP, SIP-T
• IPDC
• MEGACO, H.248
• SIGTRAN
(Signaling Transport and Backhaul)

Authentication
Server

HTTP

RADIUS

Signaling and Media
Virtual Circuits

QoS: MPLS, DiffServ — B

Troy

IP Stream Testing
RTP Jitter Analysis
Signaling Call Flows

SIP, H.323,
MGCP,
H.248, RTP,
RTCP

Feature Server -
Announcements

External DNS, LDAP, ENUM

QoS: MPLS, DiffServ — C

Media over IP

Physical Link
DS-3, OC-n, IMA

A —

Customer
Premise-SP
Connectivity

SS7 Signaling over IP
SCCP, ISUP, TCAP and
Application Parts over
TALI, MPUA, SUA

Inter-AS IP Gateway/Service Node
To Other Autonomous Systems
Voice Transcoding
T.38 Fax Gateway

SS7
Signaling
Gateway

D
SS7 Signaling

Service Control Point
(SCP)
TCAP Messaging
Intelligent Network
Queries and Responses

FIGURE 2.2 Integrated switch platform.

recovery from security breaches, such as hacking and denial of service attacks, and quick restoration of service is also mandatory for maintaining a quality presence at the access network. Exact performance measures in cps are often elusive due to the multiplicity of use cases that can be present during a measurement interval. For example, measuring the capacity of a switch in cps could

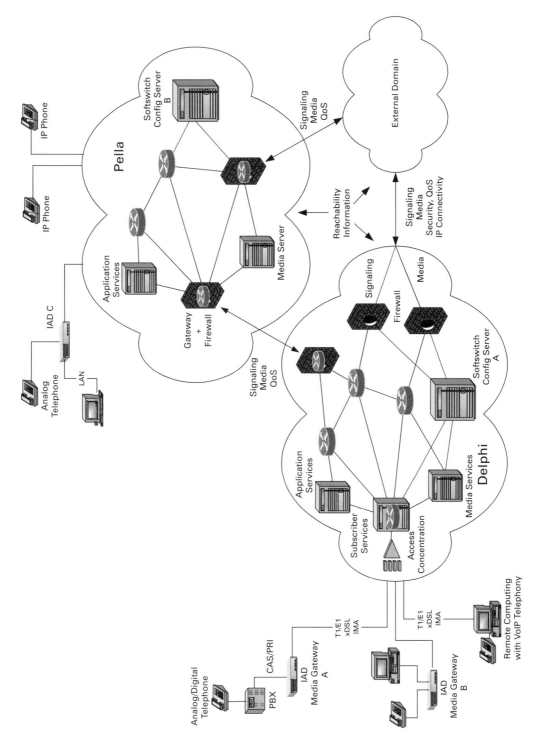

FIGURE 2.3 Cloud internals with firewalls.

yield different results, depending on how many protocols, which ones, and their instantaneous mix in the system during call setups. It is therefore wise to develop a dependency graph when addressing this issue to determine the bounds of system performance depending on capacity. Without such detailed knowledge of performance, the scalability of the platform can be miscalculated.

A different measure of performance that provides more insight to carriers is the DPM, or *defects per million,* in call attempts and failed connections after call establishment. This parameter is the "report card" of the network in general, and when it is time-stamped with a "cause" indication, it can serve as a yardstick for the specific switching platform which experienced the failed calls.

The new EO Delphi needs to interface to the PSTN via SS7 signaling (reference point **D**). In North America, the signaling standard is ANSI SS7, whereas in Europe it is a variant of the ITU SS7 specification as refined by ETSI, depending on the country of interest. Depending on domestic service needs, countries may deem it is necessary to issue a country-specific variant to the basic ITU SS7 specification, and there are a plethora of such variants, which creates homologation requirements (see references). Inside the Delphi domain, signaling to and from the gateways most likely will be some form of SS7 over IP (TALI or MPUA, from the IETF), BICC from the ITU-T (Q.1901), or a proprietary method involving a mix between a standard signaling protocol and extensions that may or may not be part of the standard at the time of network deployment—for example, SIP as defined in RFC 2543 and the draft contributions that comprise SIP-T as of this writing (SIP with telephony extensions). We are unlikely to see unilateral vendor extensions or modifications to ITU signaling specifications, such as H.323 and SS7, without consensus from standards organizations such as ETSI.

A reference sample of the Delphi EO internals is shown in Figure 2.3 Demultiplexing of incoming streams takes place at the edge of the domain, and packets will be routed according to the application (voice, data) and the current call state. For example, for voice calls during setup, signaling may take place between an IAD endpoint and the softswitch itself. It may become necessary to interact with the user via a voice server, such as in the case of credit card calls, in which case an *application server* may be injected in the path of the packet stream via a temporary call diversion. In other cases it may become necessary to play an announcement, for example, *"The number you have entered cannot be completed as dialed,"* when the switching platform determines there is something wrong with the dialing process. In general, such announcements will be played from a *media server* application, which may be hosted and accessed by the softswitch as an independent subsystem component.

The local domain contains routing equipment for steering the media and signaling packets to the proper equipment. Of special note is the use of firewalls to shield the domain and its access network from malicious and curious intruders. For purposes of generalization, we will assume there are separate firewall applications (not necessarily dedicated firewall "boxes") for signaling and data. Even within data applications, there may be separate firewalls for voice, data VPNs, voice VPNs, and other applications, such as distributed games. The firewalls need to be controlled by some component of the softswitch platform to ensure dynamic creation and deletion of access "holes" for the applications that need them. One such example is basic incoming call signaling from a calling party in attached domain *Pella*. There may be only one permanent transport address open for setting up the call, and as soon as signaling has been authenticated, additional "holes" will be opened to proceed with call establishment. Similarly, firewalls need to be protocol-savvy to know when to close the additional holes, either on their own or via command from another subsystem component or from the softswitch itself.

> Firewalls can seriously affect system capacity and performance because they are placed in the middle of the signaling and data paths, and as such, they complicate the call flows. The actual position in the network and impact of firewalls needs to be fully understood when specifying system performance and scalability requirements.

2.2.1 Core Wireline Packet Network

We will consider three types of network elements in the core packet network in the sample topology of Figure 2.4. The first is the *router*, with all the network engineering enhancement it needs to create *favorite* paths with predetermined QoS and virtual trunks to carry voice and data to edge networks, such as the one we saw at Delphi. Routers traditionally examine the Layer 3 header of the packets in order to determine which way to forward them. In Chapter 4 we will see a significant deviation from this rule with the advent of MPLS. Since the original major benefit of IP was ubiquitous access, albeit neither guaranteed to happen nor guaranteed to happen with any consideration to packet behavior, bandwidth utilization, resilience, and support for multiservice applications, changes had to be made in the manner in which IP packets are examined and forwarded through network elements. We will look at two approaches to traffic engineering in packet networks: using Differentiated Services (Diffserv), which redefines the type of service (TOS) field in the standard IP packet for purposes of packet stream classification, and, of course, using MPLS. The subject of traffic engineering is complex and will be visited within the context of call flows throughout this text, in order for the reader to appreciate when and where preferred paths need to be established,

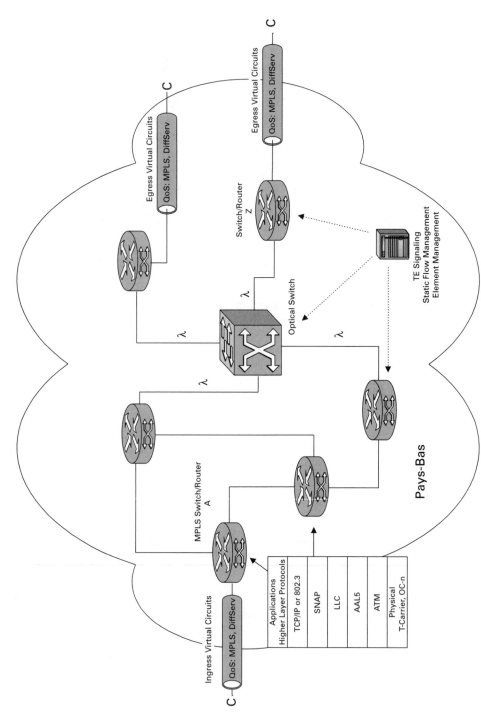

FIGURE 2.4 Core network.

the effect of switched paths on network scalability (resources, performance, etc.), and robustness questions that arise from traffic engineering of IP links.

The second element in the core packet network is the traditional *switch*. In this case our paradigm is ATM switching, which may also need to include MPLS capabilities in order to meet edge-to-edge traffic engineering requirements. Switches can deliver better performance as they perform forwarding based on link layer (Layer 2) information, such as the ATM header field. Switches require the establishment of paths in advance for the flows that will traverse them; in other words, the selection of the egress interface is predetermined for the entire flow without the need to look at the contents of each and every packet. One drawback to this type of operation may be inadequate scalability due to limitations in the static availability of virtual circuits and paths in a switch. Dynamic creation of virtual circuits and paths within a switched network is feasible but usually very costly in performance and complexity. We will concentrate our attention on the case of the preestablished paths through the switches of the network.

The third element is the optical switch. Optical switching is finding acceptance and will eventually be a dominant technology in the core switched network. An optical switch maps *lambdas* (wavelengths) at its ingress to lambdas at its egress, for optical circuits that do not require add and drop multiplexing (ADM) services in the core network. The result is faster switching operation and higher signal capacity, because the incoming signals remain optical without the traditional conversion to electrical and reconversion to optical, as has been done in conventional ADM equipment. Naturally, the issues we need to solve early on are the signaling method to establish the switching matrix of the various wavelengths and the policies that will take effect when failures occur in equipment and links.

IP packets are transported over an ATM network via one or both of the methods described in RFC 1483. One method requires the placement of an additional header in the IP frame and is known as *Sub-Network Attachment Point Logical Link Control* (*SNAP/LLC*) encapsulation, which is depicted in Figure 2.4, whereas the other method maps incoming packets to virtual circuits (VC) via payload fragmentation and is referred to as *VC multiplexing*.

A great deal of the work involved in traffic engineering takes place inside the core network, whose robustness is paramount to meeting the quality of service offered by the carrier who owns and operates it.

High performance network elements (switches and routers) perform traffic management, such as per-VC queuing or other packet forwarding discipline, inside distributed I/O cards rather than through a central computing entity in the device.

Distribution of functionality, including traffic management, serves to avoid the possibility that a single failure in a network element will affect the entire network.

2.2.2 The PSTN

It has been said by many that the PSTN will not go away any time soon. The details of call establishment, protocols, equipment, and general operation of the North American and European telephone networks have been covered in the technical literature many times. We will concern ourselves in this text with the Class 5 EO system and the Class 4 tandem nodes for purposes of explaining the interoperability of the PSTN with the new IP-based telephone networks.

Domain *Atlantis* is our local exchange carrier's EO. It serves a segment of the local population and terminates the copper whose other end is the RJ11 wall jack on our premises. It also terminates ISDN PRI trunks and PBX trunks (CAS and PRI), and switches voice circuits between users in its local serving area for local calls and between users across carrier domains for long distance calls. Long distance calls outside the local serving area are handed off to an Inter-eXchange Carrier (IXC), which operates a Class 4 tandem network. Call establishment proceeds from the calling party to its ultimate destination along hops on the tandem network, until the called user's local serving area EO is found and the call is handed to a local carrier for termination (see Figure 2.5).

Of interest to us is the possibility of using the existing Class 5 system (e.g., Lucent 5ESS, Nortel DMS100, Alcatel DEX) to offer basic telephone features to a packet-based local network. This can be accomplished with the help of a special type of equipment, the GR-303 (V5.2 for Europe) Voice Gateway. GR-303 is a Telcordia specification (V5.2 is from ETSI) that allows bundling of multiple T1s (E1s) to the local Class 5 switch, which views them as a single extended trunk group of DS0s spanning multiple facilities, all of which can be managed through a single signaling channel. The Voice Gateway has IP-based interfaces to the local network (reference point B), and voice calls are converted between packetized format and Time Division Multiplexing (TDM). The switch itself is not aware of the existence of the access packet network.

The method of employing the services of a GR-303 (V5.2) Voice Gateway can give an option to the carrier for quick deployment IP-based services, while incrementally upgrading and switching slowly to a softswitch platform maintaining the telephony features and behavior of the legacy Class 5 switch.

We will cover call establishment and control using PSTN hops, and use of conventional PSTN network elements and systems, in the context of call flows with at least one IP endpoint.

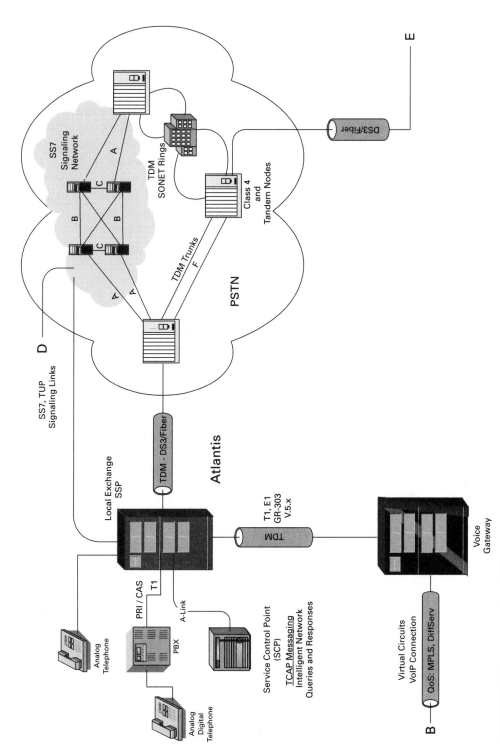

FIGURE 2.5 Hopping on the PSTN.

SS7 Signaling Network

A

TDM SONET Rings

C

B B

C

A A

A A

PSTN

Class 4 and Tandem Nodes

TDM Trunks

F

DS3/Fiber

E

D

SS7, TUP Signaling Links

Local Exchange SSP

TDM - DS3/Fiber

Atlantis

T1, E1 GR-303 V.5.x

TDM

Analog Telephone

PRI / CAS

T1

A-Link

PBX

Analog Digital Telephone

Service Control Point (SCP)

TCAP Messaging
Intelligent Network Queries and Responses

Voice Gateway

Virtual Circuits VoIP Connection

QoS: MPLS, DiffServ

B

45

2.2.3 Wireline, CATV Access Network

DSL technology for LEC-offered integrated services and POTS replacement in the access network has a competitor in the consumer market. Basic telephony service and interactive data access is also being offered by CATV operators through a fairly recent enhancement of their signal distribution system to support bidirectional data transport. CATV operators have been creating the *interface, signaling,* and *transport* specification for cable modems (CM) and multimedia terminal adapters (MTA) through the *CableLabs®* consortium. The intent of the specifications is to define a set of internal and external standard interfaces for support of real-time, packet-based integrated services, such as primary service voice telephony. It is believed that all CATV operators who adhere to the interface specifications can interconnect their packet domains directly and in an interoperable manner, thus providing end-to-end, multidomain, IP-based telephony over an increasing number of CATV serving areas.

The specification has been known as Data over Cable Service Interface Specification, or DOCSIS,[4] which is overviewed here, and one of its objectives is support of bidirectional real-time traffic. The underlying principle is simple: A DOCSIS-compliant cable modem receives its data over unused 6 MHz video channels within the cable spectrum. Upstream traffic flows to the system headend in the 5–42 MHz subsplit band (5–65 MHZ for European systems).

DOCSIS is in itself not a complete interface specification for support of voice telephony, in particular in the area of call signaling. The PacketCable® initiative from CableLabs has produced an additional set of specifications which complement DOCSIS and complete the picture of primary telephone service through a CATV operator.

Figure 2.6 serves as our example generic CATV access network for integrated services.

Domain *Zeta* is a managed IP-based network at the cable headend, which is equivalent to the LEC EO for the purpose of offering telephony service. The Call Management Server (CMS) has capabilities equivalent to a softswitch and controls the cable modem termination systems (CMTS), the proxies, firewalls, and routers, as well as the media and signaling gateways for interfacing with the PSTN. Each CMTS connects to a series of MTAs using a *common medium, hybrid fiber coax* (HFC) network, thus forming a geographically distributed LAN configuration. This means packetized voice and

---

4.   The name has since changed to the CableLabs® Certified Cable Modem Project, but we will continue to refer to it in this text with its original name DOCSIS, since it still enjoys wide recognition in the industry.

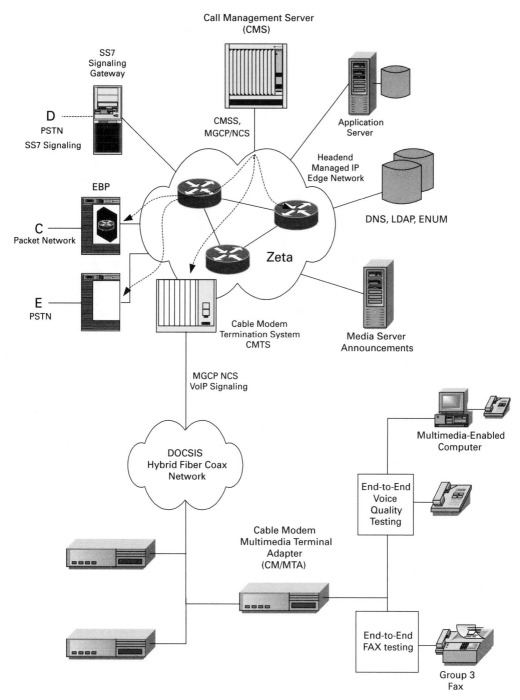

FIGURE 2.6 Cable modem access.

data to and from each subscriber MTA in an area served by a CMTS traverses a common physical link to and from the CMTS. In turn, the CMTS performs multiplexing and demultiplexing of individual packet streams for further routing through the Zeta edge network and beyond.

A CATV access network that supports interactive data services and voice telephony uses a time-slotting (TS) methodology to assign bandwidth and a timing reference for users to place their data on the upstream link. The timing reference is established via the transmission of a 3 ms time marker, either through an out-of-band (OOB) or an in-band (IB) physical layer signaling mechanism. The OOB method uses the T1 framing structure of 1.544 Mbits/s to establish the recurring 3 ms time reference every 24 frames for a downstream OOB channel of 1.544 Mbits/s, or 48 frames for a downstream OOB channel of 3.088 Mbits/s. The IB signaling method uses an embedded timing marker in an MPEG-2 transport stream packet.

Upstream rates can be 3.088 Mbits/s, 1.544 Mbits/s, or 256 Kbits/s. Data is sent in standard Ethernet frames using IEEE 802.2 LLC and ISO/IEC 8802-3 specifications. Not all data rates need to be supported simultaneously by the MTA. Data in the upstream direction is sent by MTAs in fixed time slots allocated to it by the CMTS or in time slots for which it contends for access with other users using the basic Time Division Multiple Access (TDMA) contention principle. There are three defined methods for upstream data transmission:

1. Fixed bandwidth access with reserved time slots.
2. Dynamically reserved bandwidth via request from the MTA and assignment of time slots by the CMTS.
3. TDMA contention transmission per time slot, with possible collisions with other users' data.

The time slot size is 512 bits and is independent of the MTA data rate. The number of time slots in the upstream direction, between the 3 ms time marker occurrences, depends on the MTA data rate. For the lowest rate of 256 Kbits/s, we have 3 TS; for the 1.544 Mbits/s rate, we have 9 TS; and for the highest upstream rate of 3.088 Mbits/s, we have 18 TS per 3 ms marker period. The TS principle used in data over cable is shown in Figure 2.7. The transport stream MPEG-2 packet is shown in Figure 2.8.

Downstream data is broadcast to all MTAs on the medium. Demultiplexing is based on the Media Access Control (MAC) address and the Network Services Access Point (NSAP) address assigned to the MTA by the CMTS. There are several issues of security and privacy that arise immediately when signaling and data transport from many unrelated users share a common medium and are broadcast in one direction. These concerns are addressed by the cable industry standards and will be visited in the context of call flows.

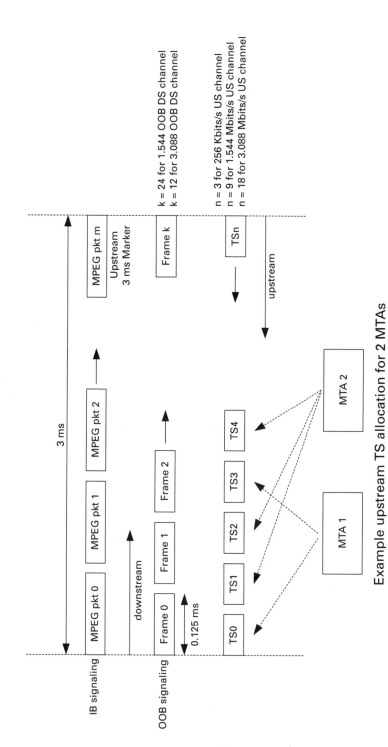

FIGURE 2.7 Data over cable TDM channel.

49

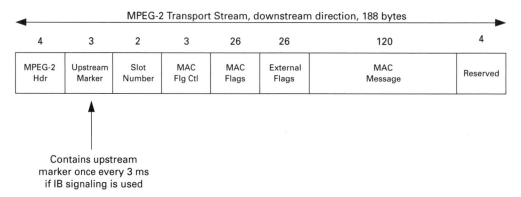

FIGURE 2.8 MPEG-2 packet.

Signaling between CMSs goes through an Exterior Border Proxy (EBP), reference point C, which may also act as a router and a firewall. The signaling protocol for CMS-CMS call establishment is based on the SIP standard, whereas the signaling protocol between a CMS and its MTAs is MGCP/NCS. Calls to another IP-based telephony infrastructure that are signaled through the EBP may require protocol translation by the Border Gateway Protocol (BGP). Calls with one leg on a CMS-controlled MTA and the other on the PSTN need to be signaled through an SS7 signaling gateway.

The MTA is analogous to the IAD Media Gateway of our wireline point-to-point example, and the same types of customer devices are expected to be attached, even though the business driver for CATV telephony is focused more to the home rather than the enterprise. End-to-end application testing between a CMS-supported environment and a softswitch access network may involve a hop on the PSTN, or traversal of an IP-based tandem core network, similar to the one we discussed earlier. As such, call setup over tandem IP arrangements may include multiple legs and be quite complex. Caution is always recommended in assuring performance is acceptable for any type of voice telephone call, any time.

Signaling for Voice over IP telephony uses the MGCP protocol between the CMS, the MTA, and the PSTN gateways, and SIP for signaling between CMSs and across domains. The protocol stack for data over cable is shown in Figure 2.9.

The ITU G-series codecs that must be supported by the MTA are similar to those in the IAD case, but note that the packetization rates may be different (faster packetization) than those in endpoints residing outside the control of the CMS, such as interdomain IP-only calls, with the intent to minimize packet delay (see Table 2.2). This could cause a conflict when codecs are negotiated and must be resolved before the call is established.

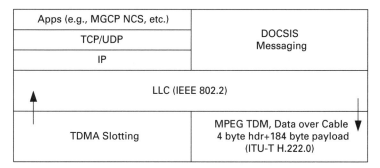

FIGURE 2.9 Data over cable protocol stack.

TABLE 2.2 MTA Codecs

MTA CODEC	PACKETIZATION RATE (MSEC)
G.728 16 Kbits/s	2.5 (codec should be supported)
G.729 Annex E 11.8 Kbits/s	10 (codec should be supported)
G.711 64 Kbits/s	2.5 (codec support is mandatory)

Given the slotted nature of the upstream channel and the possibility of TDMA conflicts, a reduction of the packetization time may make up only some of the time lost in the packet transmission from the MTA to the CMTS. Codec negotiation is simpler for *on-net* calls between CMS environments than for interdomain packet calls to non-CMS controlled endpoints, as we will see later. There is at least one mandatory and common codec to all the current implementations of IADs and MTAs: G.711 (64 Kbps A or muLaw), which at least guarantees a call cannot fail because of codec incompatibility even across non-CATV operator domains, as long as compatible rates are negotiated or the call can support asymmetric bandwidth allocation. In addition, the uncertainty arising from the type of codec each call will end up using requires careful bandwidth engineering, even at the access network. Support for legacy fax is also a challenge for VoIP telephony over CATV.

The issue of scalability often arises when a common transmission medium is shared by a growing population of users. There are concerns that as the number of users grows, performance (i.e., latency, voice quality) on the CATV access network will degrade, but these can be addressed by fixing the bandwidth to the MTA for the most time-sensitive applications, such as voice, and scaling the access network by additional CMTS/HFC deployment as the needs require.

We should not forget POTS telephony service offers access to emergency and operator services (911 dialing, operator barge-in, etc.). Any replacement to POTS service—a voice telephony service that will replace POTS as residential primary telephone service—must offer the same capability for regulatory reasons. An additional issue, the survivability of the POTS-replacement service, either by IADs or MTAs, during power blackouts, also requires serious consideration. Legacy POTS supplies the analog telephone with all the power it needs, but IADs and MTAs require wall-socket power in order to continue functioning properly. Only time and the "test" of a few adverse conditions in the serving area—ice storms, power blackouts—will tell whether the requirement for a minimum of 4 hours of battery-powered customer premise gateway operation is enough.

2.2.4 Wireless Access

The wireline networks are in the middle of massive changes to achieve multi-service integration, but the digital wireless networks are also undergoing dramatic improvements and innovations for the purpose of converging voice and data services over a single medium—the air. The big "LAN in the Sky" is being positioned to bring wireless data access at speeds that will rival those of the wireline networks we discussed earlier. The changes are taking place in the infrastructure and the access equipment (handsets and mobile terminals), as well as in new services that will eventually be offered as soon as the networks have been upgraded.

The new *wireless services* will make engineering the *wireline* networks very interesting because of their inherent user mobility capabilities. Imagine one day being able to take your laptop everywhere around the world with an immediately available 384 Kbps wireline connection wherever you go, much like the ubiquitous dialup services most of us still "enjoy" in airport terminals and hotels. If enough people can do this (and they will do this if it is made affordable), traffic engineering at the network border crossings between the wireless carrier and the packet data networks will remain an exciting problem for a long time. Also, imagine a future generation of handsets that can play full color video clips. It is in this context that a review of the current and planned capabilities of the wireless networks is necessary, before we address end-to-end signaling and traffic engineering across dissimilar multiservice networks and a plethora of backbones.

The current focus of the evolution of the digital wireless network is threefold:

1. Migration of the present TDMA digital wireless networks (IS-136, Global System for Mobile Communications [GSM]) to Code Division Multiple Access (CDMA).
2. Upgrade of the predominantly circuit-switched infrastructure to integrate high-speed packet data and voice with efficient usage of the radio frequency spectrum. This step requires new types of mobile terminals and handsets.
3. Convergence of the North American, European, and Japanese digital wireless networks to the Universal Mobile Telecommunication System (UMTS), as the objective of the Third Generation Partnership Project[5] (3GPP).

The GSM migration path is shown in Figure 2.10. We will take a high-level view at the General Packet Radio Service (GPRS) network as a reference for the requirements in signaling and traffic engineering, without loss of generality as the networks migrate towards UMTS. It is assumed there will be additional changes required to meet the final objective of UTMS, but the intermediate *network* enhancements ideally will not be made obsolete in this process.

The industry support for a common physical access method for UMTS networks is not converging into a single and universal method, but at this time it is envisioned that at least two different CDMA coding schemes will be standardized. The result will be a new generation of multimode mobile stations, but with higher functionality and international range. The upgrade in the infrastructure to support high-speed packet data is necessary for the wire-

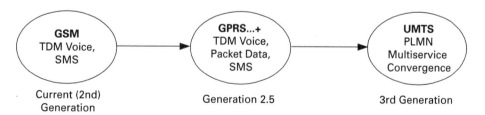

FIGURE 2.10 GSM network evolution.

---

5.   Current information about the evolution of 3GPP can be found on www.3gpp.org. The 3GPP members develop standards for the adopters of the ITU-T IMT-2000 framework. The organizational partners of 3GPP include standards associations from Europe (EISI), Japan (ARIB and TTC), Korea (TTA), and China (CWTS).

less networks to move beyond the limitations of the Short Message Service (SMS) and offer voice and broadband multiservice access from fixed or mobile wireless stations. In order for us to appreciate the impact that high bandwidth wireless data transport will have on network engineering in the wireline world, it is important first to discuss an overview of the current wireless infrastructure and see where the upgrades will eventually take us.

2.2.5 System Component Overview

Key components of the basic GSM Public Land Mobile Network (PLMN) are shown in Figure 2.11, with a simple call flow to understand call termination at a mobile system.

1. Mobile Switching Center (MSC)
2. Base Station System (BSS)
3. Mobile Station (MS)
4. Home Location Register (HLR)
5. Visitor Location Register (VLR)
6. Authentication Register (AUR)

The GPRS enhancement, also shown in Figure 2.11, introduces two additional components for routing and transport of packet data traffic.

1. Gateway GSM Support Node (GGSN)
2. Serving GSM Support Node (SGSN)

The HLR and VLR are database systems with assigned Signaling Connection Control Part (SCCP) subsystem numbers (SSN) and accessible via SCCP/TCAP (Signaling Connection Control Part/Transaction Capabilities Application Part) signaling and the Mobile Application Part (MAP). The interface between the MSC and BSS consists of one or more 2.048 Mbps E1 links with SS7 signaling shown in the protocol stack of Figure 2.12. The interface between the BSS and MS or other wireless terminal equipment is the radio frequency spectrum, with TDMA and frequency division access methods for GSM, IS-136, and GPRS. The principles of the North American and European wireless systems are very similar, but their use of the radio resources—allocated spectrum, time-slotting of RF carriers, radio channels, mapping of logical channels onto physical channels, and signaling—is quite different. The North American wireless network is expected to support GPRS.

The GGSN node is the packet access to the GPRS network. It may or may not include firewall capabilities (depending on the implementation), but a firewall is certain to exist at the access to the center hosting the GGSN node. The GGSN obtains routing information about the current SGSN of the MS from the HLR and uses this information to route packets arriving at

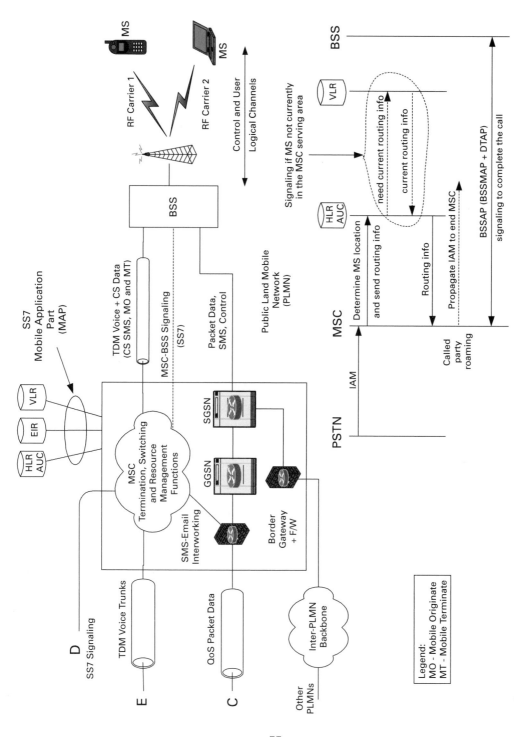

FIGURE 2.11 Wireless access network.

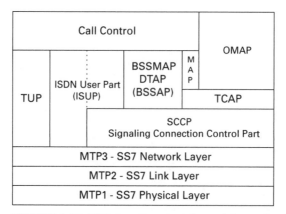

FIGURE 2.12 SS7 signaling stack for mobile applications.

ingress reference point C to the current SGSN. Packets between the SGSN and GGSN are tunneled using the GPRS Tunneling protocol (GTP) and either TCP or UDP, depending on whether reliable delivery is required.

The GPRS-capable MS is served by one SGSN at any given time while on the GPRS network. If the user is in the local serving area, it is "attached" to its home SGSN, which creates awareness of the MS's current mobility status. When roaming in the GPRS network, it is attached to the area SGSN, and mobility information is signaled to the HLR through the VLR.

Packets arriving at the home GGSN, or at GGSNs of other GPRS networks, are tunneled to the serving SGSN. From the serving SGSN, they are routed to the MS, using the GPRS transmission plane, which includes the BSS GPRS Protocol (BSSGP) between SGSN and BSS, and the encrypted, radio-interface-independent Logical Link Control (LLC) between the SGSN and the MS.

The MSC interfaces with both the PSTN and external Packet Data Networks (e.g., X.25, IP). The packet interface is either via the GGSN for external networks or via a border gateway (BG) for inter-PLMN access. The PSTN interface is via a voice switch. Voice trunks are terminated at the MSC and signaling with the PSTN is performed using standard SS7. Voice call termination into a PLMN is very similar to TDM voice call termination at a telco EO. Incoming calls from the PSTN are always first routed to the called party's MSC (the switching center that holds the called party's subscription information in its HLR). This is the terminating switch that is obtained when the calling party's carrier translates the dialed number and gets the Destination Point Code (DPC) of the home MSC serving the called party. However, the called number contains no further routing information and additional signaling may be required to obtain the current location of the MS or terminal.

Additional signaling may be intra-PLMN if the called MS is in another part of the same carrier's network, or it may be inter-PLMN if the called party is roaming and is currently being served by another carrier's network.

Once the call reaches the home MSC (that is when the IAM message is received), the MSC will consult with its HLR. If the called MS is currently registered locally (neither roaming nor in another area of the PLMN), the call will be signaled with the BSS serving the subscriber's cell, and a voice circuit will be reserved on the TDM link between MSC and BSS. Signaling will complete between the BSS and MS, and the call will be terminated at the MS.

If the party is roaming or visiting in another part of the PLMN, the HLR knows this fact already, as this event has been signaled to it by the serving VLR when it "picked-up" the "visiting" user. The HLR will signal to the serving VLR to obtain additional routing information—the end MSC information—and will return this information to the home MSC, which will then proceed to signal the call to the end MSC that is currently serving the user.

The above operation will repeat at the new MSC when it receives the IAM message, and once the serving VLR identifies the called party as currently being in its area, the call will be completed with signaling between the terminating MSC, the BSS, and the MS. To the two parties—calling and called—the additional signaling to locate the MS is seamless and imperceptible beyond some increase in post-dial delay (PDD) latency.

Call origination from an MS is the reverse process. Once the MS has signaled its intention to its current BSS and MSC to place a call, it transmits the dialed digits, which are translated at the current MSC to obtain routing information. If the called party is another MS on the same PLMN, the call is forwarded to the end MSC. If the called party is roaming, the call is forwarded and the same steps we discussed above will take place at the home MSC of the called party. The call then proceeds as before. If the called party is on the wireline network, the call is signaled to the local exchange or IXC, and signaling proceeds between the MSC and the EO until the call is terminated.

The Network Access Control function of GPRS controls the manner in which users "attach" to the network. It provides registration, authentication, admission control, message screening, packet format adaptation, and accounting and billing information.

Packet routing supports tunneling, compression, and encryption, while mobility keeps "tabs" on the current location of the user.

Logical link management controls the established link between the MS and the PLMN, and the radio resource management function manages the channels in the cell and dynamically controls the number of channels allocated for GPRS use. It also provides a mechanism to manage the path between the BSS and an SGSN, based on criteria determined by the network operator.

2.2.6 Services of the GPRS Network

GPRS offers high-quality circuit-switched voice and "always-on" data access to its users, without the need to "dial-up" a connection to the network. The network's ability to allocate previously circuit-switched radio resources in a more efficient manner, by offering "virtual connections" to multiple users, will result in higher network capacity and less complex signaling exchanges between the MSC and MS.

The GPRS network offers three mobile classes of service to the MS, as shown in Figure 2.13.

The key distinction among the classes is the degree to which the MS can have access to voice and data simultaneously. Classes A and B allow simultaneous *attach* (the MS dynamically becomes part of—or attaches to—the GPRS network), as well as activation and network monitoring. Invocation of GPRS data service is limited for Class B, which also cannot enjoy simultaneous voice and data transport. Class C requires manual selection of GPRS data service.

The GPRS services are defined in the GSM 02.60 documents and are shown in Figure 2.14. The network's functions are shown in Figure 2.15.

Point-to-point connectionless service is a basic packet-switched, datagram service, with supported confirmation delivery on the radio path. The corresponding connection-oriented service establishes a stateful connection between the communicating endpoints for reliable end-to-end transfer of transaction or interactive data. The connection state is maintained when the MS crosses cell boundaries and is released in cases of malfunction or call termination.

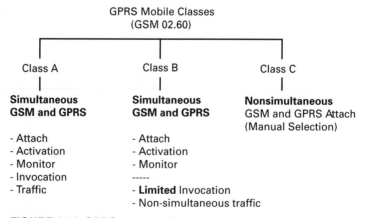

FIGURE 2.13 GPRS classes of service.

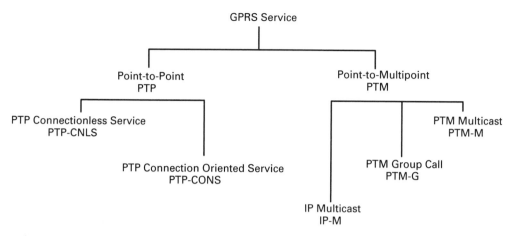

FIGURE 2.14 GPRS services.

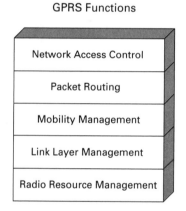

FIGURE 2.15 GPRS functions.

The point-to-multipoint services allow a user to send data to more than one recipient at the same time. Multicast service transmits packets over certain areas requested by the sender, without actually knowing the number or identity of the recipients. In contrast, Group Call sends packets only to specifically identified recipients, who may be in areas of the PLMN.

IP multicast service is defined in a manner similar to IP multicast over the Internet. The IP multicast group can be within the carrier's network or across network boundaries, including Internet.

GPRS keeps track of a mobile system's current location, and with the help of the SGSN, it performs access control and security functions.

2.2.7 Radio Resource Usage in GPRS

GSM defines two types of logical channels—the *traffic* and *control* channels—which are mapped on the physical radio channels using Frequency Division Multiple Access (FDMA) and TDMA. The GSM Logical Channels are shown in hierarchical form in Figure 2.16. The current GSM channel definition remains the same for GPRS, but the usage of the traffic and control channels for a GPRS PLMN and the handsets that support GPRS is different.

Data and voice are transported over traffic channels (TCH), using signaling on the control channels (xCCH). The latter are divided in four categories:

1. Broadcast Control Channel (BCCH)
2. Common Control Channel (CCCH)
3. Dedicated Control Channel (DCCH)
4. Cordless Telephony Control System (CTS)

The CTS category is beyond the scope of this text. The Cell Broadcast Channel (CBCH) is a downlink channel that carries the Short Message Service Cell Broadcast service (SMSCB) and uses the same physical channel as the Standalone Dedicated Control Channel (SDCCH). SMSCB should not be confused with the SMS, which we overview next in this section. SMSCB allows short messages to be broadcast to all users within an area, and they are shorter in length (82 characters) than SMS messages.

TCHs and CCHs are mapped on the Radio Frequency Channels (RFCH) that have been allocated to the cell, in predefined time-slot positions (for the nonassociated CCH) and in time slots signaled to the MS by the BSS when the call was being set up (for the TCH and Slow Associated Control Channel, or SACCH). Time slots are organized in frames, and a TDMA frame carries 8 TCHs with their associated CCHs. This is shown in Figure 2.17. A TS has a duration of 577 microseconds[6] and the frame repeats every 4.615 milliseconds. When an MS wishes to place a call, it signals to the MSC (via the BSS) for a TCH allocation. Similarly, when an incoming call is received for an MS, a TCH is allocated and signaled to the MS via a CCH.

TDMA frames are organized in multiframes of 26 frames each, only 24 of which carry traffic. The twelfth TDMA frame of the multiframe carries the Slow Associated Control Channel (SACCH, allocated to a user after the TS

---

6.   For time slots using 156.25-symbol periods, whereby one symbol period is 48/13 microseconds. The base transceiver station may use both 157- and 156-symbol periods for time slots within a frame, which gives a slight variation. The frame length is 4.615 milliseconds in either case. See reference GSM 05.10.

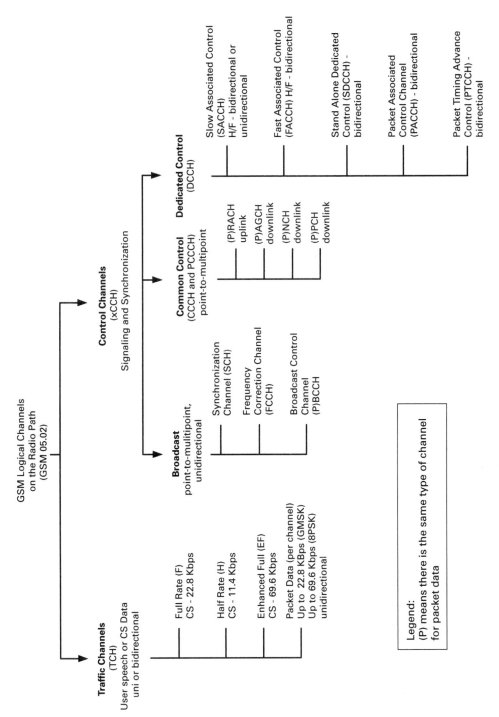

GSM Logical Channels
on the Radio Path
(GSM 05.02)

Traffic Channels
(TCH)
User speech or CS Data
uni or bidirectional

Full Rate (F)
CS - 22.8 Kbps

Half Rate (H)
CS - 11.4 Kbps

Enhanced Full (EF)
CS - 69.6 Kbps

Packet Data (per channel)
Up to 22.8 KBps (GMSK)
Up to 69.6 Kbps (8PSK)
unidirectional

Control Channels
(xCCH)
Signaling and Synchronization

Broadcast
point-to-multipoint,
unidirectional

Synchronization
Channel (SCH)

Frequency
Correction Channel
(FCCH)

Broadcast Control
Channel
(P)BCCH

Common Control
(CCCH and PCCH)
point-to-multipoint

(P)RACH
uplink

(P)AGCH
downlink

(P)NCH
downlink

(P)PCH
downlink

Dedicated Control
(DCCH)

Slow Associated Control
(SACCH)
H/F - bidirectional or
unidirectional

Fast Associated Control
(FACCH) H/F - bidirectional

Stand Alone Dedicated
Control (SDCCH) -
bidirectional

Packet Associated
Control Channel
(PACCH) - bidirectional

Packet Timing Advance
Control (PTCCH) -
bidirectional

Legend:
(P) means there is the same type of channel
for packet data

FIGURE 2.16 GPRS channel definition.

61

(GSM 05.02)

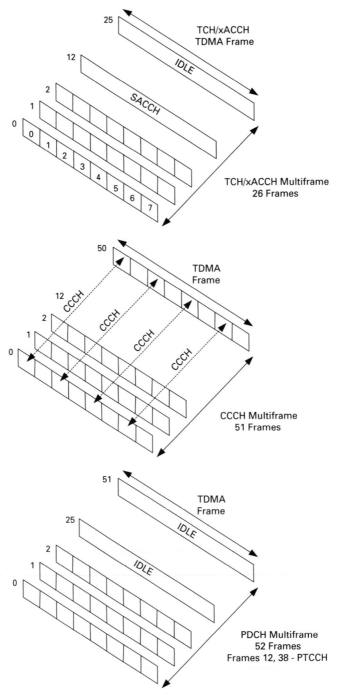

FIGURE 2.17 GSM TDMA framing.

and channel between the BSS and MS have been assigned). The twenty-sixth frame is idle. The 26-frame multiframe repeats every 120 milliseconds.

Typically, for a voice call on the GSM network, the MS will be assigned a circuit-switched TCH at full rate, which will rate-adapt the speech encoding of the 13 Kbps GSM coder to the BSS. The GPRS upgrade allows for dynamic allocation of more than one TCH (up to 8, or an entire TDMA frame), for speeds exceeding 150 Kbps per user (under GMSK modulation) or more with 8PSK modulation. The latter supports data speeds of up to 69.6 Kbps for a single channel. Since the TS allocation is on-demand, the same channel can be allocated to a voice circuit for other users, depending on need, or for the same user if simultaneous voice and data transport are permitted in the user's mobile class of service.

Control Channels and Packet Data Channels (i.e., PDCHs allocated to a physical channel) have different multiframing. The CCH multiframe cycles through a 51 TDMA frame sequence, whereas the PDCH multiframe is 52 frames long. The mapping of logical channels in the various multiframe structures is a very complex process and is explained in detail in GSM 05.02.

2.2.8 The Short Message Service and Its Evolution

SMS brought us an early but rudimentary ability to send short text messages of up to 140 user-entered characters in length to and from MS stations. The SMS service needs to be provisioned at a service center (SC), which acts as an intermediary and packet store-and-forward service in the message exchange. The store-and-forward capability of the SC is actually beneficial in that it provides a temporary "hold" period for an undelivered message if the user cannot be located. In GSM networks, SMS messages are sent to the MS using the SDCCH if a TCH has not been allocated to the MS, or via the SACCH if the MS is already using a TCH. It is apparent the bandwidth allocated for SMS is not only small, but is also shared on CCHs whose primary service is management of other resources.

There is a significant change in this area for SMS in the GPRS network. SMS messages will be transported by a Packet Data Traffic Channel (PDTCH), and as such, they will be delivered to the GPRS packet ingress. The SMS service is supported for all three GPRS mobile classes of service.

The SMS is a point-to-point service between a Short Message Entity (SME) and an MS, via an SC. The SME and SC are external to the PLMN and are not shown in Figure 2.11.

Two SMS services are defined:

1. SMS Mobile Terminate (MT), for sending messages to a MS.
2. SMS Mobile Originate (MO), for sending messages from a MS.

SMS also allows simple interworking with electronic email in both directions. Email is sent using a single SMS message or multiple concatenated SMS messages as necessary.

SMS itself is evolving to eventually bring full color animation to the MS in real time. The ultimate objective—MMS, or Multimedia Messaging Service—is a multiservice integration of text, video, and audio to a future generation of MS.

2.2.9 Voice Quality

Voice in the GSM/GPRS environment is circuit switched, but it is not toll-quality voice. Wireless networks have an additional handicap in that they have to deal with nature's elements and real-time mobility, and as a result they do not deliver consistently high-quality voice. The GSM voice coder produces a 13.2 Kbps stream of 260 bits every 20 milliseconds. The coder ranks very well under MOS and Perceptual Speech Quality Measurement (PSQM) tests. However, in an effort to further improve voice quality on the wireless network, GSM has specified a new voice coder based on Algebraic Codebook-Excited Linear Prediction (ACELP), which requires approximately the same bandwidth—244 bits per 20 ms frame, plus overhead.

One aspect you must keep in mind is the different packetization rates (frame rates) supported by a network operator and technology. Even if the coding format is the same at both ends, differences in the bit rate may cause a call to be rejected if rate adaptation is not provided at one of the ends.

2.3 CONCLUDING OBSERVATIONS

We have taken a quick tour of three dissimilar types of networks, which are evolving to support integrated services in the best way possible, given their preexisting implementation and architectural restrictions. Signaling for a simple call across the PSTN is a complex process, when looked at in detail, and is becoming increasingly complex with the development of packet-based telephony. In spite of the fact there are winners in the battle of the protocols, signaling across VoIP domains is so much more complex, as is engineering the traffic characteristics of the new multiservice networks. A key attribute of the new "composite" PSTN is support for mobility. With it, however, comes an uncertainty as to the instantaneous and time-dependent load that can be expected during peak periods, as well as the need for a new definition of the "peak" period itself.

In the last chapter of this part, we look at advances in traffic engineering in packet networks. In the remainder of the text we will examine call flows across domains we have discussed, such as Delphi, Pella, Atlantis, Zeta, and other examples.

2.4 SIGNALING, MEDIA, AND PLATFORMS: THE NECESSITIES

Network design is the process of carefully engineering the connectivity of an equipment topology for the purpose of transporting multiservice information flows with deterministic quality of service. There is a list of items we want to consider when putting such an end-to-end topology together, and a high-level sampling of them is shown in Table 2.3, Table 2.4, and Table 2.5.

TABLE 2.3 Key Signaling Plane Softswitch Considerations

THE SIGNALING PLANE	FEATURE CONSIDERATIONS
Equipment, Topology, Connectivity	The set of servers, routers, switches, firewalls, proxies, access concentrators, PBXs, IADs, telephone types, and other legacy equipment that need to be "touched" in the process to set up a voice call.
Protocols, Interworking, Interoperability	Requirements for call setup, MGC, bearer plane establishment, statistics gathering, etc. MGCP, H.323, Megaco, SS7 over IP (MPUA, TALI), SIP, and Bearer-Independent Call Control Protocol (BICC, Q.1901) in the context of call flows across domains. Homologation for country-specific signaling standards.
Call and Connection Model	Call and connection models within a domain and across provider domains may involve multiple legs in the establishment phase. Identification requirements for the supported models.
Endpoint/Server Discovery	When making a call to an endpoint hosted by a different service provider, prior to routing a call the endpoints' location needs to be determined. This process may be dynamic—with support for mobility, and presence—or static.
Call Routing	In the PSTN, routing is done with point codes of SSPs, STPs, and SCPs. For VoIP interdomain routing, routes need to be obtained via advertisement (e.g., Telephony Routing over IP, based on BGP) or preestablished fixed access to carrier networks.
Admission Control	Attempted calls may have to be rejected based on QoS issues or the lack of required resources (bandwidth, processing power, etc.).
Security	Authentication, privacy, nonrepudiation, antihacking measures.
Performance	Post-dial delay, integrated telephony feature support.
Capacity	Number of calls in signaling progress. This is related to the measure for platform capacity.
Resilience	In the call flow diagrams, the handling of a "missing arrow" and/or a "bad arrow," i.e., a message carrying bad data.
Failover/Redundancy	The protocol needs to support failover in the presence of rainy day scenarios, in order to complement the platform's failover capabilities.

TABLE 2.3 Key Signaling Plane Softswitch Considerations (continued)

THE SIGNALING PLANE	FEATURE CONSIDERATIONS
Scalability	A term often misunderstood or misused. Everything scales, given enough cost and resources. In this context, the measure of scalability for a particular design is the degree to which resource requirements and costs increase with increasing network capacities. The result is either an increasing step function with noted discontinuities or a monotonically increasing linear relationship. Linear relationships may be acceptable, depending on the gradient.
Reachability	Support for all types of calls, anywhere, any time, just like in the PSTN.
Telephony Feature Support	Filter the most common features, the ones required by regulations, and any new ones required by new applications, and select existing ones for legacy applications.
Mobility Support	The ability to dynamically register one's subscription attributes at another station/endpoint, not necessarily located within the same enterprise or home.
Multimedia and Conferencing	Requirements placed on IADs to support conferencing, bridge requirements, and dissimilar media stream mixing. Requirements for ad hoc conferencing, i.e., dynamic conversion of a point-to-point call into a conference call. Sound quality with varying delays and packet QoS from various participants across domains.

TABLE 2.4 Key Bearer Plane Design Considerations

THE BEARER PLANE	FEATURE CONSIDERATION
Equipment, Topology, Connectivity	Servers, routers, switches, access concentrators, IADs, firewalls, proxies, IP-based and legacy equipment.
Delay	Delay is due to several factors (see ITU-T Recommendation G.114). Minimization of delay is required for tandem applications.
Jitter	Jitter can be unpredictable if the various links traversed by packet flows are not engineered properly. Unpredictable jitter has a substantial negative impact on delay and can seriously affect the quality of a voice conversation.
Packet Loss	A lot of effort is being focused to traffic-engineer end-to-end, QoS-controlled paths for interdomain and intradomain routing. Traffic engineering should seek to minimize packet loss or eliminate bottlenecks that would cause packet discard for time-sensitive information, if possible.

TABLE 2.4 Key Bearer Plane Design Considerations (continued)

THE BEARER PLANE	FEATURE CONSIDERATION
Security	IPSec, H.235, and new forms of encryption and interoperability.
QoS	Mapping of generic packet flow QoS requirements to tangible benefits for the consumer. For example, percent calls dropped, noncompleted calls, objectively measured voice quality, nondisruptive support for voiceband calls (fax/modem), accurate accounting and billing, survivability (power-outages).
Protocols (Transport, QoS Routing)	RTP and Real-Time Control Protocol (RTCP) implementation. Traffic engineering, i.e., DiffServ, MPLS, and how to manage the resulting topologies.
Route Discovery, Routing	Interior Gateway Protocols (IGPs), like Open Shortest Path First (OSPF), may produce an optimum map of the Layer 3 connectivity, but the actual hand-stitched path topology may look different, depending on service and other constraints. Ability to detect and eliminate loops for traffic-engineered paths (like the IGPs themselves do for Layer 3 routing).
Failover	Requirement to keep all stable calls up while paths are reconfigured in the presence of link and/or equipment failures. Maintain network capacity and feature availability.
Voice Quality	The use of objective measurements of analog voice, and automated mappings of packet QoS to voice quality measures, such as PSQM/PAMS, PESQ, and MOS.
Image Quality	Similar arguments for motion picture quality for the subscribed QoS and network engineering of paths.
Media Encoding Types and Codec Negotiation	G.711 may be the least common denominator, but this is a complex topic requiring special attention when traversing domains. Impacts capacity planning for trunks and call setup times.
Capability Discovery and Exchange	The possibility of acquiring information about an endpoint before signaling is initiated. Some mechanisms are in place to do this, but the concern is whether ASs should expose such information to the casual inquiry.
Media Transcoding	It should be avoided while traversing packet domains, regardless of the signaling protocol in use. When entering the PSTN, conversion to G.711 is necessary. There may be cases where transcoding within packet domains is required, but it can seriously affect performance in all respects.

TABLE 2.4 Key Bearer Plane Design Considerations (continued)

THE BEARER PLANE	FEATURE CONSIDERATION
Fax, Modem, Voiceband	Support for fax in packet networks of large delays is not easy. There is one method that reverts to G.711 when fax tones are detected, but the use of T.38 has also been pursued as an alternative to fax support over packet networks. It is an issue of cost and reliability, but the requirement may be to offer fax and modem services over any RJ11 jack that can host a black phone in an IAD.
Bandwidth Requirements, Traffic Engineering	This is a topic that will keep a lot of network engineers busy for a long time. In the next chapter we will discuss MPLS, DiffServ, and issues in creating and maintaining manually routed paths in complex topologies.

TABLE 2.5 Key Softswitch Platform Design Considerations

THE SOFTSWITCH PLATFORM	FEATURE CONSIDERATIONS
Centralized vs. Distributed Platform Implementation	Scalability vs. complexity and cost of the call server for providing QoS-capable integrated services.
Call Processing Model	The AIN basic call model is used for the current set of telephony features on the PSTN, but is seriously challenged for creating and executing integrated telephony services based on packet technology.
Billing/OSS Support	Settlements with other carriers, Customer Detailed Records (CDRs), protocols for OSS system interconnect.
Fault, Configuration, Accounting, Performance, and Security (FCAPS)	This is especially important when the network is hybrid, i.e., partially IP-based with hops on internal TDM segments. Statistics collection and presentation (meaningful, real-time statistics and expert analysis on what to do).
Network and Element Management (the view from the top, while managing the individual elements)	Use of SNMP, CMIP, TL-1, EMS-specific interfaces, and integrated TMN-based NMS/EMS platforms.
Failover (methods to remain up and running in the face of equipment and facility failures)	The ability to preserve databases and call states in the presence of system component malfunctions.

TABLE 2.5 Key Softswitch Platform Design Considerations (continued)

THE SOFTSWITCH PLATFORM	FEATURE CONSIDERATIONS
Robustness (platform survivability)	The platform's ability to handle not only switch failures, but network-engineered bearer path failures in real time.
Breadth of Signaling Support	This is a measure of flexibility to access other networks, but it may create a performance tradeoff.
Features and Services	Implementation of the old and the new telephony features on the platform.
Media Services (announcements)	Mandatory for providing telephone service.
Address Translation Directory Services (who, where, subscribed services, capabilities, and permissions). Routing/Location Discovery Provisioning Facility Management	Mandatory to support ubiquitous telephony service. Dialing plans, IP and other network addresses, URL to E.164 translation and vice versa, etc. Facility and equipment configuration for voice service provisioning.
User Authorization and Authentication Messaging, Voice, and Text User Mobility	Necessary to access integrated services from a fixed location or while mobile. Portable capabilities, presence.
Performance and Capacity (calls per second, number of active calls)	Capacity vs. cost is a scalability tradeoff.
Orderly Performance Degradation	Never, ever crash the system when pushed too hard. Crashing the system takes the service provider's network down.
Government Regulations (dial tone, lawful intercept, emergency dialing, operator services [primary telephone service], service survivability, etc.)	Federal, state, and local regulations are usually not negotiable, and while the process of establishing the new regulations for the new packet-based PSTN is continuing, the majority of the old ones will hold.
Cost	If the service providers can recover their investment in a reasonable timeframe, service infrastructure build-out will continue.

References

ETSI GSM Series (www.etsi.org)

1. GSM 01.04: "Digital cellular telecommunications system (Phase 2+); Abbreviations and acronyms."
2. GSM 01.61: "Digital cellular telecommunications system (Phase 2+); GPRS ciphering algorithm requirements."
3. GSM 02.02: "Digital cellular telecommunications system (Phase 2+); Bearer Services (BS) supported by a GSM Public Land Mobile Network (PLMN)."
4. GSM 02.03: "Digital cellular telecommunications system (Phase 2+); Teleservices supported by a GSM Public Land Mobile Network (PLMN)."
5. GSM 02.04: "Digital cellular telecommunications system (Phase 2+); General on supplementary services."
6. GSM 02.06: "Digital cellular telecommunications system (Phase 2+); Types of Mobile Stations (MS)."
7. GSM 02.60: "Digital cellular telecommunications system (Phase 2+); General Packet Radio Service (GPRS); Service description; Stage 1."
8. GSM 03.03: "Digital cellular telecommunications system (Phase 2+); Numbering, addressing and identification."
9. GSM 03.07: "Digital cellular telecommunications system (Phase 2+); Restoration procedures."
10. GSM 03.20: "Digital cellular telecommunications system (Phase 2+); Security related network functions."
11. GSM 03.22: "Digital cellular telecommunications system (Phase 2+); Functions related to Mobile Station (MS) in idle mode and group receive mode."
12. GSM 03.40: "Digital cellular telecommunications system (Phase 2+); Technical realization of the Short Message Service (SMS); Point-to-Point (PP)."
13. GSM 03.41: "Digital cellular telecommunication system (Phase 2+); Technical realization of Short Message Service Cell Broadcast (SMSCB)."
14. GSM 03.60: "Digital cellular telecommunications system (Phase 2+); General Packet Radio Service (GPRS); Service description; Stage 2."
15. GSM 04.06: "Digital cellular telecommunications system (Phase 2+); Mobile Station-Base Station System (MS-BSS) interface; Data Link (DL) layer specification."
16. GSM 04.07: "Digital cellular telecommunications system (Phase 2+); Mobile radio interface signaling layer 3; General aspects."

17. GSM 04.08: "Digital cellular telecommunications system (Phase 2+); Mobile radio interface layer 3 specification."
18. GSM 04.60: "Digital cellular telecommunications system (Phase 2+); General Packet Radio Service (GPRS); Mobile Station (MS)-Base Station System (BSS) interface; Radio Link Control/Medium Access Control (RLC/MAC) protocol."
19. GSM 05.02: "Digital cellular telecommunications system (Phase 2+); Multiplexing and multiple access on the radio path."
20. GSM 05.03: "Digital cellular telecommunications system (Phase 2+); Channel coding."
21. GSM 05.04: "Digital cellular telecommunications system; Modulation."
22. GSM 05.05: "Digital cellular telecommunications system (Phase 2+); Radio transmission and reception."
23. GSM 05.08: "Digital cellular telecommunications system (Phase 2+); Radio subsystem link control."
24. GSM 05.10: "Digital cellular telecommunications system (Phase 2+); Radio subsystem synchronization."
25. GSM 08.02: "Digital cellular telecommunications system (Phase 2+); Base Station System-Mobile-services Switching Centre (BSS-MSC) interface Interface principles."
26. GSM 08.04: "Digital cellular telecommunications system (Phase 2+); Base Station System Mobile services Switching Centre (BSS-MSC) interface Layer 1 specification."
27. GSM 08.06: "Digital cellular telecommunications system (Phase 2+); Signalling transport mechanism specification for the Base Station System-Mobile-services Switching Centre (BSS-MSC) interface."
28. GSM 08.08: "Digital cellular telecommunications system (Phase 2+); Mobile Switching Centre Base Station System (MSC-BSS) interface Layer 3 specification."

Texts
1. *Signaling in Telecommunication Networks*, John G. Van Bosse, Wiley Interscience.
2. *IP Telephony: The Integration of Robust VoIP* Services, Bill Douskalis, Prentice Hall PTR and Hewlett-Packard Press.
3. *Signaling System #7*, Second Edition, Travis Russell, McGraw-Hill.

CableLabs References (www.packetcable.com)
1. "PacketCable 1.0 Architecture Framework Technical Report," PKT-TR-ARCH-V01-991201, December 1, 1999, Cablelabs.
2. "PacketCable Network-Based Call Signaling Protocol Specification," PKT-SP-EC-MGCP-I02-991201, December 1, 1999, Cablelabs.

3. "PacketCable PSTN Gateway Call Signaling Protocol Specification," PKT-SP-TGCP-I01-99991201, December 1, 1999, Cablelabs.

4. "PacketCable Event Messages Specification," PKT-SP-EM-I02-001128, December 1, 1999, Cablelabs.

5. "PacketCable Audio/Video CODECS Specification," PKT-SP-CODEC-I01-991201, December 1, 1999, Cablelabs.

6. "PacketCable Security Specification," PKT-SP-SEC-I01-991201, December 1, 1999, Cablelabs.

7. "PacketCable Dynamic Quality of Service Specification," PKT-SP-DQOS-I01-991201, December 1, 1999, Cablelabs.

3

SONET and DWDM Technology Overview: The Present and the Future

3.1 THE BASICS

SONET is optical TDM technology, which has been standardized by ANSI. It successfully addressed the issue of physical layer compatibility at the *midspan meet*, following the breakup of the Bell System in the mid-1980s. The technology was developed as a high-speed, wide area, physical transport mechanism for optical networks, which primarily carried telephone calls between central offices (CO). SONET allows for multiplexing and transport of signals from the Digital TDM hierarchy, with rates ranging from sub-DS-1 up to DS-3, as well as signals from the Synchronous Transport Signal[1] (STS-n) hierarchy. The optical carrier (OC) level of SONET begins with a line rate of 51.84 Mbps, also referred to as OC-1, and proceeds to the current top level of OC-192 at 9953.28 Mbps (51.84 x 192). A rule of thumb to determine the speed of an OC-n is to multiply the basic OC-1 rate of 51.84 Mbps by n, the OC index.

Very similar to SONET is the Synchronous Digital Hierarchy (SDH) optical transport technology, which is standardized by the ITU. Optical SDH starts at the STM-1 (Synchronous Transport Module) rate, which is equal to STS-3, and proceeds in **m increments of the STS-3 rate**, whereby **m** is the STM index. Therefore, the STM-4 signal has the same line rate as the STS-12 signal, which is 4 (the STM index) x 3 x 51.84 Mbps. The STS-192 line rate

---

1. The STS hierarchy refers to the electrical level frame structure upon the OC signal.

is the same as for STM-64. The most popular rates in the STS hierarchy are STS-3, STS-48, and STS-192, but other intermediate rates have been deployed in the wide area as well. Table 3.1 shows the popular SONET rates and overhead capacity consumed by the framing structure of the corresponding STS-n signal.

Although SONET and SDH are byte-synchronous optical transports, they allow for the multiplexing of plesiochronous[2] signals within the STS-n framing structure and the payload envelope. Through the use of simple pointers in the overhead of the frame, equipment can identify the current starting position of the multiplexed signals within the envelope. The line and section overheads in the STS-n structure consume 3.3% of the line bandwidth.

> STS-n frames are transmitted at a rate of 8 KHz, which has its origin in PCM digital voice transmission. An octet position in an STS-n frame repeats every 125 microseconds.

SONET is a layered architecture that defines three types of terminating equipment, each of which contributes information to the overhead of the STS frame structure. Figure 3.1 shows the SONET layers, whereas Figure 3.2 and Figure 3.3 show the construction of the STS-1 and STS-3 signals respec-

TABLE 3.1 Popular SONET OC-n Rates 1

OPTICAL CARRIER LEVEL	LINE RATE	SYNCHRONOUS PAYLOAD ENVELOPE RATE (MBPS)	LINE AND SECTION OVERHEAD (MBPS)
OC-1	51.84	50.112	1.728
OC-3	155.52	150.336	5.184
OC-12	622.08	601.344	20.736
OC-48	2488.32	2405.376	82.944
OC-192	9953.28	9621.504	331.776

2.   The Greek word *plesiochronous* means "close in timing," which really means that it is not synchronous, but is close enough to be placed in an SPE with the support of pointers to identify the beginning of the payload. The payload will graciously "slide" inside the STS envelope, even if both are generated at the same frame rate.

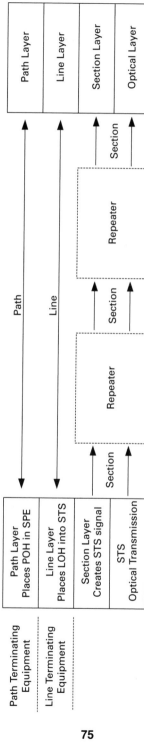

FIGURE 3.1 SONET layers.

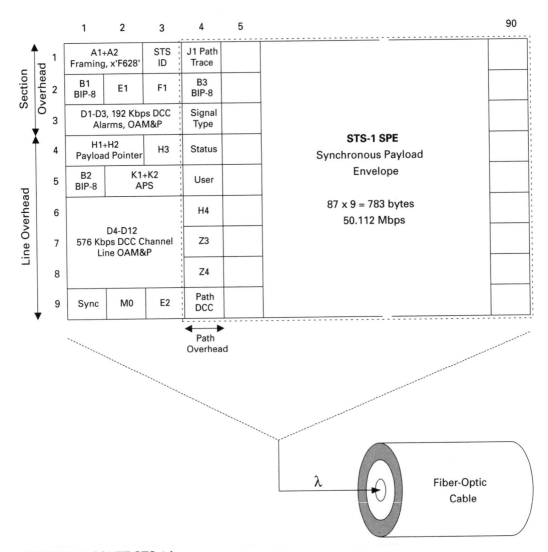

FIGURE 3.2 SONET STS-1 frame.

tively. Construction of a generalized STS-n frame scales along the format of the STS-3 frame.

The method of transporting lower rate signals within a higher rate STS-n is by *channelizing* the Synchronous Payload Envelope (SPE) and directing the multiplexing equipment to the correct starting location of each transported channel. This type of channelization is soft in that the position of the tributary signal within the SPE is not fixed and in fact it varies over time,

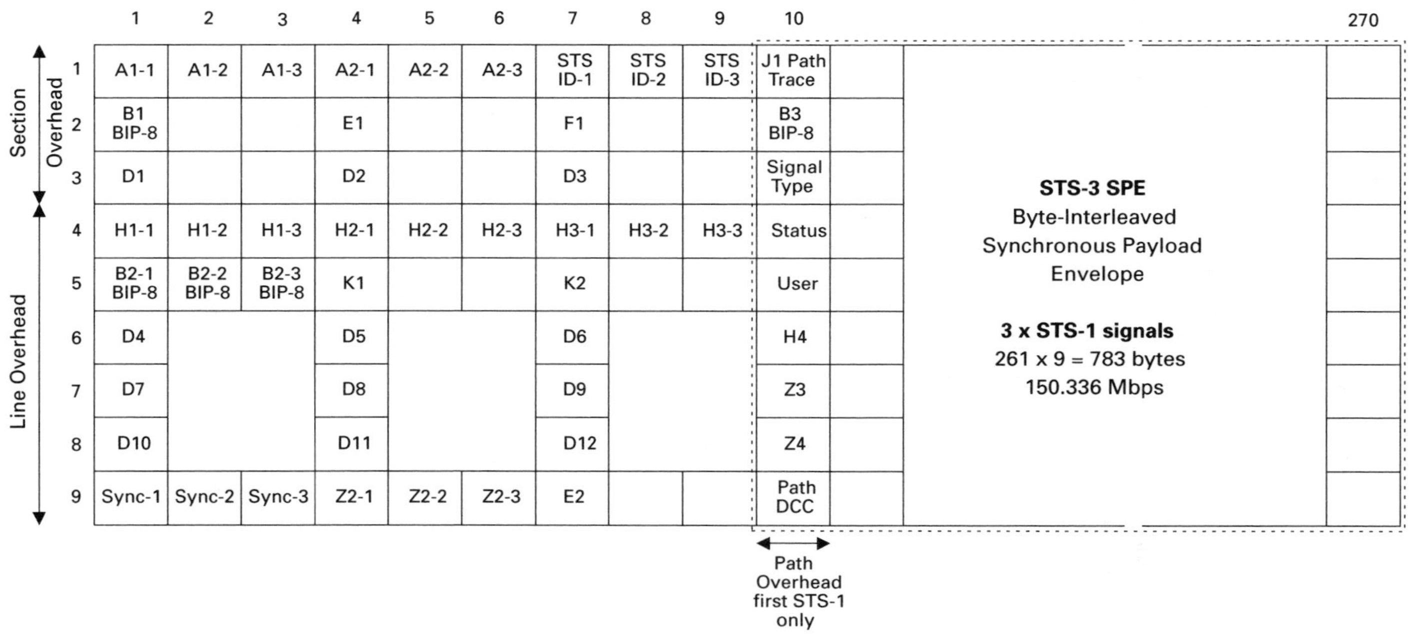

The table below represents the SONET STS-3 frame structure. The rows are numbered 1–9 on the left, and the columns are numbered 1–10 across the top (with column 270 at the far right marking the STS-3 SPE region).

	1	2	3	4	5	6	7	8	9	10		270
1	A1-1	A1-2	A1-3	A2-1	A2-2	A2-3	STS ID-1	STS ID-2	STS ID-3	J1 Path Trace		
2	B1 BIP-8	Sync-2		E1			F1			B3 BIP-8		
3	D1			D2			D3			Signal Type		
4	H1-1	H1-2	H1-3	H2-1	H2-2	H2-3	H3-1	H3-2	H3-3	Status		
5	B2-1 BIP-8	B2-2 BIP-8	B2-3 BIP-8	K1			K2			User		
6	D4			D5			D6			H4		
7	D7			D8			D9			Z3		
8	D10			D11			D12			Z4		
9	Sync-1	Sync-2	Sync-3	Z2-1	Z2-2	Z2-3	E2			Path DCC		

Section Overhead: rows 1–3, columns 1. **Line Overhead**: rows 4–9.

STS-3 SPE
Byte-Interleaved Synchronous Payload Envelope

3 x STS-1 signals
261 x 9 = 783 bytes
150.336 Mbps

↔ Path Overhead first STS-1 only

Legend:
1. A1-1 indicates the A1 byte from the first STS-1, A1-2, the first A1 byte from the second STS-1, etc.

2. Blank byte slots are N/A.

FIGURE 3.3 SONET STS-3 frame.

77

even if the SONET and tributary clock sources are fully synchronous. Lower rate signals are byte-interleaved within the frame for rates above STS-1, as shown in Figure 3.3. The demultiplexing equipment at intermediate and terminate ends can thus locate each of the embedded signals via the use of the frame payload pointers, in bytes H1 and H2. The operation of Add/Drop, then, is simply the mechanism of placing a tributary signal in the payload envelope of an STS-n signal using the means available in the frame header, and removing a transported signal at terminating equipment, thus creating a reusable "payload hole" in the envelope.

This would have been a good and perpetual solution; however, not all traffic is TDM in nature, and in fact we are moving slowly into a packet-only world for all applications. Packet payloads are self-identifying in nature, via delimiters present in the protocol encapsulation of the user data. In other words, if we look at the STS-3 frame and our objective is to pass packet data, it is not necessary (on the contrary, it is inefficient) to delimit STS-1 boundaries within the STS-3 frame, especially when there are no STS-1 signals being transported in the first place. SONET allows a slightly different frame composition at the STS-3 rate and above, known as *concatenated* STS signals, whereby four bytes in locations 4-2 (row 4, column 2), 4-3, 4-5, and 4-6 become concatenation indicators to the line terminating equipment (LTE). A concatenated STS-3 signal is thus indicated as STS-3c and carries a single SPE. ATM and IP over SONET can use such an STS-3c structure for packet flows directly, without the need for channelization.

3.1.1 Topologies

SONET and Dense Wavelength Division Multiplexing (DWDM) technologies are used to develop backbone networks in metropolitan, regional, national, and international domains. Backbone networks carry integrated traffic by default, as access circuits of all kinds—voice, data, video, voiceband—effectively merge in the backbone. SONET is avery robust transmission technology. All bits on the physical medium enjoy the same QoS with exceptional service reliability by the rules of design of optical networks. In fact, a significant portion of the effort in the deployment of optical networks centers in what we call RAS[3]—*Reliability, Availability, Survivability*. Backbone topologies need to be far more reliable than anything deployed at the access for the simple reason of taming the scale of the problem that could be caused by network outages.

---

3.   Not to be confused with the RAS protocol of the H.323 specification.

When optical transmission became possible over long hauls, it was observed that network element (NE) connectivity could be accomplished in a manner far more robust than previously accomplished with point-to-point T-carrier systems. The formidable *backhoe* and the legendary problems it has caused by severing transmission cables also had a lot to do with the pursuit of robust alternative transmission methods in the backbone. The idea of a network *ring* topology was born out of necessity, and it allowed a loop configuration of offices generating, relaying, or consuming traffic, which can belong either to the *service provider* or to the *customer*. This generic idea of ring connectivity is also found in enterprise networks using Fiber Distributed Data Interface (FDDI) LAN technology, but it is generally less reliable. The principles are similar; however, SONET takes it several steps further in creating robust and survivable paths and links between traffic endpoints.

The idea of a SONET ring is shown embedded in the core of the larger topology in Figure 3.4. Rings are normally deployed using either 2-fiber or 4-fiber links in the span between NEs. Rings can be *unidirectional* or *bidirectional*. Unidirectional rings carry traffic in one direction only. This means that two elements on the ring will experience asymmetric delays, since the **from** traffic does not flow on the same path as the **to** traffic.

The ring carrying traffic in the clockwise (CW) direction is referred to as the Working Ring (WR), and the ring carrying traffic in the opposite (counter-clockwise, or CCW) direction is the Protection Ring (PR). Unidirectional rings usually carry the *same traffic* in both directions. That is, each node places the signal on both rings (the direction is really logical and refers to the manner in which the NE transmit and receive ports are connected between adjacent nodes), and a node decides in real time which signal is best—subject to configuration restrictions.

> If the working ring fails, the nodes automatically switch to the PR and traffic can be restored within 50 milliseconds.

The main advantage of this feature is that voice and data session's stay up when a protection switch occurs, and video broadcast effects are not even perceived by the viewers in most cases. This is a good attribute, but for large geographic areas, the asymmetric delays that are introduced by the automatic protection switching can cause serious problems for applications running over time-sensitive protocols, like TCP.

Delays in 2-fiber unidirectional rings are asymmetric because the delay from site 1 to site 4 is the delay of one span, whereas the delay from site 4 to

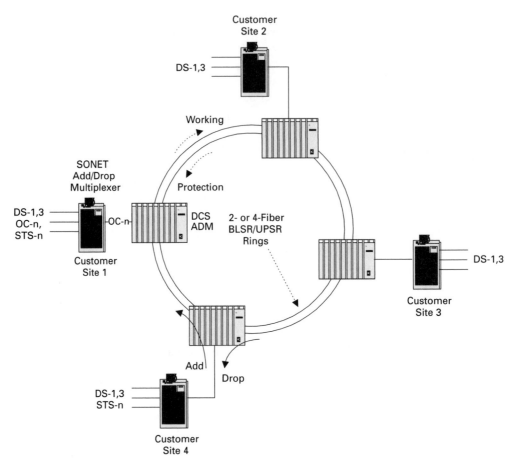

FIGURE 3.4 Basic SONET ring with add-drop multiplexers.

site 1 consists of three spans, as we move around the ring in the CW direction. Worse yet, if a protection switch takes effect, the delays reverse themselves exactly. If you are familiar with round trip time (RTT) calculations under RFC 1323 (wide pipes), you know this can be a headache of an issue.

Bidirectional rings solve the problem of asymmetric delays, but cause other management concerns. Those rings carry live traffic in both directions of the ring. This means that traffic between sites 1 and 4 flows in the CW direction, while traffic from site 4 to 1 goes the other way. Bidirectional rings, however, have provisioning considerations regarding protection switching in 2-fiber implementations. Since both sides carry live traffic, it is important to have sufficient bandwidth on the PR to effect a switch. Once a protection switch occurs, the live ring will carry all the traffic, thus reducing the asymmetric delay situation of the unidirectional ring. This can be remedied with 4-fiber implementations, whereby a protection switch preserves the bidirectional nature of the span and, the overall ring. Also, 4-fiber rings offer the most flexibility for diverse fiber routing, thus further minimizing the possibility of an accidental disruption of both the working and protection rings. However, 4-fiber rings are expensive and find most of their use in long-haul backbones.

The backbone network usually carries aggregations of T-carrier traffic, as shown in Figure 3.4, and this is the lowest visibility into the traffic streams achievable from the network perspective. DS-1 and DS-3 signals—the tributaries—are multiplexed into STS-n payload envelopes, with $1 \leq n \leq 192$ for the most part, and the resulting STS signals are placed on the ring at the origin of the aggregation, to be dropped off at an NE. NEs capable of *picking off* and *adding* payload from an STS signal are called Add/Drop Multiplexers (ADMs).

It is common practice to multiplex STS-n signals into higher speed STS-m signals, m > n, thus performing multiplexing at the STS rates.

The SONET physical layer is itself layered. The lowest layer is the *photonic layer*. The photonic layer is responsible for sending bits of the electrical frame in an optical manner; that is, it is responsible for modulation of the light wave in the fiber. Bits travel between NEs through optical repeaters when the distances between NEs require reconstruction and amplification of the optical signal.

The segment between an NE and an optical repeater, or between two optical repeaters is the *section* layer. The segment between STS-n multiplexers is the *line* layer, whereas the segment between endpoint payload multiplexers is the *path* layer. It is possible for a topology configuration to collapse the section, line, and path layers into one layer (e.g., for collocated NEs) but this is not very common, except in COs.

A special configuration of a multiple ring configuration is known as the *virtual ring* (VR) and is shown in Figure 3.5.

The basic idea of a VR is simple. A ring in a VR configuration can share a portion of another ring, using either nodes configured to operate in both rings or interconnected nodes carrying only the traffic common to both rings. Traffic from the core ring—meaning higher speed and capacity—can be transported in both rings. In essence, VRs are similar to interconnected rings, but with shared paths and without the need for matched nodes (MNs), as we will see in the next section.

In our references we will discuss interconnected rings and VRs with emphasis on requirements arising in the provisioning of circuits, fault management, and alarm surveillance.

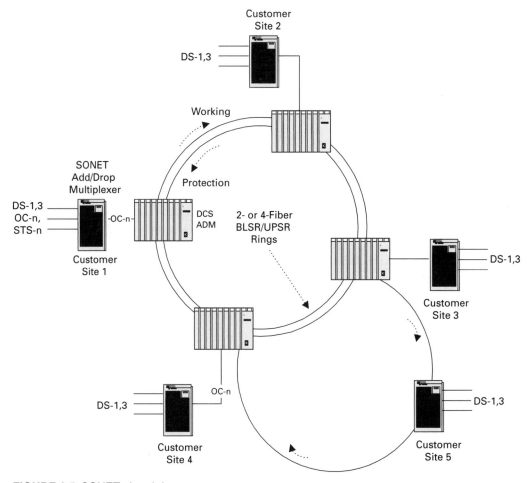

FIGURE 3.5 SONET virtual ring.

SONET rings implement either line or path switching. There are two major types of protection for rings.

1. Bidirectional Line Switched Rings (BLSR)
2. Unidirectional Path Switched Rings (UPSR)

The cases of BPSR and ULSR are less common. Any of the protection schemes can exist in 2-fiber or 4-fiber deployments.

Line switching flips the entire set of working channels to the protection fiber. Path switching is more selective and restores traffic as low as the tributary level, and in general, under the entire capacity of the channel. Path switching is gaining as the most accepted method for affording ring protection.

3.1.2 SONET Network Elements

The ADM is the fundamental generic NE of a SONET network. The main purpose of the ADM is to *groom* (pick off or split) SONET traffic and feed it to Terminal Multiplexers (TMs). ADMs on the backbone ring are Line Terminating Equipment (LTE).

The TM is also a SONET NE and is either a CPE device or an optical network endpoint in a CO. The TM connects to Remote Fiber Terminals (RFTs) and other Digital Loop Carrier DLC equipment. Most commonly, TMs aggregate T-carrier signals or subrate signals and place them in STS payload envelopes. TMs are STS Path Terminating Equipment (STS PTE).

A DLC is part of the subrate (T-carrier or below) distribution network, which forms the first point of payload aggregation in the Carrier Service Area (CSA). We will see all these devices connected in a reference configuration in the next section. Subrate multiplexing at the Nx64 level—up to DS1—inside a SONET SPE is via Virtual Tributary (VT) channels. DLCs are typically VT Path Terminating Equipment (PTE).

A Digital Cross-Connect (DCS for short) is a large ADM that can perform the add/drop functions usually down to the VT level. DCSs are LTEs on the core ring, but they can also be PTEs for some of the traffic.

These devices can all exist in a fully compatible manner on the same ring. Rings can also be interconnected via MNs. MNs are most commonly found paired in COs, connecting rings usually of different speeds.

A special case of a SONET NE is the *Drop and Continue* element (also called *Drop and Repeat*). The purpose of this NE is to pick off payload, duplicate it, and send it along two paths—the original plus a feed closer to the CSA distribution network. These types of nodes are commonly used for video broadcast distribution.

In the special case of Virtual Rings, NEs configured to operate in both rings operate either as LTEs or STS PTEs. It is the former if only ADM functionality is provided by the NEs, whereas as STS PTEs terminate the path layer as well, acting more like TMs.

STS signals carrying all types of traffic can exist on a ring topology in any portion of the backbone network. In other words, the payload type in an STS signal is of no significance from a provisioning perspective on a ring. Therefore, an STS-1 signal carrying broadcast-quality video can be configured on the same ring as signals carrying DS1 VTs, which themselves may be carrying simple PCM-based voice telephony or a PRI trunk from a PBX.

3.1.3 Common Ring Configurations: Short-to-Medium Haul

Figure 3.6 shows a typical configuration of a transport network from the distribution in the CSA through the feeder portion and into the backbone. The backbone ring in the center of the drawing is shown as a 2-fiber BLSR or UPSR (the reference is invariant to the protection mechanism implementation). Diverse fiber routing is assumed, although this is a deployment issue and not relevant to network and fault management, alarm surveillance, and circuit provisioning.

Some key observations in this drawing are the point-to-point connection between the ADM of the feeder network (top left) and the method of establishing connectivity between the backbone and secondary rings. First, the DCS equipment shown connecting the two rings may or may not connect through MNs. Second, the secondary ring in the feeder network (on the right) may not necessarily be of the same construction and protection type as the core ring. For example, a core BLSR can feed into a UPSR ring used for video broadcasting.

Legacy networks employ Fiber Optic Transmission Systems (FOTS), which use proprietary framing schemes to transport primarily DS-3 signals over fiber. DS-3 deployment is mainly optical, even though a standard of optical signal transport was never published. Therefore, there is a portion of the distribution network connected to the feeder with FOTS equipment, which requires equipment of the same type at the CO for extraction and creation of the DS-3 signal in electrical format. It can then be placed in an STS envelope for transport across the backbone.

Figure 3.7 is similar, but shows connections to an IXC or other entity, not part of the U.S. West network. This creates the mid-span meet situation, whereby equipment from different vendors is supposed to interoperate. In other words, if there are mid-span idiosyncrasies based on the interpretation of unused or undefined control fields in the SONET envelope, they will be treated and settled at the time of span installation and will not appear as an issue in the network management process.

It also assumed the mid-span meet is a point-to-point connection, whether it uses protection switching or not.

The reference drawing also shows interconnected rings via MNs. An industry view of how this is accomplished is shown in Figure 3.8.

Figure 3.9 shows the construction of a VR, which we briefly discussed in the previous section. The key consideration is provisioning traffic for two sites of customer A, which travels on Rings A and B. When VRs are provisioned and deployed, a core ring is designated.

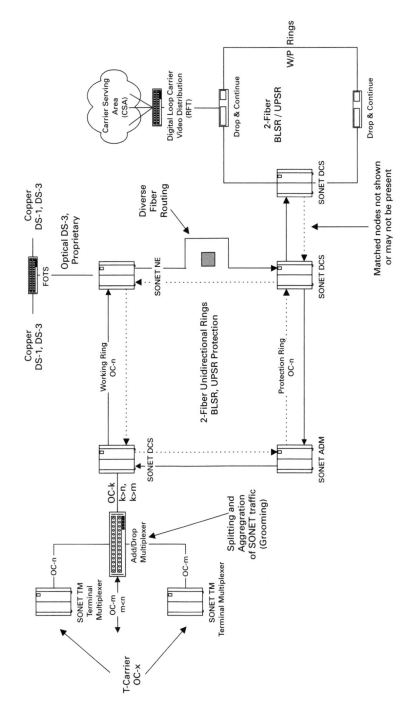

FIGURE 3.6 A transport network from the distribution in the carrier service area.

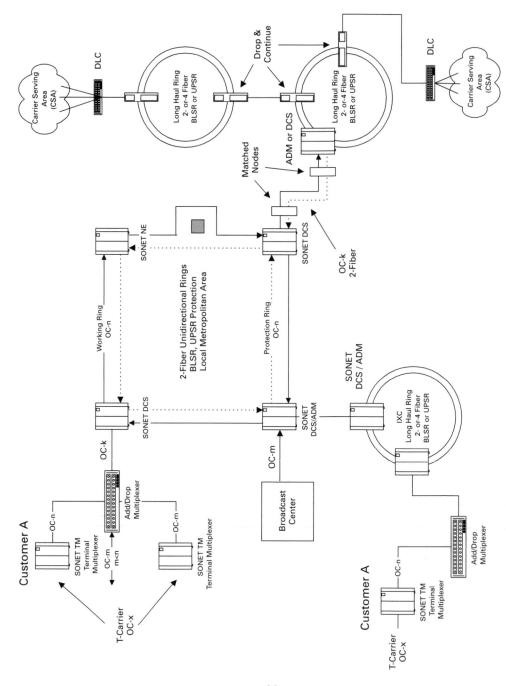

FIGURE 3.7 Core SONET network with connections to an IXC.

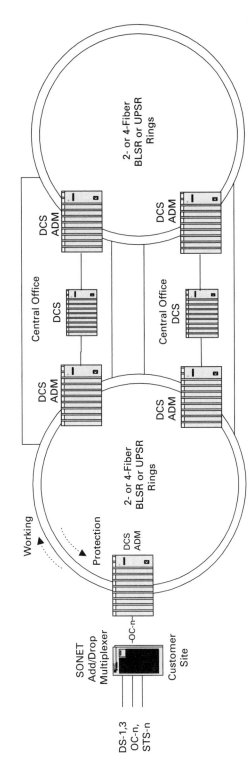

FIGURE 3.8 Interconnected rings via matched nodes.

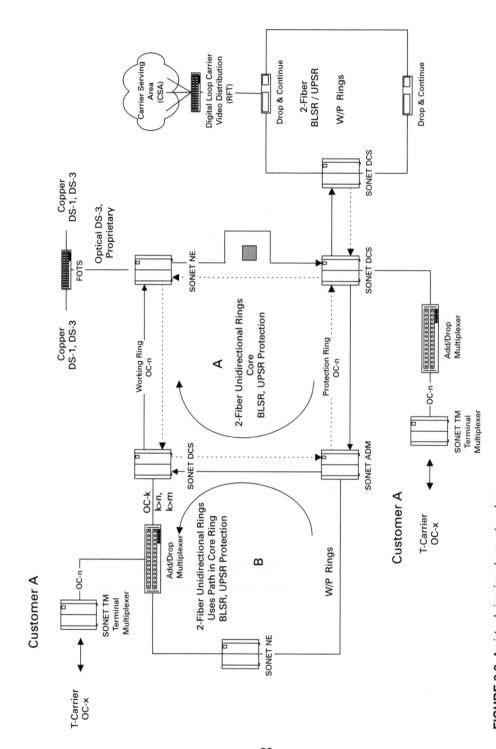

FIGURE 3.9 A virtual ring in a larger topology.

3.1.4 SONET Service Assurance

SONET Service Assurance is provided through instantaneous switching at the line or path layer, depending on the provisioning of the Ring that experienced the fault. For purposes of circuit provisioning, the WR and PR are identical.

In 2-fiber implementations, when service is restored on the WR, all newly provisioned circuits on the PR are switched onto the WR. The presence of protection switching on a span of a VR not common to both rings does not affect the operation of the ring not experiencing the protection switching. The presence of faults in point-to-point links of interconnected rings does not affect the operation of either ring.

3.1.5 WDM, DWDM, and Lambda Switching

SONET certainly met the objectives of physical layer compatibility at boundary points and high bandwidth transmission in the backbone with very high reliability and survivability. However, as more and more demand for bandwidth grew, SONET started to face the "fiber exhaustion" problem, also known as hitting the "bit rate scalability wall." In other words, within 20 years of the creation of commercially viable fiber-optic transmission, the basic premise of getting higher and higher bit rates from a single optical channel did not stand the test of time. The pursuit of higher bit rates via multiplexing of multiple wavelengths on the same fiber resulted first Wavelength Division Multiplexing, (WDM) and then in DWDM. The basic principle of optical multiplexing is shown in Figure 3.10.

Starting from basic multiplexing of 2 wavelengths and moving upwards to more than 100 wavelengths in the same medium, each of which can carry line rates of up to 10 Gbps or even more, it is easy to see why this new technology has breathed new life into fiber-optic transmission. It is desirable to use the existing fiber plant and upgrade it to achieve higher capacity, and whenever possible, this is the avenue pursued by administrators of existing installations.

WDM is really Frequency Division Multiplexing (FDM). There is an association of the wavelength of light with its frequency in the well known formula $c = \lambda f$, where c is the speed of light. Therefore, for every λ multiplexed in a channel, there is a corresponding frequency f that is being multiplexed. The optical signals being multiplexed do not even have to be of the same line rate or format. In the example shown in Figure 3.10, for $n_1 = m_1 = 48$ and $k_1 = 192$, the resulting bit rate of the multiplexed signal in the fiber is 14,929.92 Mbps. It is easy to see the way the numbers scale with increasing signal multiplex density. And since there is no restriction on the type of traffic that traverses the fiber on each multiplexed signal, it is immediately apparent why this technology is so desirable in constructing the backbone network.

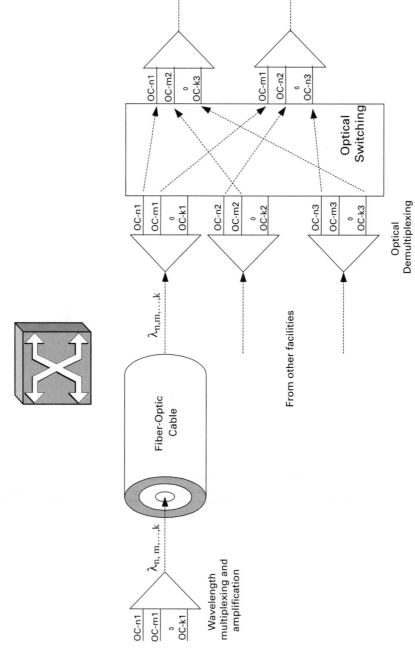

FIGURE 3.10 Optical multiplexing.

90

The benefits are obvious with higher multiplexing capacities, but DWDM has a greater appeal than mere capacity enhancement. In SONET, as in early WDM systems, the digital cross-connect of channels in the DCSs, required transforming the optical signal on the ring to electrical form, repackaging the payloads, and then inserting the new package in another optical channel for propagation around the ring. This *OEO* transformation, as it is known, is costly in many ways, and it slows the add, drop and continue operations by performing unnecessary intermediate operations at the physical layer. The more desirable solution is to stay at the optical level as we traverse each DCS and not convert to an electrical representation until it is absolutely necessary, and as close as possible to the ultimate destination of the payload. The way to accomplish this is via switching the λs in each fiber, thus converting the DCS systems into λ routers (or switches, depending on your point of view). This method is also shown in Figure 3.10. The positive effects and potential applications of λ switching are enormous, and we will revisit this topic later in the text in the specific context of QoS in the backbone.

DWDM, λ switching, and SONET are not exactly compatible technologies with the current state of the art in networking equipment. Carriers still implement SONET and DWDM solutions, while λ switching is expected to start making its impact over the next couple of years. A lot of questions around λ switching still need to be addressed before it becomes ubiquitous in the backbone, especially in the area of robustness, survivability, and interoperability with the existing optical transmission systems. SONET and DWDM optical technologies still have the upper hand in the construction of the core network, and administrators have acquired extensive management, configuration, and maintenance experience in these technologies.

3.1.6 Early Performance Considerations

The overhead of an STS-n signal, not including the Path Overhead (POH) content, is 3.3% regardless of the line rate. POH occupies one column of the STS-n frame regardless of n, which means its impact to the overall overhead is diminishing as the rates get higher. The question becomes, then, how much more overhead is associated with user information before we get to meet the first customer data bit? In the TDM world, transmission overhead is associated primarily with framing and maintenance channels for alarms and statistics exchange between equipment. In the packet world, overhead increases with the number of protocols in which the customer information is wrapped before it is sent on its way. We will expand on the topic of trading the "rigidity" and "unfriendliness" of TDM with the flexibility and voracious appetite for bandwidth of packet-based service multiplexing later in the text.

References

1. *SONET, A Guide to Synchronous Optical Networks*, Walter J. Goralski, McGraw Hill.
2. GR-253, Bellcore (Telcordia)
3. *Fiber Optics, Theory and Applications*, Chai Yeh, Academic Press.

4

The Pursuit of QoS in Packet Networks

4.1 FROM BEST EFFORT SERVICE TO PREDICTABLE PERFORMANCE

We have known from the beginning of packet-based telephony that to get the same performance from statistically multiplexed, packetized streams as TDM data, we would be facing a daunting task. IP networks have been around for a long time (e.g., the Internet), but they have been built to carry data in a "best effort" manner, using a suite of protocols that can either guarantee delivery (TCP) or operate in "black hole," datagram mode (UDP). Even if delivery is guaranteed, timeliness of delivery is rarely an issue with plain old data applications (e.g., FTP). Tardy data transport may affect congestion window sizes in TCP, but the data will get to the other end, one way or the other. VoIP, on the other hand, is a lot less tolerant to delay and delay variation (jitter). Packets carrying digitized voice samples must get to their destination with strict timing constraints, or they are as good as lost if they arrive outside a tolerance window. Lost or very late voice packets cannot be retransmitted, and the impact of lost packets on voice quality can be perceived by the talking parties and become annoying. Furthermore, delay variation is a packet flow parameter that must be minimized because it affects interactive applications through increased delay due to buffering at de-jitter points in the network (points where asynchronous packet streams meet synchronous TDM hops, as in the case of a PSTN gateway, looking towards the PSTN). In other words, the behavior of packet flows with respect to strict timing constraints is a key requirement for support of voice and video applications over packet networks.

The nature of standard Layer 3 packet switching presents an issue in meeting performance objectives on the timeliness front. If all packetized data that converges on a network routing element is supposed to receive equal treatment, such as forwarding based only on a lookup of the IP Destination Address, it is almost impossible to predict the behavior of any stream in terms of individual packet latency and delay variation. It is also just as difficult to predict packet loss in cases of network congestion, or even to predict when and where congestion will occur. In other words, IP data routers, which utilize standard Layer 3 packet forwarding techniques, are not entirely adequate to support time-sensitive flows constrained by low loss, jitter, and latency requirements mandated by the application.

The only way we can minimize packet delay and instill interarrival predictability into a packet flow is by minimizing the random attributes of the flow through network nodes. And the only way to remove randomness is to forward every packet that belongs to a constrained stream in a predictable and *load-invariant* manner. This simple observation leads to some early conclusions.

1. For time-critical applications, packet forwarding cannot be based only on IP address lookup in the routing table if the network is supposed to scale. This is also true for virtual routing tables used in constructing VPNs.
2. Packet forwarding in each network node must become context-aware and knowledgeable of the QoS constraints on a per-individual stream or aggregate stream basis.
3. Packet flows must become path-oriented if we must control the behavior of each end-to-end flow.

Path-oriented IP[1] has been studied extensively for the last few years with the objective to develop equipment that can distinguish packet flows with special treatment requirements from packets that are not associated with a service constraint. There are two primary approaches to creating a path-oriented packet flow:

1. Implicit path creation—that is, inclusion of sufficient information in the packet header to "force" routing of qualified packets over physical interfaces meeting QoS criteria for the particular flow, and treatment of packets according to specified rules for queuing, forwarding, and discard probability. Routers run interior route discovery protocols (IGPs), which can be rudimentary (e.g., request in progress, or RIP) or more

---

1.   Path-oriented IP is not a standard term, but I use it here to distinguish basic Layer 3 packet switching from packet forwarding over predetermined end-to-end paths.

sophisticated to include link "costs" in the advertisement of paths to their neighbors (e.g., OSPF, ATM P-NNI). Border routers connecting adjacent autonomous systems (AS) may advertise aggregate paths into their domains, but for purposes of routing a packet to an adjacent AS, the idea is the same as in the IGP case. This routing information is used by all the nodes in a topology to develop a "tree" view of the meshed physical connectivity. Packets can then be routed using "least cost" algorithms, which set the routes dynamically in the routing table, or they can be explicitly source-routed if the network operator feels comfortable circumventing the automated process and is aware of the properties of the chosen physical end-to-end path.

2. Explicit virtual path creation, whereby sufficient information is placed in a header (a new packet header or an interpretation of the standard header, depending on the type of packet technology) to switch the packets to a predetermined outbound interface, with queuing and forwarding meets the required QoS for the flow. This approach is quicker than Layer 3 packet switching, because routing tables need not be consulted to send a packet on its way. Once such a path has been created for a flow, the process of packet forwarding becomes in effect equivalent to Layer 2 switching.

The first approach to meeting QoS requirements for a flow is best served with DiffServ architecture, described in IETF RFC 2475. This is a highly scalable approach for establishing *per-hop behavior* (PHB) for individual packet flows and packet flow aggregates, without the explicit creation of logical end-to-end paths for the flows. PHB is simply the way packets of a classification will be queued, forwarded, and considered for discard, with respect to all streams routed through the node. The actual queuing scheme employed by a node for each of the packet classifications is not specified in the architecture and depends on the implementation.

The second approach led to the development of MPLS, an evolution of Cisco's "Tag" switching. MPLS is not a new idea per se, as frame relay and ATM in effect use a "label"—the Data Link Connection Identifier (DLCI) and VPI/VCI (Virtual Path Identifier/Virtual Circuit Identifier) header fields, respectively—to switch packet streams with minimum overhead, but those fields take on a special meaning if interpreted in the context of an MPLS switching environment, which may include both switches and routers in the end-to-end path from source to destination.

Of course, once a label-switching approach has been chosen as the most desirable to deliver predictable QoS, nothing prevents the network operator from adding DiffServ constraints upon the virtual MPLS paths, on a per-path and (individual or aggregate) flow basis, provided both techniques are supported by the equipment. In fact, this is what may happen in many cases to improve our visibility into a packet stream's behavior during node traversal. The creation of QoS-constrained MPLS paths is far from trivial, as we will see shortly.

Equipment that supports DiffServ and MPLS switching has been available in the market, but network engineering of large distributed topologies using these two techniques is still on the learning curve. We will first take a quick look at DiffServ and MPLS, and then at a combination of both approaches in the reference topologies of the previous chapter. In the call flows of the second part of this text, we will place the MPLS and DiffServ methods in context as we create paths for routing voice calls and try to place a call across autonomous systems.

4.1.1 An Overview of Differentiated Services

The DiffServ architecture specifies the TOS bits in the standard IP packet header to define classes of "service," that is, the method by which packets of a classification will be *queued, forwarded,* and/or considered for *discard* during congestion, when they reach a DiffServ node. The TOS field has been renamed *Differentiated Services Code Point* (DSCP) and uses only the six most significant bits (MSBs) of the TOS. The two least significant bits (LSBs) are currently unused. The evolution of the IP packet header for DiffServ is shown in Figure 4.1 and a decoded IP header is shown in Figure 4.2.

Packet flows receive queuing and forwarding treatment according to the setting of the DSCP code in one direction only, and if symmetric behavior is desired, flow classifications must be set up *explicitly* and *separately* in each direction.

Expedited Forwarding
Expedited Forwarding (EF, RFC 2598) is the highest priority class, and packets with DSCP=EF proceed to an output queue of higher priority than all other output queues in the node; however, EF support is not mandatory for DiffServ compliance.

EF flow classification can be used to ensure the minimum possible jitter and latency through nodes configured for EF support, but use of the EF class must be done with caution. When implementing EF, the network operator must carefully police the flows and must also be careful not to aggregate too many flows with EF classification into each node. The latter would nullify the impact of expedited forwarding and reduce the output operation to simple first in, first out (FIFO) and possibly even stagnate flows from the AF classes.

Occasionally, flows need to be tunneled through transit domains, which may or may not be Differentiated Services (DS) compliant. If the transit domain does not support DiffServ, there can be no guarantees regarding classes of service, unless the domain supports some other method of flow

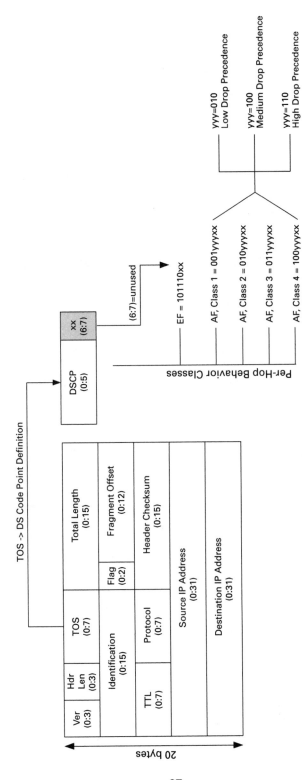

FIGURE 4.1 DSCP definition.

classification, such as MPLS. If the transit network supports DiffServ, then the following rule ensures uniformity in treatment for the EF flows:

> When EF-classified packets must be tunneled through a transit DS network, the tunneling flows must also be assigned to the EF class.

From the attributes of the EF class of service, it would be tempting to assign all VoIP bearer channels to the this class, but such a decision is not simple and depends on a lot of other factors, such as size and scalability of the network topology, the QoS capabilities of adjacent and transit domains, and other considerations.

Assured Forwarding

Assured Forwarding (AF, RFC 2597) defines a higher resolution of service classification and drop precedence. There are four classes with three prioritizations within each class, which dynamically share the resources—bandwidth—of the node. All AF classifications receive lower priority forwarding treatment than the EF class. AF=1 with yyy=010 is the highest priority and lowest drop precedence class, as shown in Figure 4.1.

Tunneling is also a possibility in reasonable scale networks, and the following rule ensures predictability of behavior across and through different networks:

> When AF-classified packets must be tunneled through a transit DS network, the tunneling flow must be assigned to at least the same AF class as the tunneled packets.

Various queuing schemes can be implemented in a DS node to support AF and EF, but a key question in the implementation is which packet and from which class to drop first when congestion is detected. EF is virtually assured to avoid packet discard, unless the congestion is so severe and there are so many flows assigned to the EF class that there is no other option. The statistical behavior of a node during congestion will be measured over a time interval, which needs to be large enough to obtain a meaningful sample of the PHB of the various flows. The idea of the tiered classification in AF is to assign a forwarding probability to each packet as it enters its output queue, which decreases with decreasing priority classification.

```
------------ ETHER Header ------------
ETHER: Destination: 00-02-16-C2-E9-50
ETHER: Source: 00-30-94-92-5E-F2
ETHER: Protocol: IP
ETHER: FCS: 370905CD

------------ IP Header ------------
IP: Version = 4
IP: Header length = 20
IP: Differentiated Services (DS) Field = 0x88
IP: 1000 10.. DS Codepoint = Assured Forwarding - Class 4 - Low Drop Prec
IP: .... ..00 Unused
IP: Packet length = 200
IP: Id = e48
IP: Fragmentation Info = 0x0000
IP: .0.. .... .... .... Don't Fragment Bit = FALSE
IP: ..0. .... .... .... More Fragments Bit = FALSE
IP: ...0 0000 0000 0000 Fragment offset = 0
IP: Time to live = 253
IP: Protocol = UDP (17)
IP: Header Checksum = 6586
IP: Source address = 192.168.255.6
IP: Destination address = 192.168.200.254

------------ UDP Header ------------
UDP: Source port = 17800
UDP: Destination port = 200
UDP: Length = 3656
UDP: Checksum = 0
UDP: 192 bytes of data


00 02 16 c2 e9 50 00 30  94 92 5e f2 08 00 45 88    .....P.0 ..^...E.
00 c8 0e 48 00 00 fd 11  65 86 c0 a8 ff 06 c0 a8    ...H.... e.......
c8 fe 43 e6 48 6a 00 b4  00 00 80 00 1d 51 7c fc    ..C.Hj.. .....Q|.
27 a5 06 95 ff 06 71 78  f7 ee f6 76 59 f9 e8 78    '.....qx ...vY..x
f1 e6 6d 5d 6f 6c 5f e9  e7 fd e5 f5 ee 64 f4 db    ..m]ol_. .....d..
ec 79 e7 ea 70 ff 68 71  e7 fa f9 5f 73 ed 6f 7e    .y..p.hq ..._s.o~
6e 65 6e ff 67 74 fa 7d  f7 e0 e9 eb 7c 79 76 77    nen.gt.} ....|yvw
f5 73 f5 f0 72 f7 f1 f9  f1 7e 72 72 74 77 73 6f    .s..r... ~rrtwso
f5 f3 6e 60 f9 f0 65 e8  e8 6c fa ef 7b 6a 6d 76    ..n`..e. .l..{jmv
e8 7c 66 f7 6a 66 df de  72 66 f8 e1 fa df 69 6d    .|f.jf.. rf....im
df f8 ed eb 7b 76 fb 6f  65 6e 7e 67 6b 6d 64 6c    ....{v.o en~gkmdl
de 79 79 f1 6a ed f5 f5  f9 ea f0 ec de ef f2 6c    .yy.j... ........l
73 df f5 fc ee ef 6a 77  f4 67 ff 77 67 59 5d 71    s.....jw .g.wgY]q
5e 70 7b 7d de fd 37 09  05 cd                      ^p{}..7. ..
```

FIGURE 4.2 Ethernet IP packet with TOS (decoded by Agilent Advisor).

Figure 4.3 shows an example merging of eight DS flows into an output link. If EF traffic is not properly shaped and policed, and the EF queue is always serviced when there is at least one entry in it, there is a danger of stagnating service to the AF queues for extended burst periods. The result would be wide variations in delay and jitter for the AF classes, which would defeat the purpose of supporting multiclass service through the node. Proper design techniques, with policing at the ingress and shaping at the egress of each network node, would guarantee the worst-case performance parameters of the EF flows, without denying service to the AF queues. It is thus important to set

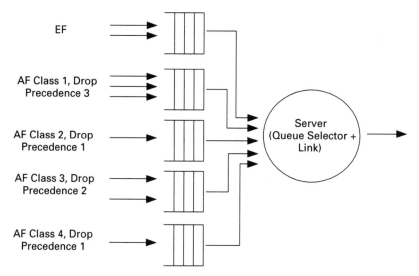

EF

AF Class 1, Drop
Precedence 3

AF Class 2, Drop
Precedence 1

AF Class 3, Drop
Precedence 2

AF Class 4, Drop
Precedence 1

Server
(Queue Selector +
Link)

FIGURE 4.3 DiffServ EF and AF queueing.

the range of parameter tolerances to realize the performance characteristics of lower priority queues when multiservice flows converge in the network.

DiffServ networks can recover from link and node failures quickly because no explicit path setup is necessary when traffic is rerouted due to recalculation of the tree view of a traffic source to its reachable destinations. In other words, the danger of "oscillation" of the logical connectivity between a source and a sink of a flow is neither diminished nor augmented as a result of using DiffServ flow classification.

4.1.2 An Overview of MPLS

ATM and frame relay are two technologies that switch packets based on Layer 2 information. ATM switches cells based on a lookup of the VPI/VCI field, and frame relay uses the DLCI field of the packet to switch frames. IP, on the other hand, is by definition a routed network layer (Layer 3) protocol, and if QoS requirements are to be imposed on a topology, a faster method of packet forwarding is required. QoS in this context refers primarily to controlling packet flow parameters, such as delay, jitter, and discard probability. There are also derivative parameters, such as nondisruptive flow rerouting in the presence of network malfunctions, which we will examine in context. MPLS is the method that accomplishes this task via explicit controlled path creation between a source and a destination of a packet flow, and its idea is relatively simple, although network engineering of MPLS networks is not a simple matter.

For Ethernet networks, MPLS defines a new label for IP datagrams, to be inserted between the Ethernet frame header (6 bytes of destination address + 6 bytes of source address + 2 bytes of protocol type) and the IP datagram. This is shown in Figure 4.4 and a decoded packet is shown in Figure 4.5. Note that the IP protocol value of 0x800 cannot be used for MPLS packets over Ethernet.

> Ethernet defines two new protocol types for transporting MPLS packets. The value of *0x8847* is reserved for MPLS Unicast, and *0x8848* is reserved for MPLS Multicast.

We will concentrate on MPLS Unicast mode in this overview.

The label is a 32-bit quantity, of which the 20 MSBs comprise the actual label and the least significant 8 bits are the time to live (TTL) field. Since IP itself is not visible through MPLS topologies until it reaches the egress MPLS node, a special consideration for the TTL value was necessary to ensure that loops are caught when they are not detected by other means and that packets do not "live" forever. There are also three experimental (EXP) bits and one stops bit on the MPLS label. There is a suggested use of the EXP bits for DiffServ-aware MPLS implementations. The S bit signifies the last label when set to 1. It is useful when label "stacking" is in effect, as we will see shortly.

MPLS Nomenclature

It is helpful to familiarize yourself with some important MPLS terminology, listed in Table 4.1, so that subsequent discussions on its operations in the call signaling and bearer transport context are easier to follow.

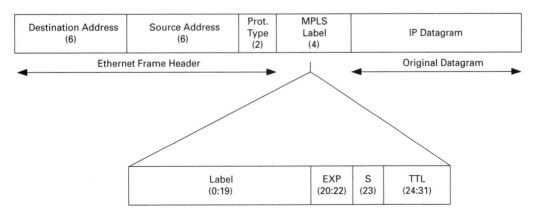

FIGURE 4.4 Ethernet IP frame with MPLS label.

TABLE 4.1 Key MPLS Terminology

TERM	DEFINITION
abstract node	A group of nodes whose internal topology—number of nodes and connectivity among them—is not visible to the ingress node of the LSP. An abstract node is referred to as *simple* if it contains only one physical node.
adjacency	Two label switching routers (LSRs) that run a label distribution protocol to exchange label information between them are label distribution peers, and are referred to as adjacent.
DLCI	Data Link Connection Identifier, used in frame relay networks to identify frame relay circuits. In an MPLS topology, it can be interpreted as an MPLS label.
Forwarding Equivalence Class (FEC)	A flow whose packets are forwarded in the same manner— for example, with the same queuing mechanism and ranges of delay and jitter required for the QoS assigned to the flow.
frame merge	Label merging for frame-based flows, such as frame relay.
label	A short fixed-length field used to identify a FEC whose value is of local significance, but whose QoS meaning is global from the network operator's perspective.
label merge	The replacement of multiple incoming labels for a particular FEC with a single outgoing label.
label swap	Incoming label replacement with a new outgoing label with the same QoS meaning for the downstream MPLS node.
Label Switched Path (LSP)	The path through one or more Label Switched Routers (LSRs) at one level of the hierarchy followed by a packets in a particular FEC.
Link State Advertisement (LSA)	Each router in a topology is responsible for describing its view of its local routing topology. Descriptions are sent in LSAs. These LSAs are distributed to all the routers in the topology. The collection of the LSAs generated by all the routers is known as a Link State Database.
explicitly routed LSP	An LSP established by a means other than normal IP routing.
Label Switching Router	A router capable of MPLS packet forwarding.
loop detection	A method of detecting when packets have traversed a node more than once.

TABLE 4.1 Key MPLS Terminology (continued)

TERM	DEFINITION
loop prevention	A method of preventing routing loops. In some implementations loops are allowed to be created (there may be no other choice due to lack of information at path creation time) and be detected and eliminated later.
MPLS domain	A contiguous set of MPLS nodes within an AS, or through contiguous MPLS AS that have established continuous and uninterrupted MPLS LSPs between them.
MPLS edge node (or router)	An MPLS node that connects an MPLS domain with a node that is outside the domain.
MPLS egress node	The last MPLS node in an LSP, which delivers the original IP packet to its neighbor.
MPLS ingress node	The first MPLS node in an LSP, which receives the original IP packet and inserts an MPLS label.
MPLS node	A node running MPLS. An MPLS node may also act as a Layer 3 router for non-MPLS flows.
traffic trunk	A set of flows aggregated by their FEC type and then placed on an LSP or set of LSPs called a traffic-engineered tunnel.
VC merge	Label merging where the MPLS label is carried in the ATM VCI field (or combined VPI/VCI field) so as to allow multiple VCs to merge into a single VC.
VP merge	Label merging where the MPLS label is carried in the ATM VPI field. This allows multiple VPs to be merged into a single VP. In this case, two cells would have the same VCI value only if they originated from the same node. Cells from different sources are distinguished via the VCI.

Label-Switching Operation

MPLS defines FECs for flows through transit nodes. A FEC is a classification of treatment by the transit node, with respect to QoS parameters such as queuing, scheduling, ranges on delay, and delay variation and discard probability in cases of node congestion.

The binding of a packet flow to an LSP of a FEC is done at the ingress to the MPLS network by assignment of a label whose QoS meaning has global, end-to-end significance for the network operator, although the value itself has local significance between adjacent MPLS nodes. Labels have to be requested and assigned to a flow. The assignment process is called *binding* of the stream to the LSP associated with the label.

A network operator needs to decide whether LSPs will be created automatically, based on information supplied by the IGP (e.g., OSPF), or explicit path creation will be forced regardless of "least cost" paths that may have been calculated by the network nodes. The explicit path creation is a little dangerous because it cannot dynamically bypass node and link failures. The automatic LSP creation is of more interest in the context of this overview.

Before we examine label requests and assignments, let's look at the operations involved in an LSP to process incoming packets when a packet arrives at the ingress LSR. See Figure 4.5.

Figure 4.6 shows how a physical connectivity of the topology is translated into a set of nodes with primary and alternate routes to reach their neighbors. Here, primary means of "lesser cost" than all the "alternate" routes. This cost usually refers to the loading of the link and the downstream neighbor's ability to process incoming packet flows, among other parameters. Costs are unidirectional: The cost from Node B to Node C along the primary route is not necessarily the same in the reverse direction.

Cost adjustments inside the abstract node (G) are insignificant as long as the aggregate LSA advertised by G does not change. Domain G's internals are not visible to our example domain, but its neighbors have received the advertised cost of traversing the domain, for example, along the primary route from C to G.

When all the costs of all the nodes of the topology are gathered by a node via LSAs from its neighbors, a logical least cost path is calculated for each of the reachable nodes in its topology. We will assume LSPs between a source and sink of a flow will be built along the least cost path between the ingress and egress LSR. As the dynamics of the network change, costs along routes may change as well, which can force a new calculation of the least cost path between ingress and egress. LSPs may then be either left alone, if QoS parameters can still be met in the new reality, or automatically rerouted.

Figure 4.7 shows flow TF_n generated by Node N and terminated at Node M. Ingress Edge LSR A receives an unlabeled IP flow and places Label **a** on each incoming packet. It also sets the label **a** S bit to 1 to signify the bottom of the label stack. The ingress LSR may or may not know whether there will be tunneling involved along the LSP. The QoS context for this flow has been preestablished when the label negotiation and assignment took place. Following the label insertion, the packet is appropriately queued and scheduled for transmission.

When a labeled packet now reaches LSR B, the process at B involves looking up the context of incoming label **a** and swapping the label with a new label **b**. The new label context **b** specifies the flow treatment, and the packet is queued and scheduled for transmission.

```
------------ ETHER Header ------------
ETHER: Destination: 00-30-94-92-5E-F2
ETHER: Source: 00-02-16-C2-E9-50
ETHER: Protocol: MPLS_UCAST
ETHER: FCS: E1C90068

------------ MPLS Header ------------
MPLS: Label Stack Entry[1] = 0x006601FE
MPLS: 0000 0000 0110 0110 0000 .... .... .... Label = 1632
MPLS: .... .... .... .... .... 000. .... .... Experimental Use = 0
MPLS: .... .... .... .... .... ...1 .... .... Bottom Of Stack (S Bit) = TRUE
MPLS: .... .... .... .... .... .... 1111 1110 Time To Live = 254

------------ IP Header ------------
IP: Version = 4
IP: Header length = 20
IP: Differentiated Services (DS) Field = 0x00
IP: 0000 00.. DS Codepoint = Default PHB (0)
IP: .... ..00 Unused
IP: Packet length = 200 (4 bytes missing)
IP: Id = 9c6a
IP: Fragmentation Info = 0x0000
IP: .0.. .... .... .... Don't Fragment Bit = FALSE
IP: ..0. .... .... .... More Fragments Bit = FALSE
IP: ...0 0000 0000 0000 Fragment offset = 0
IP: Time to live = 254
IP: Protocol = UDP (17)
IP: Header checksum = D663
IP: Source address = 192.168.200.254
IP: Destination address = 192.168.255.6

------------ UDP Header ------------
UDP: Source port = 18538
UDP: Destination port = 17382
UDP: Length = 180
UDP: Checksum = 0
UDP: 168 bytes of data
```

FIGURE 4.5 Ethernet IP packet with TOS and MPLS header (decoded by Agilent Advisor).

These steps will repeat at every intermediate node and abstract node until the egress edge LSR D is reached, which will look up the incoming label **d**, and the context will specify the end of the line for this packet flow. The label will be popped, which leaves the original unlabeled IP packet to be delivered to destination Node M.

Labels are not only swapped at each node, but in certain cases they may be pushed on top of existing labels **a** and stacked, as we will see shortly. We will also discuss with issues of failover and recovery.

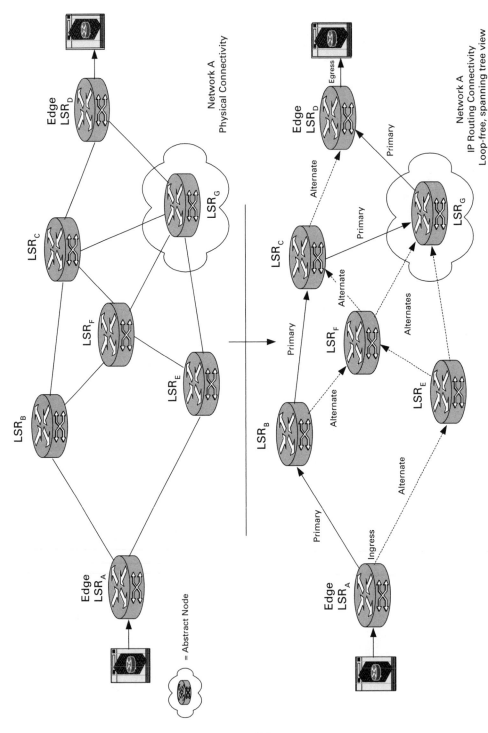

FIGURE 4.6 From mesh topology to least cost tree view.

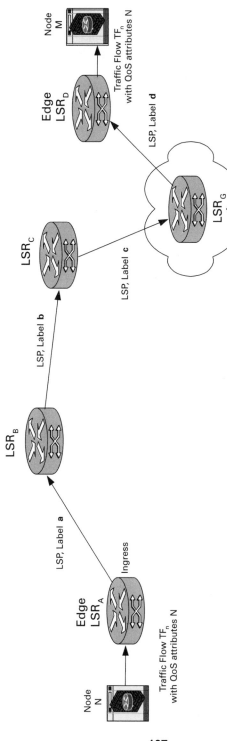

1. Establish LSP by requesting and obtaining labels; establish adjacencies, if applicable; configure LSP attributes and protection, if applicable.

2. Switch ingress label with egress label for all MPLS packets.

3. Perform failure recovery per configured protection procedures.

FIGURE 4.7 Label switching through an LSP.

Following are some points to remember:

1. If a transit LSR happens to be an ATM-LSR, as in the case of connecting an Ethernet domain to an MPLS-aware ATM switch, the incoming label will be mapped either to the VPI/VCI or only to the VPI.
2. Traffic conditioning must be done at the ingress LSR (shaping and policing) to within the traffic parameters of the flow for sustained and peak flow rates. This will ensure that downstream LSRs will receive a well-behaved stream and thus minimize the probability of packet discard, as well as meet intermediate requirements for delay and jitter.
3. In cases of link failure between adjacent LSRs, the LSP's new physical route may need to be recalculated, and no traffic will flow between the affected LSRs until there is routing convergence and the LSR is ready to forward the flows along the new path.

RSVP Label Distribution Method

Using MPLS labels is a lot easier than distributing them to the nodes of an LSP. The primary methods used are through extensions to the Resource Reservation Setup Protocol (RSVP), the Label Distribution Protocol (LDP) and its extensions, and via the BGP. Regardless of the label distribution protocol used to distribute labels, the LSRs must agree on the QoS meaning of each label. Labels offer higher resolution QoS classes (up to 2^{20}), but in reality only a few FECs are expected to be implemented for typical multiservice networks.

Figure 4.8 shows in summary the steps involved to obtain labels with the extended RSVP.

LSP control can be either *independent* or *ordered*. In independent LSP control, an LSR decides unilaterally how to bind the flow to a label for the specified FEC: It "picks" the label, and advertises it to the requesting upstream LSR. In ordered control, the label binding begins at the egress LSR and proceeds upwards towards the ingress LSR. The only independent decision for label mapping is made by the egress LSR. All other upstream LSRs wait until they receive the label value from the downstream neighbor before they do the mapping and proceed to advertise a label in the upstream direction. Ordered control is better suited for avoiding routing loops. The two LSP control methods are not interoperable for all practical purposes.

Ordered control can be implemented with either RSVP or LDP.

RSVP defines three reservation styles and operates on top of UDP.

1. Fixed Filter (FF)
2. Shared Explicit (SE)
3. Wildcard Filter (WF)

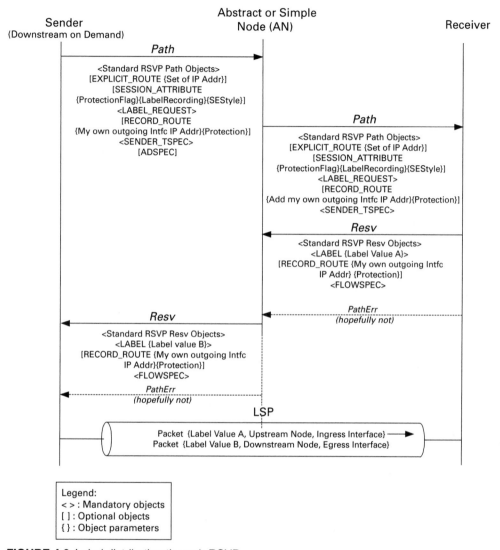

FIGURE 4.8 Label distribution through RSVP.

Of the three styles, only SE and FF are of interest for the purposes of traffic engineering of multiservice, nonsimultaneous flows traversing MPLS nodes. In the FF style, a different reservation is made for each and every sender. Reservations and labels are not shared, and therefore the reserved bandwidth through the node is the sum of bandwidths for each reservation. This is the simpler of the two styles of interest for traffic engineering, but it is rigid in that it does not allow bandwidth sharing.

The SE style, in effect, bundles senders into a reservation at the discretion of the receiver. However, different labels can be assigned to each sender, and the LSP for each one can thus be different.

The extension to RSVP defines five new "objects" to deal with requesting and receiving labels.

1. LABEL_REQUEST
2. LABEL
3. EXPLICIT_ROUTE
4. RECORD_ROUTE
5. SESSION_ATTRIBUTE

Only LABEL_REQUEST and LABEL are mandatory when using RSVP as the label distribution protocol. The LSR requesting a label formats an RSVP packet with the standard RSVP "objects" and includes a LABEL_REQUEST and, optionally, either or both of the RECORD_ROUTE and SESSION_ATTRIBUTE objects.

The EXPLICIT_ROUTE object, if included, carries an ordered list of nodes over which the LSP will be created. This requires knowledge of the topology at the ingress edge LSR and the current capabilities and operating capacity of each node. Use of EXPLICIT_ROUTE results in manual setup of the LSP,and care must be exercised when accounting for link and node failures in intermediate LSRs.

The RECORD_ROUTE object is a request for the created LSP node list to be propagated upstream to the requesting node. It can be useful for troubleshooting medium-and-large scale topologies by having quick access of the current LSP physical routes.

The SESSION_ATTRIBUTE object contains information regarding the priority of this LSP setup session over others in progress, the local switching protection required to reroute around failed links, and the preemption priority of this session from others in progress. It can also signify whether labels should be recorded when recording routes.

The *Path* message arrives at the neighboring downstream node, which will make a reservation for the requested Class of Service and propagate the Path message downstream. The expected flow characteristics and Class of Service requested by the sender are contained in the SENDER_TSPEC object. The desired reservation style is included in the SESSION_ATTRIBUTE object, and in the example signaling diagram, we show a reservation with the SE style.

When the egress edge LSR is reached, it will assign a label and begin a backwards process of sending the *Resv* message. The Resv message contains the label value to be used by its immediate upstream neighbor and any other information that had been requested by the included optional objects in the Path message. It also contains the FLOWSPEC object, which is part of the flow descriptor list and sets the flow specification as it travels upstream. The FLOWSPEC object has identical format to the downstream propagated SENDER_TSPEC (sender traffic specification).

When the *Resv* message is received from downstream, the recipient will record the downstream label and bind it with an upstream, which it will include in a Resv message it sends upstream, together with any additional information it needs to add to those received from the downstream LSR.

This process of label binding repeats until the ingress LSR is reached, at which time the unidirectional LSP is considered to be in place.

Exception conditions include the following:

1. If a node cannot do label binding for any reason, including internal failure, it responds with *PathErr* to the upstream node. This ends the attempt to use RSVP for LSP creation through that node.
2. PathErr is sent if there are no labels available. This is hard to believe for most topologies, but it could happen.
3. If the EXPLICIT_ROUTE object is not supported by a downstream router, it sends a PathErr message. This precludes explicit routing through that node.
4. Routing loops should be signaled with PathErr messages.

At the end of the label assignment and binding process, we have created a unidirectional LSP from Node N to Node M. LSPs in the opposite direction must be set up using the same procedures, but in the reverse direction. Note that it is possible for the same FEC in the reverse direction to create a different physical path between Nodes M and N.

RSVP maintains a "soft reservation state," which needs to be refreshed periodically. Refreshing is done with Path and Resv messages. If the "soft state" timer for the reservation expires before a refresh message has been received, the reservation is removed. This requirement is one of the criticisms regarding the scalability of RSVP for microflow reservations (for example, on a per-call basis). Due to the nature of FEC aggregation and the fairly static nature and longevity of the created LSPs, the extended RSVP approach for MPLS LSP setup is more scalable than RSVP reservation setup on a per-microflow basis.

LDP Label Distribution Method

A competing method for label distribution is the LDP protocol and an extension known as Constraint-Based LDP or CR-LDP. LDP is a stateful protocol and establishes reliable transport connections (TCP) with its adjacent LSRs. The protocol uses explicit LSR discovery procedures. We will overview LDP in the context of the signaling diagram of Figure 4.9.

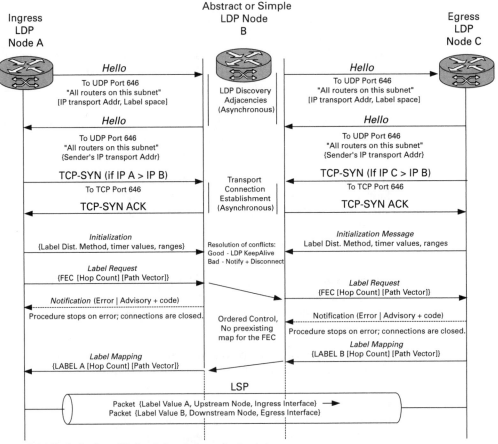

Ingress
LDP
Node A

Abstract or Simple
LDP Node
B

Egress
LDP
Node C

Hello
To UDP Port 646
"All routers on this subnet"
[IP transport Addr, Label space]

LDP Discovery
Adjacencies
(Asynchronous)

Hello
To UDP Port 646
"All routers on this subnet"
[IP transport Addr, Label space]

Hello
To UDP Port 646
"All routers on this subnet"
{Sender's IP transport Addr}

Hello
To UDP Port 646
"All routers on this subnet"
{Sender's IP transport Addr}

TCP-SYN (if IP A > IP B)
To TCP Port 646

Transport
Connection
Establishment
(Asynchronous)

TCP-SYN (If IP C > IP B)
To TCP Port 646

TCP-SYN ACK

TCP-SYN ACK

Initialization
{Label Dist. Method, timer values, ranges}

Resolution of conflicts:
Good - LDP KeepAlive
Bad - Notify + Disconnect

Initialization Message
Label Dist. Method, timer values, ranges

Label Request
{FEC [Hop Count] [Path Vector]}

Label Request
{FEC [Hop Count] [Path Vector]}

Notification (Error | Advisory + code)

Procedure stops on error; connections are closed.

Ordered Control,
No preexisting
map for the FEC

Notification (Error | Advisory + code)

Procedure stops on error; connections are closed.

Label Mapping
{LABEL A [Hop Count] [Path Vector]}

Label Mapping
{LABEL B [Hop Count] [Path Vector]}

LSP

Packet {Label Value A, Upstream Node, Ingress Interface} →
Packet {Label Value B, Downstream Node, Egress Interface}

Label Distribution Control Modes: independent vs. ordered control
Label Advertisement Methods: downstream unsolicited vs. downstream on demand
FEC Element: Per LDP (all modes) or CR-LDP (donwstream on demand, ordered control mode only) definition
CR-LDP Label Request: LSP-ID, FEC [ER (ER-HOP), PDR, PBS, CDR, CBS, EBS]
PDR: Peak Data Rate; **PBS**: Peak Burst Size; **CDR**: Committed Data Rate; **CBS**: Committed Burst Size; **EBS**: Excess Burst Size

FIGURE 4.9 LDP signaling for label distribution.

LDP needs to discover its LSR adjacencies, which it does by sending LDP-HELLO messages to UDP port 646 at the "All Routers on this Subnet" well-known IP multicast address (224.0.0.2). Extended procedures for discovery of not directly connected adjacent LSRs have also been defined, and LDP-HELLO packets are sent to the same UDP port and the specific IP address of the queried LSR.

HELLO messages optionally carry the IP transport address of the sending LSR to be used for the next step in the label distribution process, the opening of a reliable connection between them via TCP. LSR adjacencies discovered via HELLO messages are valid for the time period specified in the message, after which they may expire, unless the time period is set to infinity or another HELLO message from the LSR is received before the timer expires.

After the HELLO messages from the peers have been exchanged and adjacencies have been recorded, the peers establish a TCP connection on port 646. The session is initiated by the LSR whose transport address is less than its peer's when the IP addresses are compared as long integers. This means an intermediate LSR may send TCP-SYN to some of its neighbors, while it will wait to receive TCP-SYN from others. The session establishment among peers is not synchronized among the LSRs, and the LSR that initiated the TCP connection is the *master* of the session.

Following establishment of the TCP connection, an INITIALIZATION message is sent by the master LSR. This message advertises the desired label distribution discipline, label ranges for ATM (VPI/VCI) and frame relay (DLCI), a KeepAlive timer value, and other parameters.

There are two methods specified for label distribution.

1. Downstream unsolicited (or unsolicited downstream).
2. Downstream on demand.

The first distribution method binds labels to FECs unilaterally, without an explicit label request from an upstream LSR, and advertises the labels and FECs to its LDP peers. In the second method, an FEC label binding is performed after a specific request from an upstream LDP peer.

The independent and ordered LSP control methods we discussed in the RSVP case hold true in the case of LDP as well.

The session initialization phase is completed with both LSRs exchanging KeepAlive messages. Unresolved conflicts and incompatibilities result in an error notification by the LSR and session disconnection. Notifications are denoted with dotted lines in the signaling diagram.

An LSR can now request a label by sending a Label Request (LR) message. The LR message contains a maximum hop count to prevent the "forever" looping of the request in possible routing loops downstream. A mandatory parameter of the LR is the FEC being requested and specifies the packets that will be mapped to a particular LSP. It may also include a path vector element, which is the list of all the LSRs that have been traversed by this LR message.

At this time, if a node experiences difficulties (incompatibilities, unavailable resources, etc.) a notification will be sent to the requesting upstream LSR, and it will propagate to eventually reach the ingress edge LSR. All connections between LSRs on the path will be torn down.

If the LR message eventually reaches the egress LSR (for ordered LSP control) a Label Mapping message will be generated, which contains the

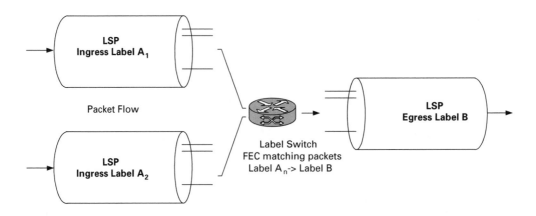

Notes:
FEC specification differs between LDP and CR-LDP.
CR-LDP includes traffic parameter specification for the LSP.
CR-LDP may include DiffServ specification element.

FIGURE 4.10 LSR actions for matching FEC.

label value of local significance with the upstream LSR. If all upstream LSRs are successful with the FEC bindings, the LSP is considered in place when the ingress edge LSR processes the Label Mapping message it receives from its downstream neighbor.

The primary difference between LDP and CR-LDP is in the encoding of the FEC parameters. In the CR-LDP case, the LR message may contain a DiffServ element as well, as we will see shortly. Figure 4.10 shows a typical label merge of matching FECs.

CR-LDP supports the following constraints in setting up an LSP:

- Strict and loose explicit routing
- Specification of traffic parameters, such as peak rate and committed rate.
- Route pinning—fixing the path of a loosely routed LSP, even when a better one becomes available.
- CR-LSP preemption—whether existing routes can be preempted if the current request cannot be serviced due to insufficient resources.
- New status codes for handling failures.
- LSPID, a unique identifier of the CR-LSP in the network.
- Resource class per the network administrator's definitions.

LDP (and its CR-LDP extensions) uses several other messages to control the setup of LSPs, not all of which are within the scope of this text. Table 4.2 shows a summary of the defined LDP messages and a brief description of their use.

TABLE 4.2 LDP Message Summary

LDP MESSAGE	DESCRIPTION
Label Request	Requests a label from the downstream LSR.
Label Mapping	Returns a value to the requesting LSR (in either independent or ordered LSP control).
Label Abort Request	Used to abort (cancel) an outstanding label request message.
Label Withdraw	Used to tell the LDP peer that the FEC-to-label mapping for this label is no longer desired.
Label Release	Used to withdraw previously requested FEC and label mappings.
Initialization	Used as part of the session establishment, and its primary function is to set the label distribution procedure.
Hello	Used as part of the LDP peer discovery mechanism. Exchanged periodically to maintain adjacencies during an LDP session.
Notification	Advise peer LSRs of malfunction and failure events or the status of processing LDP messages.
Address	An LSR advertises the transport addresses of its active interfaces with Address messages.
Address Withdraw	Used to inform peer LSRs that the contained transport addresses are no longer available.
KeepAlive	The KeepAlive keeps the LDP session active.

Tunneling through MPLS Domains

MPLS tunnels can get arbitrarily complex through LSP tunneling. If an operator must tunnel an MPLS LSP inside another, then the flow acquires a label stack, which is an ordered set of "shim" headers. See Figure 4.11.

In such a case, MPLS labels are "pushed" at the ingress to each tunnel and "popped" at the tunnel's egress. The last label from the stack will be popped when the edge LSR for the ultimate destination for the flow is reached. A decoded MPLS packet with a two-deep label stack is shown in Figure 4.12.

MPLS and DiffServ Together

Proposed extensions to both RSVP and CR-LDP will allow inclusion of DiffServ information to be included in the respective label distribution protocol messages. There are two types of DiffServ-aware LSPs that can be created

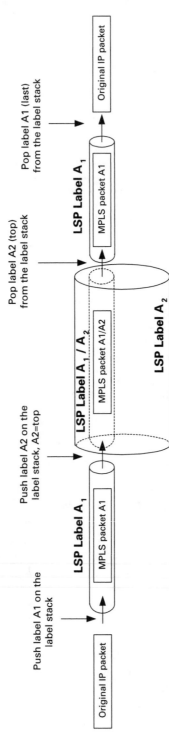

FIGURE 4.11 Tunneling through LSPs.

```
----------- MPLS Header -----------
MPLS: Label Stack Entry[1] = 0x238E1010
MPLS:      0010 0011  1000 1110  0001 ....  .... .... Label = 145633
MPLS:      .... ....  .... ....  .... 000.  .... .... Experimental Use = 0
MPLS:      .... ....  .... ....  .... ...0  .... .... Bottom Of Stack (S Bit) = FALSE
MPLS:      .... ....  .... ....  .... ....  0001 0000 Time To Live = 16
MPLS: Label Stack Entry[2] = 0x4D1111A2
MPLS:      0100 1101  0001 0001  0001 ....  .... .... Label = 315665
MPLS:      .... ....  .... ....  .... 000.  .... .... Experimental Use = 0
MPLS:      .... ....  .... ....  .... ...1  .... .... Bottom Of Stack (S Bit) = TRUE
MPLS:      .... ....  .... ....  .... ....  1010 0010 Time To Live = 162
```

FIGURE 4.12 Decoded MPLS label stack.

and two types of LSP tunnel modes, as shown in Figure 4.13 LSP types depend on the meaning and usage of the EXP label bits.

In the E-LSP (Exp-Inferred LSP) case, the EXP subfield of the DSCP is mapped to PHB of the flow. Up to eight behavioral aggregates can be supported. In the L-LSP (Label-Inferred) case, the PHB context is retrieved with the label lookup, whereas the EXP subfield maps to the drop precedence of the PHB.

There are two operating modes for DiffServ-aware MPLS nodes. The first one is the *Pipe Model*, whereby the intermediate nodes are hidden from Diff-Serv. In essence, the DiffServ information itself is tunneled across the LSP and is not looked at again until the MPLS packet arrives at the egress LSR.

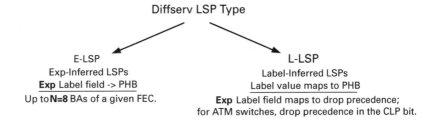

FIGURE 4.13 Diffserv-aware LSPs.

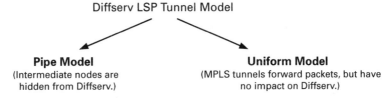

In the second approach, which is referred to as the *Uniform Model*, the MPLS tunnel is a side effect of the end-to-end path, from the standpoint of DiffServ. At any given time, a packet contains exactly one piece of DiffServ information, which is meaningful at the current node, and is always encoded in the outer-most label entry. At the egress LSR, the packet is sent unlabelled, and the DiffServ information appears in the IP DSCP.

Recovery Techniques for LSPs

Failures can and will happen in the network, and it is best if we are prepared to take specific action to specific events, as close to real time as possible. Under normal IP routing rules, if there is more than one way to get to a destination and the preferred way experiences a problem, packets will be rerouted to other outbound interfaces and nodes towards the ultimate termination of the flow. Standard Layer 3 routing does not preserve any intermediate data that may have been queued on the node experiencing the problem and in fact queues may be flushed in the rerouting process until new routing convergence is reestablished. Route discovery and convergence are the job of the IGP of the domain (OSPF, RIP) and variants of BGP between interconnected domains.

In contrast to Layer 3 routing, MPLS is path-oriented IP switching, whereby LSPs traversing specific nodes in a specific sequence and through specific interfaces have been established and are carrying packet streams. Once an LSP is set up and a failure occurs on any physical link between two LSRs, or if an intermediate node goes down, the best strategy is to have an alternate LSP to accept the packet flow and reroute traffic around the failure. Furthermore, if a "make before break" policy is used—that is, the standby LSP is preestablished and may be dormant or passing other traffic under normal operation—there is a strong possibility rerouting of LSPs can be done in real time without loss of data. It is a tall order, but it can be done in a well-engineered network. The "make before break" LSP setup method is shown graphically and in simple notation in Figure 4.14. This approach, in fact, is not much different in principle than the path protection switching mechanism used in SONET.

An LSR that generates both the working and recovery LSP is referred to as the *Path Switch* LSR (B). An LSR that sees both the working and protection LSR is referred to as the *Path Merge* LSR (C). LSRs B, C, and F comprise a protection domain, as they contain both the working and protection path. LSR F is considered an *intermediate* LSR in this nomenclature.

In a lot of cases, setting up protection paths requires redundant links if there is only one way to get between any two adjacent LSRs. In order to create a fully recoverable MPLS architecture, it will be necessary to account for all possible reroute configurations and establish protection paths, which is an often expensive proposition.

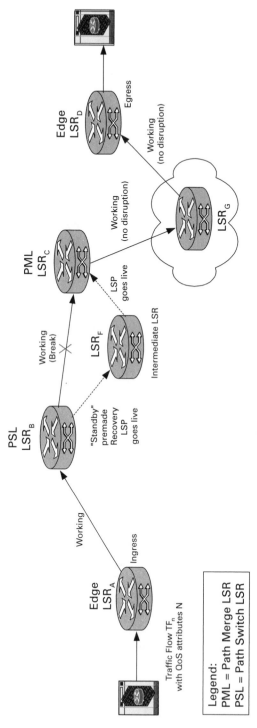

FIGURE 4.14 Failure workaround for LSPs.

Legend:
PML = Path Merge LSR
PSL = Path Switch LSR

119

If the protection required is 1:1, the protection paths must be able to carry the entire traffic of the working path, in all cases and under all circumstances. Alternatively, existing working LSPs for unrelated flows can be engineered to carry excess capacity and thus accept only the highest priority traffic of the working path upon failure. It is expected some traffic may be corrupted in the switchover process, but in general the switch to the protection path can be executed quickly, depending on the signaling mechanism used.

4.2 CONCLUDING COMMENTS

Although the MPLS and DiffServ overviews we presented are more descriptive than specific, it should make evident the size of the task involved with traffic engineering even a simple network that supports multiservice flows with wide-ranging requirements. The task becomes harder when we cross domains and the network scales to handle thousands of microflows of low bandwidth each, rather than a few megaflows of moderate to large bandwidth. We will return periodically to the traffic engineering aspect of a multiservice VoIP topology in the signaling discussions in the second part of this text.

LSP tunnels have various uses. They can be created to accommodate data flows through routing control or to employ measurement functions. For the latter, an LSP tunnel could be used to capture path statistics between its endpoints by associating performance and fault management functions with an LSP tunnel. For example, an LSP tunnel can exist solely for the purpose of capturing statistics between two LSRs.

For routing control, LSP tunnels are used to forward subsets of traffic through paths that are independent of routes computed by the conventional route discovery means of IGP, such as OSPF. This feature introduces significant flexibility (also some degree of risk) that allows policy implementation that will optimize the performance of the network. As we discussed earlier in this chapter, traffic can be routed to uncongested network resources that can absorb the rerouted traffic without adversely affecting the QoS of the included data flows. Load balancing policies can be implemented in a similar manner, as long as the lurking risk of managing the tunnels manually or semiautomatically remains manageable. If tunnels are instantiated along consistent optimum routes with the ones computed by the IGP, and if due to congestion or other issues rerouting becomes necessary, there could possibly be two images of the route topology for a period of time: one computed by the IGP and one computed by the tunnel management functions.

Recovery from topological changes must also be handled carefully if tunnel management is loosely tied to IGP route calculations. The tunnel management function must employ enough hysteresis to avoid route oscillations, while the image computed by the IGP itself is stabilizing. When the original view of the topology is restored by the IGP, the tunnels should optimally find themselves along their original routes.

References

Please note that IETF drafts are works in progress and may not be renewed when they expire.

1. IETF Draft: "Multiprotocol Label Switching Architecture," *draft-ietf-mpls-arch-06.txt*, Rosen, et al.
2. IETF Draft: "Extensions to RSVP-TE and CR-LDP for support of Diff-Serv-aware MPLS Traffic Engineering," *draft-ietf-mpls-diff-te-ext-00.txt*, Le Faucher, et al.
3. IETF Draft: "MPLS Support of Differentiated Services," *draft-ietf-mpls-diff-ext-07.txt*, Le Faucher, et al.
4. IETF Draft: "Requirements for support of Diff-Serv-aware MPLS Traffic Engineering," *draft-ietf-mpls-diff-te-reqts-00.txt*, Le Faucher, et al.
5. IETF Draft: "Extensions to RSVP-TE for MPLS Path Protection," *draft-chang-mpls-rsvpte-path-protection-ext-00.txt*, Huang, et al.
6. IETF Draft: RSVP-TE: "Extensions to RSVP for LSP Tunnels," *draft-ietf-mpls-rsvp-lsp-tunnel-07.txt*, Awduche, et al.
7. IETF Draft: "Carrying Label Information in BGP-4," *draft-ietf-mpls-bgp4-mpls-04.txt*, Rekhter, et al.
8. IETF Draft: "LDP State Machine," *draft-ietf-mpls-ldp-state-03.txt*, Boscher, et al.
9. IETF Draft: RFC 2702: "Requirements for Traffic Engineering Over MPLS," Awduche, et al.
10. IETF Draft: "Fault Tolerance for LDP and CR-LDP," *draft-ietf-mpls-ldp-ft-00.txt*, Farrel, et al.
11. IETF Draft: "Framework for MPLS-based Recovery," *draft-ietf-mpls-recovery-frmwrk-01.txt*, Sharma, et al.
12. IETF Draft: "Generalized MPLS—Signaling Functional Description," *draft-ietf-mpls-generalized-signaling-01.txt*, Ashwood-Smith, et al.
13. IETF Draft: "Generalized MPLS Signaling—CR-LDP Extensions," *draft-ietf-mpls-generalized-cr-ldp-00.txt*, Ashwood-Smith, et al.
14. IETF Draft: "Generalized MPLS Signaling—RSVP-TE Extensions," *draft-ietf-mpls-generalized-rsvp-te-00.txt*, Ashwood-Smith, et al.
15. IETF Draft: "A Path Protection/Restoration Mechanism for MPLS Networks," *draft-chang-mpls-path-protection-01.txt*, Huang, et al.
16. RFC 2205: "Resource ReSerVation Protocol (RSVP)," R. Braden, et al.
17. RFC 1700: "Assigned Numbers," J. Reynolds and J. Postel.

18. IETF Draft: "RSVP-TE: Extensions to RSVP for LSP Tunnels," *draft-ietf-mpls-rsvp-lsp-tunnel-07.txt*, Awduche, et al.

19. IETF Draft: "MPLS Label Stack Encoding," *draft-ietf-mpls-label-encaps-08.txt*, Rosen, et al.

20. *OSPF, Anatomy of an Internet Routing Protocol*, John T. Moy, Addison Wesley.

21. *Quality of Service in IP Networks*, Grenville Armitage, MacMillan Technical Publishing.

PART 2

Gateway Management and Call Signaling

In the second part of the text we will concentrate on advanced call signaling and media gateway control protocols. In the past couple of years a lot of emphasis and consideration has been given to the support of telephony features similar to those of the AIN model. The intent of the evolution of the various protocols is for service providers to offer seamless integration of next-generation services while maintaining the "look and feel" of basic telephony service of the circuit-switched network. In some cases, this effort is being driven by economic reasons, such as the desire by the providers to reuse existing AIN equipment and services whenever reengineering of the network is neither practical nor associated with a potential of increase in revenue.

We will take a look at the continuing evolution of H.323, SIP, MGCP, and the new Megaco/H.248 call model. We will also do an "in context" review of signaling-adapted SS7 for completion of calls with hops on the PSTN using the IETF M2UA, M3UA models and the Transport Adapter Layer Interface Protocol (TALI). Throughout the call flow analysis we will be discussing issues with QoS, firewalls, performances, and general configuration aspects of softswitch domains.

5

H.323: The Next Generation

H.323 is now in its fourth version and offers advanced capabilities for streamlined signaling with reduced overhead. While most of the implementations still revolve around version 2 and elements of version 3, the new version fills in gaps associated with topological robustness, resource usage reporting and additive registrations of gateways with multiple aliases. Support is provided for IETF RFC 2833 for in-band transport of DTMF tones and events, and endpoint capacity reporting allows for more detailed description of available resources. H.323v4 provides transport-level QoS via the use of RSVP, which we have already seen in the context of constructing MPLS tunnels. H.245 procedures can now be initiated in parallel with *fastStart*, thus establishing an early H.245 session and reducing the number of signaling exchanges even in the case where fastStart is rejected by the called endpoint. H.323v4 also introduces URL-type accessing of endpoints, in a manner similar to other IP-based signaling protocols.

5.1 PROTOCOL OVERVIEW

The general case of H.323 signaling involves a *zone* controlled by a GK function in a softswitch platform and gateways connecting the zone to other segments of the same provider or enterprise network, as well as with foreign networks in peer-to-peer arrangements. This is shown in summary detail in Figure 5.1. A *zone,* in our context, is logical and can contain endpoints or

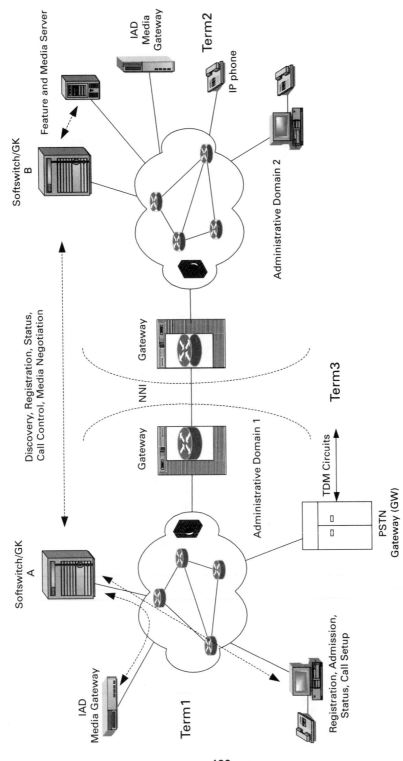

FIGURE 5.1 H.323 signaling routing models.

gateways, or both, which may not be controlled by the H.323 protocols, while the provided GK functionality is only a portion of the signaling capabilities of the softswitch.

We briefly mentioned in Chapter 1 the various signaling models in an H.323 environment, and we show them here again for reference in Figure 5.2. Even in moderate complexity topologies, with endpoints and gateways from multiple vendors and of varying capabilities, the signaling protocols and permutations that must be supported simultaneously by the GK can be numerous. In the case of supporting a public H.323 interface, interoperability specifications (i.e., the actual implementation of the various aspects of the H.323 set of specifications, the equipment it was tested with, and the test methodology) are of paramount importance. Surprises from protocol messages that cannot be properly decoded or from signaling exchanges that cannot be understood by one or both signaling entities are unwelcome, especially when they are discovered in a deployed network.

A performance goal of every platform implementation is the streamlining of signaling exchanges required to establish and maintain a call. This is mandatory in order to maximize the platform's capacity in calls-per-second, and can be accomplished by minimizing the messages required in the call establishment phase to the degree allowed by the individual protocols. The H.323 protocol in versions 2 and beyond support such streamlined signaling procedures, while also allowing the flexibility to revert to explicit signaling for logical channel control when the need arises, as deemed necessary by the GK or the endpoints in the call. However, the more flexibility and modes of operation that are added to a signaling protocol, the more important it becomes to fully test it for equipment interoperability and true conformance with the specifications, which can be a lengthy and complex task. This is a major obstacle in specifying the performance operating points of an implementation, which makes scalability a

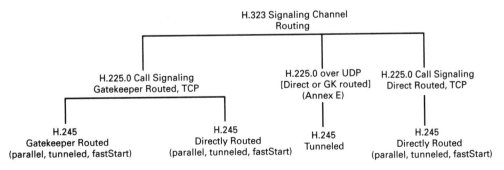

FIGURE 5.2 H.323 signaling routing modes.

must requirement in a call-processing platform design. Scalability can be the savior when parameters from an actual call mix have been measured and happen to fall a little short of the original expectations.

In our H.323 analysis, we will begin with a discussion on RAS and proceed with examples for basic and feature call flows. The softswitch of an administrative domain has signaling connectivity to other VoIP domains and to Class 4 and Class 5 systems on the PSTN, and can establish calls in a transparent manner.

5.2 REGISTRATION, ADMISSION, STATUS (RAS)

H.323 endpoints in the domain controlled by a GK need to register their presence and capabilities (see Figure 5.3). They must also receive permission to initiate and accept calls, either on a per-call basis or via preauthorization granted by the GK for all calls made and received during the lifetime of the endpoint's registration.

RAS messages and procedures are described in ITU-T Recommendation H.225.0, and a brief description of each message is given in Chapter 1. RAS communication between endpoints and the GK is performed over UDP to the IP address of the GK on the well-known unicast UDP port number (number **1719**). Before an endpoint registers with a GK, it may first need to discover which GK to register with. There are manual methods (e.g., a preconfigured GK IP address at the endpoint) and automatic methods using IP multicast. If the GK has been preconfigured in the endpoint, registration is a simple exchange of GRQ and GCF messages, if the GK is present.

A RAS GRQ message can be sent to the discovery multicast address **224.0.1.41** and UDP port number **1718**, in effect asking, *Who is my gatekeeper?* It may receive one or more positive responses, one or more rejections from active GKs, or no response at all. The more interesting scenario is when multiple GKs respond and indicate they can act as the endpoint's GK. Then a decision has to be made by the endpoint as to which GK to register with and how to act in failover situations with respect to registration. If no response is received, this is taken to mean no GK is active in this domain, and direct signaling procedures will be followed for call setup and logical channel control without the use of the RAS channel.

Let's look at the discovery process in the context of two simple call flows.

5.2.1 Discovery, Registration, and Admission Procedures

There are two types of discovery of interest using RAS:

1. gatekeeper
2. endpoint

```
------------ RAS Header ------------
RAS: RAS Message Type = Registration Request
RAS: | Request Sequence Number = 9885
RAS: | Protocol Identifier = 0.0.8.2250.0.2
RAS: | Discovery Complete = 1 (TRUE)
RAS: | Call Signal Address[0]
RAS: | | Transport Address Type = IP Address
RAS: | | | Address = 192.168.200.254
RAS: | | | Port = 1720
RAS: | RAS Address[0]
RAS: | | Transport Address Type = IP Address
RAS: | | | Address = 192.168.200.254
RAS: | | | Port = 55879
RAS: | Terminal Type
RAS: | | Gateway Info
RAS: | | | Supported Protocols[0]
RAS: | | | | Voice Caps
RAS: | | | | | Supported Prefixes[0]
RAS: | | MC = 0 (FALSE)
RAS: | | Undefined Node = 0 (FALSE)
RAS: | Terminal Alias[0]
RAS: | | E.164 Address = 7186253000
RAS: | Terminal Alias[1]
RAS: | | E.164 Address = 7186253001
RAS: | Terminal Alias[2]
RAS: | | H.323 ID = IAD_2
RAS: | GK Identifier = <GK Name>
RAS: | Endpoint Vendor
RAS: | | H.221 Non Standard
RAS: | | | T.35 Country Code = 181
RAS: | | | T.35 Extension = 0
RAS: | | Manufacturer Code = 18
RAS: | Keep Alive = 0 (FALSE)
RAS: | Will Supply UUIEs = 0 (FALSE)
```

FIGURE 5.3 RAS Registration Request message.

A GRQ needs to be sent by each endpoint served by a gateway, in a typical signaling exchange shown in Figure 5.4. The endpoint supplies its *RAS signaling TA* in **rasSignalAddress**, the type of endpoint and its aliases, and other nonstandard information, such as the country code.

The **GKID**, which is an optional parameter, is the name of the GK from which the endpoint would like to receive a response, whereas the **supports-AlternateGK** parameter (for version 4 of the protocol, shown in the call flow) indicates whether the registering endpoint supports the alternate GK procedures for load balancing and failover situations. Other parameters passed with the GRQ include the endpoint's capabilities in authentication and encryption and the version of the H.225 protocol being used.

```
------------ RAS Header ------------
RAS: RAS Message Type = Registration Confirm
RAS: | Request Sequence Number = 9885
RAS: | Protocol Identifier = 0.0.8.2250.0.3
RAS: | Call Signal Address[0]
RAS: | | Transport Address Type = IP Address
RAS: | | | Address = 192.192.1.7
RAS: | | | Port = 1721
RAS: | Endpoint Identifier = IAD_2
RAS: | Will Respond To IRR = 0 (FALSE)
RAS: | Maintain Connection = 0 (FALSE)
```

FIGURE 5.4 RAS Registration Confirm message.

The GK will respond with a GCF (Confirm) or GRJ (Reject). In the latter case, a reason will be supplied for the failure to accept the registration in the message. Reasons can include a terminal's permission to register with the GK, invalid protocol revision, rejection on the basis of security, and denial based on generic data supplied in the GRQ request.

If a GCF is returned, the GK will supply it own RAS signaling TA, a list of alternate GKs and their signaling addresses (if the feature is supported by the endpoint), and any nonstandard data meaningful to the endpoint and the GK, and not controlled by the H.323 specification.

Following successful discovery of the GK, the endpoint must now register with the RRQ/RCF message exchange, which is also shown in the same figure with decoded example packets in Table 5.1.

The RRQ message supplies the endpoint's **call signaling** address, its **RAS signaling** address (this is necessary if a GK discovery process was not necessary and did not happen), the **terminal type** (MCU, Gateway, simple endpoint, etc.), and a list of **aliases** for this terminal, such as E.164 number and H.323 ID.

The field **supportedH248Packages** indicates which H248/Megaco packages are supported, while the endpoint also indicates its capability to report **capacity reporting** information as well as its current call **capacity**.

The GK may request that the endpoint supply Q.931 messages exchanged during call processing between endpoints in the User-User Information Element (**UUIE**) of **IRR** (Information Request) packets. At registration time, the endpoint indicates in the **willSupplyUUIEs** field its ability to support this feature. The **keepAlive** field indicates a "lightweight" RRQ is being sent to indicate the endpoint is still active. The GK that receives the **keepAlive** message ignores most fields and simply notes the endpoint that sent the message.

The GK will respond with an RCF (Registration Confirm) or RRJ (Registration Reject) or in cases of malfunction, no response may be received. The

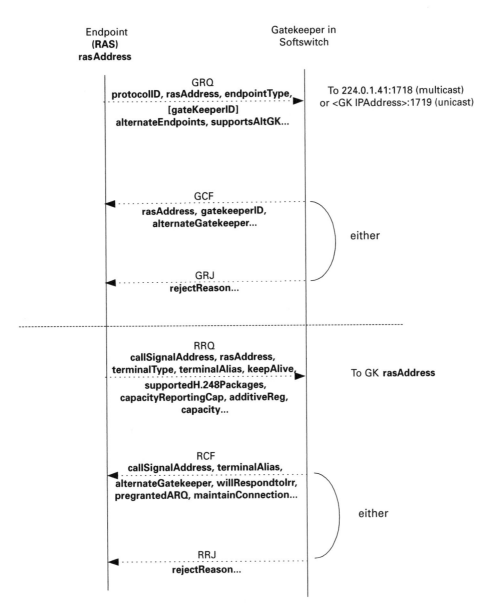

FIGURE 5.5 Gatekeeper discovery procedures.

latter case calls for the implementation to reattempt the registration procedures and take actions outside the scope of the H.323 specification. In general it is a hard troubleshooting problem when no response is received after sending an RRQ, but in a lot of cases it can be traced to parameters in the message that are not understood by the GK.

If an RRJ is received, the reason for the registration rejection is also included in the message. Examples of registration rejection reasons include invalid or duplicate aliases used by the endpoint, invalid transport addresses placed in the message, and attempts to perform additive registration when the feature is not supported.

If the RRQ is accepted by the GK, it will return an RCF. It includes the call signaling addresses for the GK, a list of prioritized alternate GKs, the TTL for the registration, an indication whether the GK will respond to IRR messages sent by the endpoint with IACK or INACK, and a list of events for which the GK grants authorization in advance (pregranted ARQ) to the endpoint. Those are **Make Call**, **Answer Call**, bandwidth limits, and the transport protocol to be used to set up calls. The GK may also be capable of keeping a signaling connection alive when there are no calls present (**maintainConnection**).

The pregranted ARQ is a very important feature because it reduces the signaling steps required when making calls, thus improving the performance of the entire system.

An endpoint or a GK can remove an active registration by sending a URQ (Unregistration Request). The GK may accept the URQ and return a UCF, or deny it and return URJ and a reason. When the GK initiates a URQ, the endpoint must accept it and process it. It may attempt to reregister with the same or another GK at a later time.

Following the registration steps, the endpoints are ready to make and receive calls. Receiving calls and making calls to other endpoints in the domain are rather easy procedures, as we will see in the following call flows, but making a call to an endpoint whose location is not known (i.e., the identifier of the endpoint is not sufficient to make the call and requires some form of translation by the GK) requires endpoint discovery procedures. A simple call flow for locating an endpoint is shown in Figure 5.6. Endpoint location discovery can be accomplished only if there is a GK that can receive an LRQ with the information about the destination endpoint and return an LCF when translation is performed successfully, or an LRJ when the operation cannot be performed.

The destination information can be a list of aliases, an E.164 number, other dialed string of digits, or an H.323 ID. The desired protocols are also signaled in the LRQ, along with the address to which to send the LCF (it will almost always be the RAS signaling address of the sender) and the circuit information, if the call is routed over the PSTN. The GK will respond with the RAS and call signaling, and supported protocols addresses of the located endpoint.

Note that some requests may take longer to execute than allowed by system timers. In order to avoid a timer expiration, an RIP (Request in Progress)

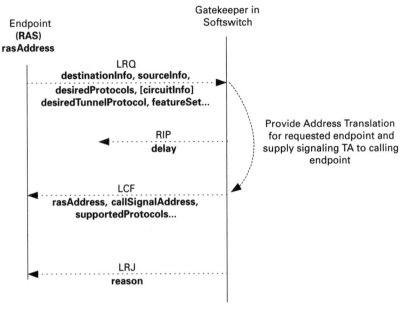

FIGURE 5.6 H.323 endpoint location discovery procedures.

message can be sent, which will indicate how long it will take to generate the real response. When the information for the response is available, the message is sent without further delay. A location request may generate this kind of intermediate response, depending on the time it will take to access data bases to perform the translation.

5.3 CALL SETUP AND TERMINATION

After registration is complete, we are ready to make and accept calls. Call setup in H.323 is divided into phases, which tend to become blurred based on the type of signaling model that will be followed in the signaling process. Phase A is the call setup; Phases B, C, and D are the logical channel control signaling and signaling for additional services. Under expedited signaling, known as **fastStart** and **Tunneling** of logical channel control signaling, portions of Phases B, C, and D can be included in Phase A.

The call termination Phase E consists of simple signaling exchanges to ensure the parties understand the media channels are closed and the call is terminated, as we will see in the call flows of the next section.

5.3.1 Basic Call Flows

The first step in the process of call setup is to establish a reliable connection[1] over TCP with the called endpoint, or with the GK that will act as proxy, as shown in Figure 5.7. As soon as we have the reliable connection in place, an H.225.0 SETUP message is sent by the calling endpoint.

This is the most important message in the process, not only because it contains the vital information about the call, but because it also proposes the signaling model for the setup process. The choice between explicit H.245 procedures, fastStart with or without Tunneling, and possibly performing early H.245 signaling (before call setup is completed) begins with this message.

The only mandatory Information Elements (IEs) in the SETUP message are the Protocol discriminator, the call reference, the message type, and the bearer capability, all of which are adaptations of the Q.931 protocol IEs. Conditionally, the calling and called party subaddress are also mandatory if PSTN hops are present in the call setup, but not otherwise. All other parameters are contained in the UUIEs of the SETUP message. The UUIE is mandatory in H.323.

As shown in the call flow, the caller indicates whether it supports opening of an early H.245 connection prior to the completion of the call setup. It also provides the TA for such a connection. If the fastStart parameter is set, the caller wishes to forego explicit H.245 signaling, while it may additionally request parallel H.245 control (simultaneous logical channel signaling; see Figure 5.8), and may include H.235 structures from Master-Slave Determination and Terminal Capability Set (MS/TCS).

A partially decoded H.323 SETUP message is shown in Figure 5.9 and Figure 5.10.

If the caller wishes to establish identical audio capabilities in both directions, it can indicate it in the **symmetricOperationRequired** parameter.

The called endpoint, proxy GK, or intermediate H.323 gateway can optionally send CALL PROCEEDING, indicating the call setup has been received and no more setup information for this call should be sent. Similarly, a gateway may send PROGRESS to indicate the call setup is in progress, especially if there is interworking with the PSTN. Either of these messages can indicate acceptance or refusal of the fastStart and Tunneling requests, as well an H.245 TA for early media control signaling.

---

1.   Annex E of H.323 allows for call signaling to be performed over UDP. This will be discussed later.

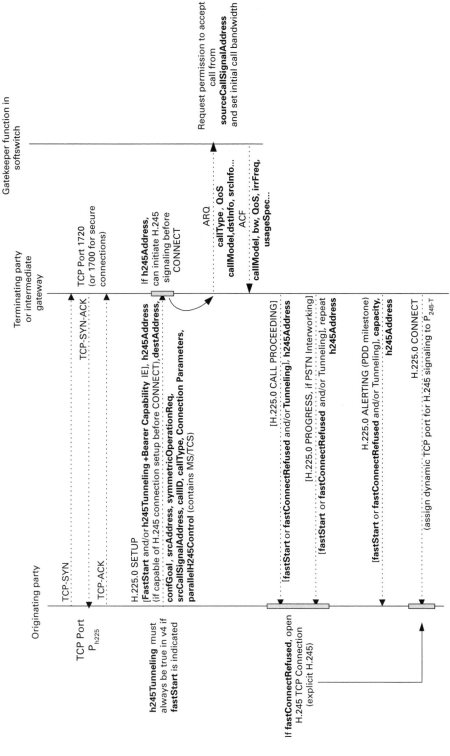

FIGURE 5.7 H.323 call setup.

135

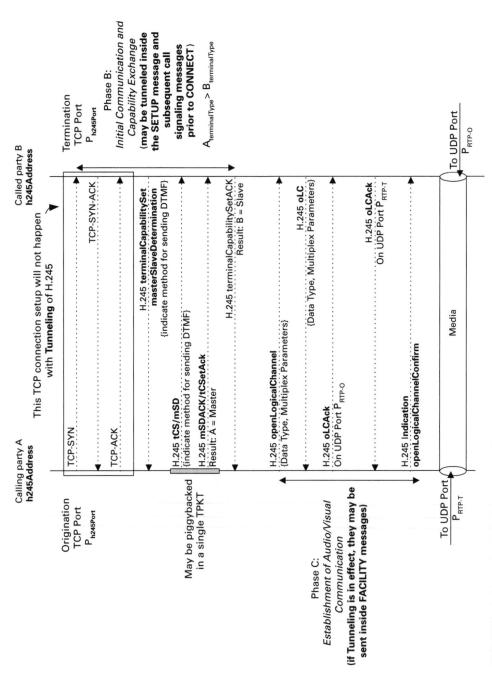

FIGURE 5.8 H.323 logical channel signaling.

```
Q931: Setup UUIE
Q931: | Protocol Identifier = 0.0.8.2250.0.2
Q931: | Source Info
Q931: | | Gateway Info
Q931: | | | Supported Protocols[0]
Q931: | | | | Voice Caps
Q931: | | | | | Supported Prefixes[0]
Q931: | | MC = 0 (FALSE)
Q931: | | Undefined Node = 0 (FALSE)
Q931: | Active MC = 0 (FALSE)
Q931: | Conference ID = EFBB3157C90301C7000000000ABE8A80
Q931: | Conference Goal = Create
Q931: | Call Type = Point To Point
Q931: | Source Call Signal Address
Q931: | | Transport Address Type = IP Address
Q931: | | | Address = 192.168.100.254
Q931: | | | Port = 11069
Q931: | CallIdentifier
Q931: | | GUID = EFBB3157C90301C8000000000ABE8A80
Q931: | H.245 Fast Start[0]
Q931: | | Logical Channel Number = 1
Q931: | | Forward Logical Channel Parameters
Q931: | | | Data Type = Audio Data
Q931: | | | Audio Capability = G.711 Ulaw 64k -- Parameter = 20
Q931: | | | Multiplex Parameters
Q931: | | | | H.225.0 Logical Channel Parameters
Q931: | | | | | Session ID = 1
Q931: | | | | | Media Control Channel
Q931: | | | | | | Transport Address Type = Unicast Address
Q931: | | | | | | | Address Type = IP Address
Q931: | | | | | | | | Address = 192.168.100.254
Q931: | | | | | | | | Port = 18989
```

FIGURE 5.9 Partially decoded fastStart with pre-version 4 SETUP, part 1 (no Tunneling).

The endpoint receiving the SETUP needs to get approval to accept the call if it does not already have a pregranted ARQ. The endpoint informs the Gkvia an ARQ of the bandwidth requirement for the call and its capability to manage QoS. The GK responds in the ACF with the frequency at which the endpoint should supply IRRs to the GK, guidance in handling the QoS for the call, and the usage information the endpoint should supply to the GK for the call.

Following a successful ARQ/ACF exchange, the endpoint can now send back ALERTING to the caller to indicate the call setup has been delivered and the (virtual) phone is ringing. As in the case of PROGRESS and CALL PROCEEDING, the fastStart and Tunneling requests can be accepted or rejected and an H.245 TA can be supplied for early media control signaling.

```
Q931: | H.245 Fast Start[1]
Q931: | | Logical Channel Number = 1
Q931: | | Forward Logical Channel Parameters
Q931: | | | Data Type = Null Data
Q931: | | | Multiplex Parameters
Q931: | | | | None
Q931: | | Reverse Logical Channel Parameters
Q931: | | | Data Type = Audio Data
Q931: | | | | Audio Capability = G.711 Ulaw 64k -- Parameter = 20
Q931: | | | Multiplex Parameters
Q931: | | | | H.225.0 Logical Channel Parameters
Q931: | | | | | Session ID = 1
Q931: | | | | | Media Channel
Q931: | | | | | | Transport Address Type = Unicast Address
Q931: | | | | | | | Address Type = IP Address
Q931: | | | | | | | Address = 192.168.100.254
Q931: | | | | | | | Port = 18988
Q931: | | | | | Media Control Channel
Q931: | | | | | | Transport Address Type = Unicast Address
Q931: | | | | | | | Address Type = IP Address
Q931: | | | | | | | Address = 192.168.100.254
Q931: | | | | | | | Port = 18989
Q931: | Media Wait For Connect = 0 (FALSE)
Q931: | Can Overlap Send = 0 (FALSE)
Q931: H.245 Tunneling = 0 (FALSE)
```

FIGURE 5.10 Partially decoded fastStart with pre-version 4 SETUP, part 2 (no Tunneling).

When the call is answered, the CONNECT message is dispatched, and it also indicates whether fastStart and tunneling are supported, the current call capacity of the endpoint, and a H.245 TA for explicit media control signaling procedures.

If early H.245 procedures are initiated, this must be done before the CONNECT is sent by the sender. Failure to establish fastStart signaling will result in a subsequent call flow, as shown in Figure 5.8.

Explicit H.245 signaling requires another TCP connection (socket), which affects the scalability, performance, and robustness of the signaling platform. When specifying performance for a design, we must be careful to include the possibility of opening explicit H.245 signaling connections in midcall (for whatever reason), which reduces resource and call capacity availability.

During the MS/TCS phase, the endpoints negotiate the preferred method for sending DTMF tones in the Multiplex Stream Capabilities, as well as the master of the call. Tones can be sent in Real-Time Protocol (RTP) payload types as in-band events or tones, per IETF RFC 2833, or as alphanumeric strings inside tunneled or explicit H.245 **userInputIndication** messages. Once the MS/TCS exchange is complete, the endpoints can proceed to open the logical channels that will carry the media.

During a stable call, there may be a need to modify the bandwidth used by the call. Usually the case will be to request more bandwidth, although it is strongly recommended for endpoints not to request more bandwidth than is necessary to carry the media reliably. Modifications to call parameters occur in Phase D.

Bandwidth modification requests are made via RAS signaling, as shown in Figure 5.11. Affected logical channels will be closed by the endpoint and reopened with the new bandwidth parameter. The recipient endpoint must go through its own BCR/BCF exchange in order to continue with the call and accept the logical channels with the different characteristics.

Figure 5.12 shows another potential modification to the characteristics of the call relating to flow control of a logical channel. The maximum bit rate is sent to the far endpoint with a flow control command after obtaining permission for the new parameter from the local GK. The recipient endpoint must go through its own BCR/BCF process if it is on another GK, close the logical channel(s) affected, and reopen them with the new characteristics.

Usage information can be reported to the GK during the call either via polling by the GK in IRQ/IRR exchanges or via unsolicited IRRs from the endpoint if this had been requested by the GK. The GK may or may not acknowledge the IRRs, per the indication given to the endpoint in the RCF message. See Figure 5.13.

Proper call termination (Phase E) calls for closing all open logical channels by the party terminating the call, sending an H.245 **endSessionCommand** to the far end, and possibly sending a RELEASE COMPLETE H.225.0 message. However, the termination of a call is frequently done simply with the **endSessionCommand**. See Figure 5.14.

5.3.2 Methods for Logical Channel Control: fastStart and Tunneling

Significant performance improvement is gained when the MS/TCS exchange is performed either with the establishment of an early H.245 signaling connection or through fastStart and Tunneling of H.245 messages in the UUIEs of H.225.0 call signaling messages. For example, if the MS/TCS is sent by the caller in the SETUP message, by setting **h245Tunneling** to TRUE, together with fastStart,[2] the called party will respond with **terminalCapabilitySetAck** in the message that either accepts or refuses the fastStart command, as we discussed earlier. The response from the called endpoint that

---

2.   In version 4 of H.323, use of fastStart also requires Tunneling.

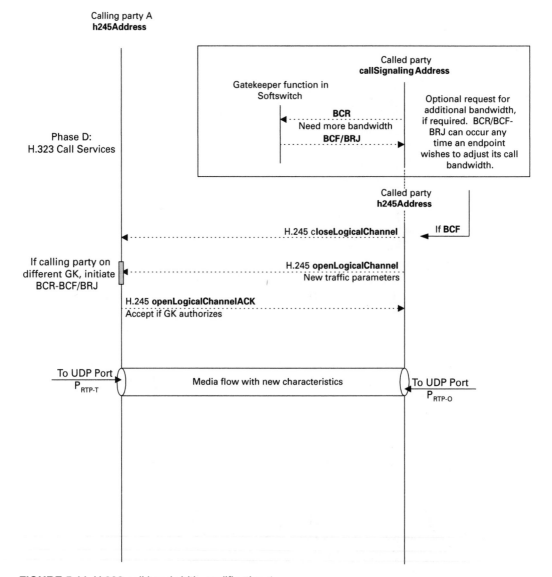

FIGURE 5.11 H.323 call bandwidth modification 1.

wishes to acknowledge parallel H.245 signaling can be in the CALL PRO-CEEDING, PROGRESS, or any other message prior to sending CONNECT.

If the CONNECT message is received by the caller without the **terminalCapabilitySetAck** response having been received in a previous call signaling message, it will be assumed that parallel H.245 control has failed and explicit serial signaling procedures will be initiated, as shown in the previous call flows.

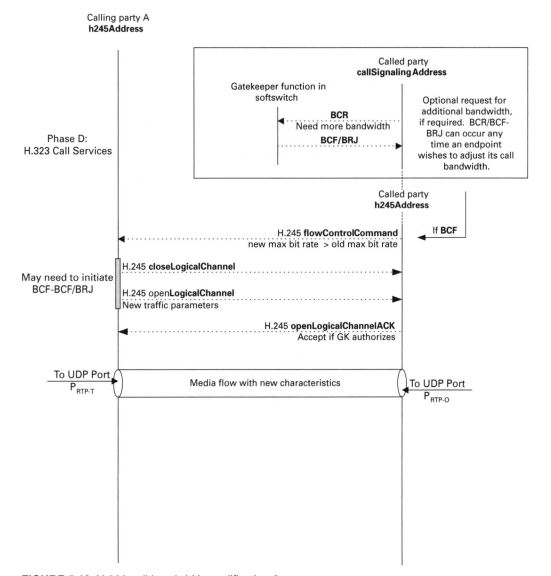

FIGURE 5.12 H.323 call bandwidth modification 2.

Tunneled H.245 signaling can be sent in the UUIE of FACILITY messages if another H.225.0 message is not scheduled to be sent. The FACILITY message is instrumental in the implementation of tunneled signaling and enhanced services in H.323.

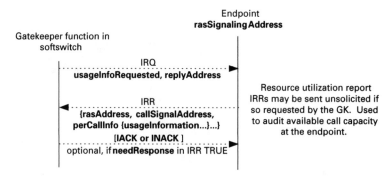

FIGURE 5.13 H.323 resource utilization reporting.

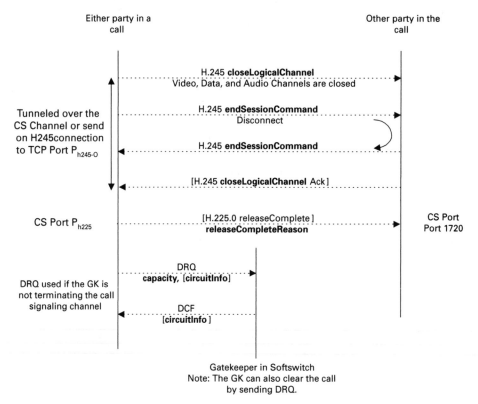

FIGURE 5.14 H.323 call termination.

In order for Tunneling to remain active for the duration of the call, the **h245Tunneling** flag needs to be set in the SETUP message and in every H.225.0 call signaling message thereafter. Note that provisional responses to a tunneling request may be sent by intermediate GKs in the GK routed model, until the endpoint's capability to support this feature has become known to the remote GK.

> The presence of tunneled H.245 messages in the initial SETUP command will override fastStart, if both Tunneling and fastStart are being requested simultaneously.

Once the MS/TCS has been settled between the endpoints in tunneled signaling, open logical channel (OLC) control can be initiated with the exchange of FACILITY messages, or explicit H.245 signaling procedures (see Figure 5.15). In either case, the content of the OLC structures is the same, but there is a major benefit in the use of the single reliable connection, i.e. the TCP socket of the call signaling H.225 channel, and avoid opening a separate H.245 connection.

In summary, Figure 5.9 shows the SETUP UUIE, indicating fastStart with the forward and reverse logical channel parameters the caller is proposing; Figure 5.16 shows the contents of the ALERTING message with the accepted parameters; and Figure 5.17 is the final connect message.

When a caller indicates fastStart, it must be able to receive media on all the channels it is proposing to the called party, immediately.

5.3.3 Codecs, DTMF Tones, and Signal Events

Codec negotiation in fastStart is a one-pass operation. The SETUP command will carry a list of options in forward and reverse channels, and the remote endpoint will select the set that it can support, based on its capabilities and current service level agreement (SLA) in effect. The SLA issue is far from trivial in packet-based communications. There are scenarios of a single GK controlling a single zone, which are rather easy to guarantee and enforce, while other cases involving multiple domains and GKs are not as obvious. Figure 5.18 highlights some of the requirements for codec negotiation and test points for bandwidth calculations.

An intradomain call between A and B or A and C (e.g., fax) involves resource allocation in the up and down links between the respective IADs and the access concentrator-switch-router internal equipment chain. A fax call that does not involve fax relay service (i.e., T.28 fax support), but instead relies on the upspeed[3] method, will have an impact on per-assigned bandwidth on the

---

3.   The upspeed method is a protocol mechanism to change the media format of an open logical channel, from any type of compressed format to G.711, upon detection of a fax tone after the call is set up.

```
H245: Multimedia System Control Message Type = Request
H245: | Request Type = Open Logical Channel
H245: | | Logical Channel Number = 257
H245: | | Forward Logical Channel Parameters
H245: | | | Data Type = Data
H245: | | | | Application Type = T.120
H245: | | | | | Separate LAN Stack
H245: | | | | | Max Bit Rate = 0 (100 bits/s)
H245: | | | | Multiplex Parameters
H245: | | | | H.225.0 Logical Channel Parameters
H245: | | | | | Session ID = 0
H245: | | Reverse Logical Channel Parameters
H245: | | | Data Type = Data
H245: | | | | Application Type = T.120
H245: | | | | | Separate LAN Stack
H245: | | | | Max Bit Rate = 0 (100 bits/s)
H245: | | | Multiplex Parameters
H245: | | | | H.225.0 Logical Channel Parameters
H245: | | | | | Session ID = 0
H245: | | Separate Stack
H245: | | | Distribution = Unicast
H245: | | | Network Address Type = Local Area Address
H245: | | | | Transport Address Type = Unicast Address
H245: | | | | | Address Type = IP Address
H245: | | | | | | Address = 146.82.186.80
H245: | | | | | | Port = 1503
H245: | | | Associate Conference = 0 (FALSE)
H245: TPKT Protocol Version = 0x03
H245: TPKT Reserved = 0x00
H245: TPKT Packet Length = 25
H245: Multimedia System Control Message Type = Request
H245: | Request Type = Open Logical Channel
H245: | | Logical Channel Number = 258
H245: | | Forward Logical Channel Parameters
H245: | | | Data Type = Audio Data
H245: | | | | Audio Capability = G.723
H245: | | | | | Max Al Sdu Audio Frames = 1
H245: | | | | | Silence Suppression = 0 (FALSE)
H245: | | | Multiplex Parameters
H245: | | | | H.225.0 Logical Channel Parameters
H245: | | | | | Session ID = 1
H245: | | | | | Media Guaranteed Delivery = 0 (FALSE)
H245: | | | | | Media Control Channel
H245: | | | | | | Transport Address Type = Unicast Address
H245: | | | | | | | Address Type = IP Address
H245: | | | | | | | | Address = 146.82.186.80
H245: | | | | | | | | Port = 49597
H245: | | | | | Media Control Guaranteed Delivery = 0 (FALSE)
H245: | | | | | Silence Suppression = 1 (TRUE)
```

FIGURE 5.15 Partially decoded H.245 openLogicalChannel structure.

```
Q931: Alerting UUIE
Q931: | Protocol Identifier = 0.0.8.2250.0.2
Q931: | Destination Info
Q931: | | MC = 0 (FALSE)
Q931: | | Undefined Node = 0 (FALSE)
Q931: | CallIdentifier
Q931: | | GUID = EFBB3157C90301C8000000000ABE8A80
Q931: | H.245 Fast Start[0]
Q931: | | Logical Channel Number = 1
Q931: | | Forward Logical Channel Parameters
Q931: | | | Data Type = Audio Data
Q931: | | | | Audio Capability = G.711 Ulaw 64k -- Parameter = 20
Q931: | | | Multiplex Parameters
Q931: | | | | H.225.0 Logical Channel Parameters
Q931: | | | | | Session ID = 1
Q931: | | | | | Media Channel
Q931: | | | | | | Transport Address Type = Unicast Address
Q931: | | | | | | | Address Type = IP Address
Q931: | | | | | | | | Address = 192.168.255.10
Q931: | | | | | | | | Port = 18902
Q931: | | | | | Media Control Channel
Q931: | | | | | | Transport Address Type = Unicast Address
Q931: | | | | | | | Address Type = IP Address
Q931: | | | | | | | | Address = 192.168.255.10
Q931: | | | | | | | | Port = 18903
Q931: | H.245 Fast Start[1]
Q931: | | Logical Channel Number = 1
Q931: | | Forward Logical Channel Parameters
Q931: | | | Data Type = Null Data
Q931: | | | Multiplex Parameters
Q931: | | | | None
Q931: | | Reverse Logical Channel Parameters
Q931: | | | Data Type = Audio Data
Q931: | | | | Audio Capability = G.711 Ulaw 64k -- Parameter = 20
Q931: | | | Multiplex Parameters
Q931: | | | | H.225.0 Logical Channel Parameters
Q931: | | | | | Session ID = 1
Q931: | | | | | Media Channel
Q931: | | | | | | Transport Address Type = Unicast Address
Q931: | | | | | | | Address Type = IP Address
Q931: | | | | | | | | Address = 192.168.100.254
Q931: | | | | | | | | Port = 18988
Q931: | | | | | Media Control Channel
Q931: | | | | | | Transport Address Type = Unicast Address
Q931: | | | | | | | Address Type = IP Address
Q931: | | | | | | | | Address = 192.168.255.10
Q931: | | | | | | | | Port = 18903
Q931: H.245 Tunneling = 0 (FALSE)
```

FIGURE 5.16 H.225 FastStart ALERTING.

```
Q931: Connect UUIE
Q931: | Protocol Identifier = 0.0.8.2250.0.2
Q931: | Destination Info
Q931: | | Gateway Info
Q931: | | | Supported Protocols[0]
Q931: | | | | Voice Caps
Q931: | | | | | Supported Prefixes[0]
Q931: | | MC = 0 (FALSE)
Q931: | | Undefined Node = 0 (FALSE)
Q931: | Conference ID = EFBB3157C90301CB000000000AC0441C
Q931: | CallIdentifier
Q931: | | GUID = EFBB3157C90301CC000000000AC0441C
Q931: H.245 Tunneling = 0 (FALSE)
```

FIGURE 5.17 fastStart CONNECT.

trunks for voiceband calls and the Call Admission Control (CAC) algorithms in effect, if neither endpoint had a G.711 SLA for voice calls.

The QoS that is achievable within a domain is easier controlled to a large degree because operating points in bandwidth utilization can be obtained from the compression algorithms in use and the list of SLAs in place. Even so, when, for example, A uses G.723.1 and B uses G.711 and has also subscribed to a higher QoS, a decision needs to be made whether A will receive higher bandwidth and its call will be bumped up to G.711, or B will receive lower bandwidth and its call will be dropped to G.723.1. Several schools of thought exist on this subject, regarding QoS for a call between endpoints with different SLAs. The network engineering problem is concentrated between test points 1, 2, and 3.

The issue becomes more complex when a call is placed to an external packet network from endpoints with high QoS SLAs, and when low quality calls are received from outside through gateways that have the ability to transcode to a higher quality voice encoding scheme. A few things must be kept in mind:

1. Transcoding from a higher compression rate, which used perceptual weighting, to a higher bandwidth encoding will not necessarily improve voice quality. The reason is that perceptual processing removes important spectral information from the analog voice signal, so when it is reconstructed (in PCM or other high-quality format), these frequency components cannot be inserted.

2. Transcoding to and from G.711 of calls through the PSTN takes place by default at the PSTN gateway; therefore it is a rather easy decision to deliver the SLA-guaranteed QoS to the calling or called endpoint of a call with one leg on the PSTN.

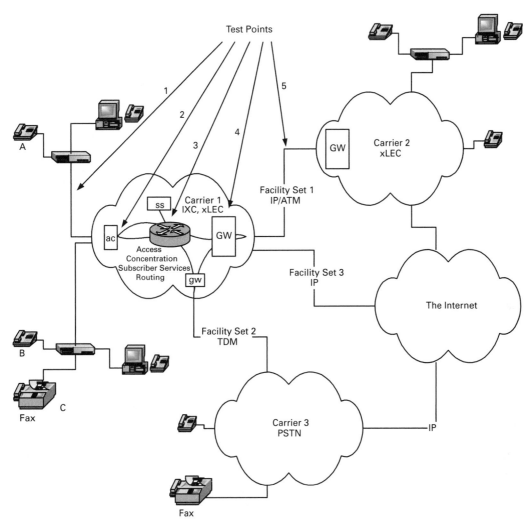

FIGURE 5.18 Codec negotiation considerations.

Case 1 involves test points 1 through 4 and whatever agreement exists for bandwidth allocation between the peer packet networks. Case 2 can be treated as a subset of the intradomain call we discussed previously, whereby one (intermediate) endpoint in the call is a G.711 gateway and will or will not perform transcoding, depending on the SLA of the local endpoint.

Once codecs have been negotiated, media will flow in RTP packets, with Real-Time Control Protocol (RTCP) packets providing a glimpse of information into the QoS being experienced during the call (jitter, packet loss). Call statistics are also obtained by the protocol containing **RTPsession** information in the **perCallInfo** field of IRR messages. However, bandwidth and QoS are not the only issues facing media transport in the packet network. A major issue is the transport of telephony tones (DTMF), analog signals, and trunk events in a timely and accurate manner.

RFC 2833 specifies RTP packet formats for transporting DTMF tones, line and trunk signals as *named telephone events*, and additional packet formats for transporting the general *characteristics* of multifrequency tones. It is a matter of implementation choice, with several implementations preferring the *named event* approach. The quality of transport of general-purpose tones in IP telephony is extremely important to emulate basic telephone services such as facsimile. The main issue with tone transport in packet-based voice telephony has been the use of compression with perceptually weighted coders. With G.711 encoding, tones can be sent transparently in the audio stream as voice band data in RTP packets, without any additional effort expended by either party. Perceptual weighting, however, is preferential to the frequency spectrum of digitized signals, and tones are not guaranteed to survive intact if passed through a codec.

Once a sender's gateway device (e.g., IAD) is detecting the presence of a DTMF tone in the outbound direction, one of three approaches can be pursued under H.323.

1. The DMTF tone will be interpreted and sent, ASCII-encoded, in an H.245 message as **userInputIndication**. If Tunneling is used, this will prompt the sending of a FACILITY message.
2. The tone will be interpreted and a named event will be sent as a specific payload type in the RTP stream. The tone may or may not be sent as voiceband data through the codec while the tone is in the process of being recognized by the sender.
3. Once the coder detects a non-speech signal (DTMF tone, fax signal, trunk events, etc.), it will be analyzed and its properties will be sent as an RTP payload type. These properties include the frequency content, volume, and duration of the signal, which will be updated at periodic intervals. The tone can then be reconstructed and interpreted at the remote end.

For example, when a call turns out to be a fax call, the answer tone could be encoded as a named event (event number 34, per RFC 2833) and sent inside an RTP packet, using the same timestamp and sequence base as the regular audio stream. This will allow quick interpretation of the event by the equipment on the path of the call for adjusting to the new requirements, such as the disabling of echo cancellers.

A method for fax support in IP infrastructures is available with the H.323 protocol if the terminals are communicating through gateways which are capable of T.38[4] procedures. If the equipment supports T38 mode, this capa-

---

4.   The T.38 real-time fax relay method is discussed in Chapter 9.

bility should be indicated during the Terminal Capabilities Exchange (TCE), by setting the **t38fax** field in the **DataApplicationCapability** structure. When the fax tone is detected and *unidirectional* voice channels have been set up, a **requestMode** H.248 command can be sent indicating **t38fax** (which is a Data Mode), and after it is acknowledged with **requestModeAck**, the currently open voice channel must be closed and a T38 channel must be opened in its place. The procedure consists of simply sending a **closeLogical-Channel** (for the audio), followed by an **openLogicalChannel** (for the t38 channel) after the **closeLogicalChannelAck** is received from the far end. If explicit H.245 procedures are in use, these messages will travel over the H.245 reliable connection. If Tunneling is in effect, the messages will be included in a H.225 FACILITY commands. For *bi-directional* voice channels the procedure is a little simpler and does not require sending the **request-Mode** command, i.e. the device that detects the fax tone will close its bidirectional voice channel and open a bidirectional t38 channel in its place.

A different approach to real-time fax support over H.323 compliant gateways is through **requestMode** again when the fax tone is detected, but the new requested mode is simply a G.711 audio logical channel to allow for uninhibited transport of tones over the RTP stream. The **requestMode** H.245 message will be sent in the same manner we discussed in the previous paragraph for T38. No other signaling is necessary. The original audio channel must be closed.

When named telephone events are sent, support for the extended DTMF keypad is mandatory. This includes the numbers 0 through 9, plus #, *, A, B, C, and D. All other named DTMF events are optional.

Tones can be tricky because their exact duration may not be known when the first RTP packet is sent. The user may simply press a DTMF key for an entire second, and it is not acceptable to wait until the event has stopped in order to send the first packet indicating its presence. This requires the ability to send quick packets announcing the event, and if the event still persists when the packet is transmitted, the ability to send intermediate updates stating the signal duration.

Implementation constraints may result in the audio channel carrying an encoding of the same tone as the RTP packets are carrying as a named event, at least for a period of time until the audio stream at the sender is blocked. This could cause the same event to be detected via two means by the remote end, but it is recommended the endpoints use the named event rather the contents of the audio stream,as the indication of a tone.

Named events should be sent immediately, as soon as they are recognized by the sender, and every 50 ms afterwards, or at the interval of the audio packetization rate.

Packet loss can cause some problems when tone transport is in progress. Particularly dangerous is the loss of the RTP packet that indicates the end of a tone. Retransmission of the last packet may be implemented by the sender and, in general, tones at the receiving end should not be extended beyond three packetization periods of the audio stream.

5.3.4 Routing calls

When calling endpoints outside the local zone of a GK, information about the called party needs to be obtained before the SETUP message can be issued, so that the local GK can route the call to the proper egress gateway, in case there are multiple connection points between the networks.

As a first step, the local GK must determine the network to which it needs to route the call. In other words, some number translation is necessary to a set of {GK, trunk ID}, but not all translation information may be available locally. At minimum, the network of the remote endpoint must be known, such that additional information can be obtained via LRQ/LCF.

As an example, consider the two cases in Figure 5.1. Caller Term1 in Administrative Domain 1 dials a digit string (the telephone number), which GK A knows is an endpoint in Administrative Domain 2. GK B supplies the location (TA of Term2), which may involve an intermediate gateway, and GK A can then complete routing the call.

Similarly, if caller Term1 calls Term3 (across the PSTN), GK A will steer the call to an appropriate PSTN gateway along the path of the call by supplying its TA in the LCF.

5.4 H.323 OVER UDP

A further improvement in performance can be realized by allowing the call signaling protocol to operate over UDP. The less reliable operation may be an issue, but it is easier to account for failover conditions when signaling is done over UDP than it is in the TCP case. Call setup and the calls-per-second performance of a platform are improved by eliminating the initial TCP connection. Annex E of the H.323 specification describe's procedures for operating H.323 over UDP, as well as the multiplexing of PDUs from various protocols in the same message.

Following are important notes to consider when operating over UDP.

1. An acknowledgment mechanism may be required to ensure delivery of the PDUs to the remote endpoint. An acknowledgment may thus be requested by the sender (ACK/NACK). Lost packets need to be retransmitted.

2. TCP by default sends KeepAlive messages to ensure that the connection between the signaling endpoints is up. Such a method does not exist in the UDP protocol; therefore application-level "I am Alive" messages need to be sent periodically by the master of the session.

3. Multiplexed PDUs, per Annex E, may be sent over TCP as well. Annex E operation supports well-known UDP/TCP port **2517**.
4. Annex E specifies a "restart" message to indicate a fresh start for the endpoint and that all previous sessions and state information have been terminated.

When fastStart with Tunneling are combined with Annex E UDP operation, the result is very streamlined signaling, which can deliver maximized performance enhancement.

5.5 AD HOC CONFERENCING

H.323 allows for point-to-point calls to be converted to conference calls. There are two cases to consider. One of the endpoints contains a Multipoint Contol Unit (MCU), or the call needs to be diverted to an MCU in a transparent manner. In addition, we need to consider whether some or all the different calls are already active.

The call flow of Figure 5.19 shows the details of an ad hoc conference when there is already a stable call between endpoint A, which contains an MCU, and endpoint B. When endpoint A decides to conference in C, it sends a SETUP command, with **conferenceGoal** parameter set to **create**, and the conference ID.

The allowed encodings of conferenceGoal are as follows**:**

1. *create*
   When a point-to-point call is expanding into a multipoint conference.
2. *join*
   When an endpoint calls into an endpoint already in a conference
3. *invite*
   When an endpoint in a conference calls into an endpoint, asking it to join.
4. *capability-negotiation*
   To negotiate capabilities for a conference to bet set up later.
5. *callIndependentSupplementaryService*
   For the transfer of supplementary services application PDU.

Call setup for the additional calls proceeds as in the case of point-to-point calls, but all the endpoints are aware they are in the same conference via the **ConferenceID** parameter.

5.5.1 Centralized Versus Decentralized Conferencing

When an endpoint is capable of providing media mixing and packet switching, it may select the centralized conference model, whereby the serving endpoint does all the media work.

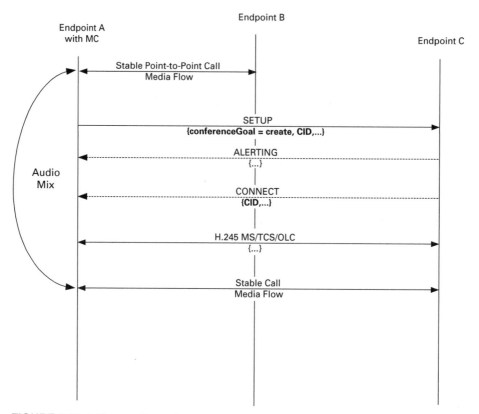

FIGURE 5.19 Ad hoc conferencing.

If the endpoint has access to an MCU/conference bridge that it needs to insert in the call to process the media, then it sets up a call with the bridge. It will drop its existing active calls, and send a SETUP command to the bridge with enough information in the **conferenceGoal=Invite** message for the bridge to call the various endpoints. Each participating endpoint requires a separate **conferenceGoal=Invite** message.

Decentralized conferencing uses multicast methods among the participating endpoints and the MCU, and thus its scope and scalability may be limited.

5.6 FEATURE CALL FLOWS

Call features in H.323 are specified in the generic H.450.1 document, along with individual specifications that define and describe the feature and the methods to invoke it. The generic feature-support mechanism is shown in the simple call flow of Figure 5.20.

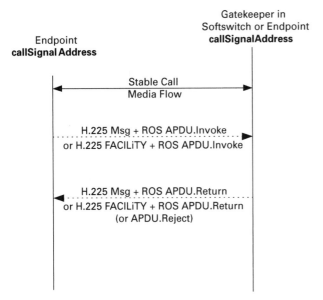

FIGURE 5.20 H.450 generic feature support mechanism. (ROS - Remote Operations Service.)

Some features can be invoked during a stable call—for example, transfer and hold, among others—while some features are invoked in a static manner and remain in effect until they are revoked. One example of the latter feature is call forward, in one or more of its flavors (always, on busy, or no answer). Telephony features are a key component of the revenue stream of service providers, and in the packet-based incarnation of the new PSTN, it is important that

1. The most popular and important telephony features are supported.
2. Each telephony feature interworks with the same feature of AIN of the PSTN.

Table 5.1 lists some popular telephony features.

The implementation of these features utilize the FACILITY command of H.225.0, with varying parameters. A feature invocation is simply sent by the activating party and may be accepted or rejected by the far endpoint.

It is unlikely for feature call flows to be implemented in the direct-routed signaling model, and we will consider the case of a softswitch receiving calls in a proxy position for the different cases.

5.6.1 Call Forward: Unconditional, Busy, No Answer

The call forward unconditional and busy (CFU and CFB) feature call flows are very similar, with the exception that the busy determination has to be

TABLE 5.1 Popular Telephony Features

FEATURE	COMMENT
Call Hold	Places an existing call on hold.
Call Transfer	Transfers the other party to another endpoint.
Call Waiting	Delivers an indication (via an audio signal and/or visual indication) that a call is incoming.
Call ID	Delivers the number and possibly the name of the calling party.
Call Forward	Always, busy, or no answer. May also be invoked remotely.
Do Not Disturb	Requires a PIN to get through and deliver the call to the subscribing endpoint. If no PIN is supplied, the call is sent to the subscriber's voice mail at the CO.
Three-Way Calling	Allows a limited ad hoc conference of three endpoints. Larger conferences may be supported, depending on the capabilities of the IAD.
Call Blocking	Blocks outgoing and incoming calls from certain numbers (e.g., 900 toll numbers).

made by the signaling platform before the call is diverted. In the case of call forward no answer (CFNR), the call will be delivered and a timer will be started. The GK will return ALERTING to the caller, but when the timer expires, the call will be diverted to the new far endpoint and a FACILITY message will be sent along indicating this is a diverted call. If the call is delivered successfully, either the ALERTING message will be resent or no action will be taken, while the call attempt to the original endpoint will be dropped and a FACILITY message, indicating the call is being diverted, will be sent to the caller.

When the call is finally answered by the new remote endpoint, the CONNECT messages are exchanged as if it were the intended endpoint of the call.

The basic flow is shown in Figure 5.21.

In the case of CFB, the remote GK will receive RELEASE COMPLETE with reason=busy when it delivers the SETUP, at which time the call will be diverted in the same manner as before, except that a RELEASE COMPLETE from the GK now is not necessary.

When a GK encounters CFU, the call is diverted immediately and proceeds in normal call setup to the new endpoint. A FACILITY message to the caller will indicate the call is being forwarded.

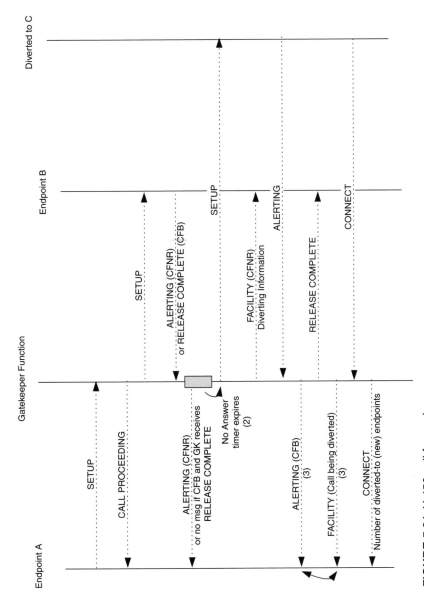

FIGURE 5.21 H.450 call forward.

5.6.2 Call Transfer

Call transfer involves the case where the call between the transferring endpoint and the transferred-to endpoint exists already or where an unconditional transfer is taking place. A composite call flow covering both cases is shown in Figure 5.22.

In the first case, a FACILITY message to the transferred-to party is sent, identifying the transfer operation. Then another FACILITY message to the transferred endpoint is sent to invoke the transfer. The transferred endpoint sets up the new call and drops the original call if successful. If an error occurs, a reason is returned to the transferring party. Finally the call between the transferring party and the transferred-to party is released.

In the latter case, the FACILITY message invoking the transfer is sent to the transferred party, which is expected to take over and establish the new call. When done, it releases the call to the transferring party.

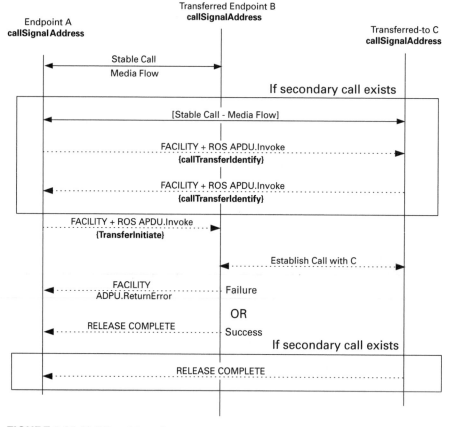

FIGURE 5.22 H.450 call transfer.

5.6.3 Call Waiting

When call waiting has been activated as a feature and a new call is delivered to the caller, the ALERTING message also contains **callWaiting**. If the called party wishes to take the incoming call, it places the existing call on hold with a **holdNotification** Application Protocol Data Unit (APDU). It then proceeds to accept the new call and, when it has ended, the original call can be retrieved with a **retrieveNotification** indication in an APDU.

A call flow for call waiting is shown in Figure 5.23.

5.7 FIREWALLS

When all is said and done about signaling, along comes a firewall to mess things up. Firewalls can modify signaling exchanges, sometimes extensively,

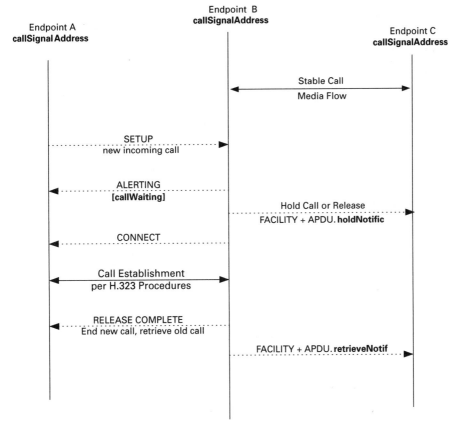

FIGURE 5.23 H.450 call waiting.

depending on implementation. We look at generic support for firewalls in the call flow of Figure 5.24.

Perhaps the greatest challenge with firewalls is that they may be programmed to perform Network Address Translation (NAT) and Port Address Translation (PAT). There are choices that need to be made, some of which reduce the effectiveness of the firewall. For example, if NAT is taking place, well-known ports may need to be left open because they cannot be translated when signaling messages are delivered; that is, the recipients expect to see signaling to certain port numbers. Similarly, discovery multicast addresses, such as when discovering the GK with a GRQ to IP address 224.0.1.41, need to be left open if the scope of multicast addresses extends outside the firewall.

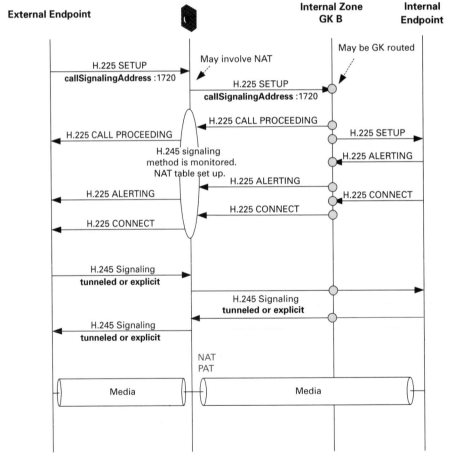

FIGURE 5.24 H.323 signaling through a firewall.

Of paramount importance in an implementation is whether an intelligent firewall is employed or firewall control is performed by an outside entity. In the former case, the firewall needs to understand and execute the protocols being signaled through it, such that transport addresses can be understood and proper "holes" can be dynamically opened at the beginning of the call and closed when the call ends. This may sound desirable, but it requires smarts in the firewalls, which may be prohibitive in cost and performance.

In the latter control model, the firewall receives its control information (i.e., open and close ports and IP addresses) from a signaling entity, which is the initial recipient of all signaling from the outside. This model suffers from performance issues as well, but the control functionality can be included in elements of the architecture that hosts the actual protocol stacks and thus minimize the cost of the implementation, depending on the scale of the design. An additional benefit of this approach is the distributed ability required when signaling and media do not traverse the same firewalls, as in cases of failover due to a malfunction in a gateway or the firewall itself. In other words, the challenge is to keep all the active calls up while rerouting through a new set or a backup set of firewalls in real time.

Lastly, let's not forget that firewalls need to be very expedient in their qualification of a packet. It would be immaterial and irrelevant to create elaborate MPLS tunnels and take other QoS measures if the first firewall on the path of the call destroys jitter and delay characteristics. It is thus imperative to ensure packets in a domain do not accidentally traverse multiple firewalls by design.

Ironically, when using security protocols like the IPSec suite, we may be experiencing the least security through a firewall. That's because both the Authentication Header (AH) and the Encapsulation Security Payload (ESP) methods hide the ports which would force the platform to deliver the packets to the intended destination, thus exposing the system to a potential denial-of-service attack.

References

1. ITU-T Recommendation H.225.0 (1999), "Call signaling protocols and media stream packetization for packet based multimedia communication systems."
2. ITU-T Recommendation H.245 (2000), "Control protocol for multimedia communication."
3. ITU-T Recommendation H.323 (1998 and 2000 pre-pub), "Packet-based multimedia communications systems."
4. ITU-T Recommendation H.450.1 (1998), "Generic functional protocol for the support of supplementary services in H.323."

5. ITU-T Recommendation H.450.2 (1998), "Call transfer supplementary service for H.323."

6. ITU-T Recommendation H.450.3 (1998), "Call diversion supplementary service for H.323."

7. ITU-T Recommendation H.450.4 (1999), "Call Hold Supplementary Service for H.323."

8. ITU-T Recommendation H.450.5 (1999), "Call Park and Call Pickup Supplementary Services for H.323."

9. CCITT Recommendation G.711 (1988), "Pulse Code Modulation (PCM) of voice frequencies."

10. CCITT Recommendation G.722 (1988), "7 kHz audio-coding within 64 kbit/s."

11. ITU-T Recommendation G.723.1 (1996), "Speech coders: Dual rate speech coder for multimedia communications transmitting at 5.3 and 6.3 kbit/s."

12. CCITT Recommendation G.728 (1992), "Coding of speech at 16 kbit/s using low-delay code excited linear prediction."

13. ITU-T Recommendation G.729 (1996), "Coding of speech at 8 kbit/s using Conjugate Structure Algebraic-Code-Excited Linear-Prediction (CS-ACELP)."

14. ITU-T Recommendation H.261 (1993), "Video codec for audiovisual services at p x 64 kbit/s."

15. ITU-T Recommendation H.263 (1996), "Video coding for low bit rate communication."

16. ITU-T Recommendation T.120 (1996), "Data protocols for multimedia conferencing."

17. ITU-T Recommendation H.320 (1997), "Narrow-band visual telephone systems and terminal equipment."

18. ITU-T Recommendation H.321 (1996), "Adaptation of H.320 visual telephone terminals to B-ISDN environments."

19. ITU-T Recommendation H.322 (1996), "Visual telephone systems and terminal equipment for local area networks which provide a guaranteed quality of service."

20. ITU-T Recommendation H.324 (1996), "Terminal for low bit rate multimedia communication."

21. ITU-T Recommendation H.310 (1996), "Broadband audiovisual communication systems and terminals."

22. ITU-T Recommendation Q.931 (1998), "ISDN user-network interface layer 3 specification for basic call control."

23. ITU-T Recommendation H.323 "Annex E: Framework and wire-protocol for multiplexed call signaling transport."

24. RFC 2833: "RTP Payload for DTMF Digits, Telephony Tones and Telephony Signals," H. Schulzrinne, et. al.

25. *IP Telephony: The Integration of Robust VoIP Services*, Bill Douskalis, Prentice Hall PTR, Hewlett-Packard Press.

6

Media Gateway Control Protocol

We have already discussed the basics of MGCP signaling with some ordinary call flows in my previously published book, and in this chapter we revisit MGCP (which is specified in RFC 2705) to look further into details of call setup in realistic situations. The protocol has continued to gain momentum and acceptance in signaling applications that do not require the endpoints to contain session "smarts." It has been stated in standards groups that MGCP will eventually be obsolete and replaced with the Megaco protocol. However, as equipment proliferation based on MGCP continues, it warrants a close look at the MGCP RFC standard and some of its applications.

Several enhancements have been made to the protocol from the early draft proposal versions, and we briefly list its commands and supported parameters in order to examine signaling in our specific topological context. The focus of this chapter is to provide additional detail into the characteristics of MGCP and discuss the real-life situation of signaling in domains that employ multiple call control protocols in a softswitch and dissimilar endpoint types. Such networks also use location discovery techniques across administrative domains. Finally we will summarize the various signaling event "packages" that can be implemented in gateways.

6.1 PROTOCOL OVERVIEW

As its name indicates, MGCP is a *Media Gateway Control Protocol*. It is low-level and rudimentary in its capabilities, and relies heavily on an external signaling entity for procedures dealing with the topology discovery, bandwidth management, and traffic engineering issues associated with call processing. The external entity is usually a softswitch with the ability to act as a call agent for MGCP endpoints. Endpoints thus need to be "paced" through the steps of a call by the call agent entity in the softswitch.

MGCP uses a connection model in which the basic abstractions are endpoints[1] and connections[2]. Endpoints are sources, or sinks, of data and can be physical or virtual. An example of an endpoint is an interface on a gateway that terminates a trunk connected to a PSTN switch (e.g., Class 5, Class 4, etc.), or an interface in Media Gateway/Integrated Access Device (MG/IAD) connected to a black phone (i.e., a POTS phone). Other basic endpoint types include DS0s on a T-carrier, analog lines, endpoints in announcement servers, interactive voice response (IVR) systems, conference bridges, packet relays, wiretap devices, and Asynchrorous Transfer Mode (ATM) trunk side networks. Virtual endpoints are found in media servers, where they can be dynamically created under software control.

In the MGCP model, the gateways are responsible for the audio signal translation function from analog or digital representation to some type of compressed digital format, while the softswitch acts as the signaling agent and call processor. In that capacity, the softswitch implements the layers of all the signaling protocols supported by the switching platform, including MGCP.

A connection under MGCP is created in a few simple steps.

1. The softswitch asks the first gateway to create a connection on the first endpoint. The gateway allocates resources to that connection and responds to the command by providing a session description in the form of parameters coded per the Session Description Protocol (SDP, RFC 2327). The session description contains the information necessary for a third party to send packets, such as IP address, UDP port, and packetization parameters, towards the newly created connection.

2. The softswitch then asks the second gateway to create a connection on the second endpoint. The command carries the session description provided by the first gateway. The gateway allocates resources to that connection, and responds to the command by providing its own session description.

3. The softswitch uses a modify connection command to provide this second session description to the first endpoint. Once this is done, communication can proceed in both directions.

---

1.   The term endpoint is used in the same context by almost every IP-based signaling protocol, although Megaco/H.248 alters the terminology slightly.

2.   Note the redundancy in the definition of the connection model.

Distributed softswitch implementations, which use multiple elements in the platform as signaling managers, can control connection establishment between endpoints controlled by each element as long as they can synchronize their actions through internal signaling.

Once established, the connection parameters can be modified at any time by a "modify connection" command. The softswitch may, for example, instruct the gateway to change the compression algorithm used on a connection, or to modify the IP address and UDP port to which data should be sent. The softswitch removes a connection by sending to the gateway a "delete connection" command. The gateway may also, under some circumstances, inform the softswitch that a connection could not be sustained and issue an unsolicited "delete connection" message to the softswitch.

The softswitch provides instructions for resource allocation to a connection by sending two sets of parameters to the gateway:

1. *Local directives* instruct the gateway on the choice of resources that should be used for a connection.
2. When available, the *SDP* provided by the other end of the connection.

The local directives specify such parameters as the mode of the connection (e.g., send only, send-receive), preferred coding or packetization rate, and usage of echo cancellation or silence suppression. Based on the value of the local directives, the gateway determines the resources, such as a DSP or a fraction of a DSP, allocated to the connection.

Once the resources have been allocated, the gateway will compose an SDP that describes the way it intends to receive packets. For example, if the gateway is capable receiving several compression algorithms, it can provide a list of them in the SDP.

There are pluses and minuses to implementing a nonsophisticated protocol for VoIP endpoints. One plus, in the eyes of this author, is the flexibility to map individual signaling steps in the process of establishing a call to the AIN call model. It is then easy to achieve a degree of integration of VoIP technology with existing PSTN topologies and equipment, from the service provider's perspective. One minus is the number of signaling steps and extensive interaction required on the part of the softswitch to stitch together call legs in semicomplex call flows, such as those found in support of telephony features. The number of signaling steps can be large, especially when dealing with a call that spans administrative domains and requires interworking with other signaling protocols. Indeed, we examine closely the interworking of MGCP with an H.323 endpoint across domains, and we will discuss issues arising in the performance of the platforms involved and other QoS concerns.

The call flow of this section is on the topology of Figure 6.1. We have two administrative domains, controlled by two softswitches and connected

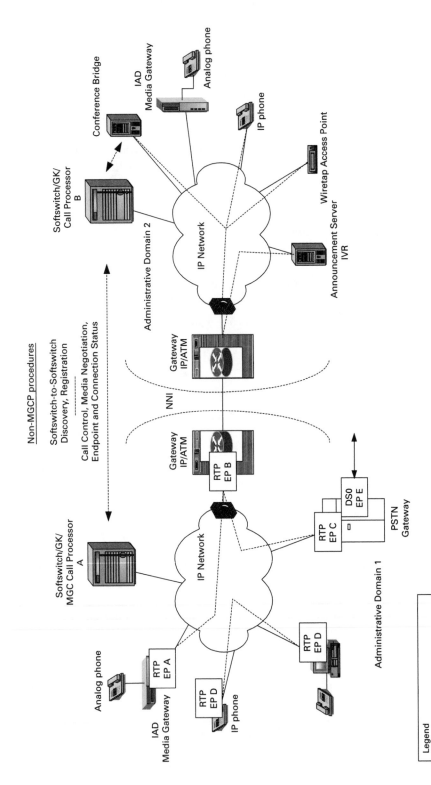

FIGURE 6.1 MGCP signaling domain context.

via gateways which pass signaling and media packets. The topology is generic and presents the types of equipment a network engineer will possibly have to deal with when charged with creating a specific call flow that spans a specific set of nodes. For example, some architectures may implement different gateways for signaling and media, and firewall topologies may be overlays on the transport network or one-to-one arrangements.

The reference signaling architecture for MGCP in this discussion is shown in Figure 6.2, which also shows the major endpoint types we are most likely to find in a service provider network. The reference has been augmented to show connectivity to both trusted and untrusted packet domains, the latter of which requires firewall deployments in key ingress points of the overall network. The ingress points and the firewall topology are determined by the scalability and cost requirements of the network architecture, and can range from rudimentary one-to-one arrangements to distributed many-to-one topologies that are very complex in the design. We will address the firewall presence with the observations in the example call flow of this section.

MGCP is a text-based protocol, which evolved into nine messages and one proposed command, as shown in Table 6.1. Transactions are simple and consist of a message sent by the softswitch as text payload on top of UDP.

The default UDP port for MGCP is 2427, for both the softswitch and the endpoint/IAD.

Messages can be *commands* or *notifications*:

1. *CreateConnection* (CRCX). Always sent by the softswitch to create a connection between a named endpoint in the MG/IAD and a remote endpoint, which can be the destination endpoint, a multiplexed port in a PSTN gateway, or a packet port in a gateway connecting domains. There is a special case for CRCX for connections involving endpoints in the same MG/IAD, whereby the command can create a connection between two endpoints in the same device.

2. *ModifyConnection* (MDCX). Sent by the softswitch to modify the parameters of an established connection, such as the remote TA and codec selection. It may also affect local connection parameters (e.g., packetization rate).

3. *DeleteConnection* (DLCX). Sent by the softswitch at the termination of call. Can also be sent by the MG/IAD endpoint when the call has been abnormally terminated in the view of the endpoint. Example of abnormal termination is loss of the RTP media stream for a period exceeding a timer value.

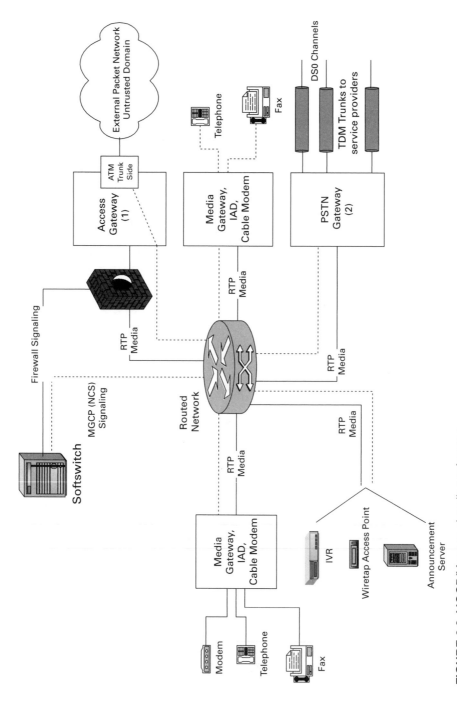

FIGURE 6.2 MGCP/Megaco signaling reference.

4. *NotificationRequest* (RQNT). Sent by the softswitch to request notification for a specific event or list of events, and also to request the MG/IAD endpoint to play signals and tones. Notification requests can be embedded in other commands to reduce signaling overhead.

5. *Notify* (NTFY). Sent by the endpoint to indicate a previously requested event has been detected.

6. *AuditEndpoint* (AUEP). Sent by the softswitch to obtain the status of an endpoint.

7. *AuditConnection* (AUCX). Sent by the softswitch to obtain the status of a connection. A useful attribute of this message is that the inquiring MGC in a distributed platform can obtain the identity of the signaling entity that is handling the call.

8. *ReStartInProgress* (RSIP). Sent by the MG/IAD to indicate some or all of its endpoints are in the process of being taken out of service, or that it is being rebooted.

9. *MoveConnection* (proposed Command MOVE). Has the same parameters as the MDCX command (which can be used as the command to move a connection), with the addition of a second endpoint ID in the same MG/IAD. Used to streamline signaling for calls involving endpoints on the same device.

Responses to all messages and commands require an acknowledgement (ACK) from the entity that received them. The references in Tables 6.1 through 6.4 offer a summary view of the MGCP messages and the required and optional parameters that can be sent in each of them by the signaling entities. In a softswitch environment, MGCP will most likely be one of the signaling protocols, because it requires additional "smarts" in the softswitch to establish multilegged, multiprotocol calls and to manage sessions.

When a connection is deleted by the softswitch, the ACK returned by the endpoint contains connection parameters, as shown in Table 6.3. Connection parameters are also optionally sent upstream to the softswitch in a DLCX command from the endpoint when it determines it is no longer possible to keep the call active (e.g., loss of RTP connectivity).

In response to MGCP commands, the softswitch can a receive a ***provisional response,*** a ***successful completion response,*** a ***transient error response,*** or a ***permanent error indication.*** The assigned codes are listed in Table 6.4. A provisional response indicates the recipient of the command wants to acknowledge receipt and successful recognition of the contents of the message, but that it's execution will take a little longer. A successful or unsuccessful response will follow later. This frees up the sender to continue other operations, which can be executed in parallel. Reaction to error responses is an attribute of softswitch architecture and design.

TABLE 6.1 MGCP Commands

VERB*	CODE†	DIRECTION	PARAMETER	RETURN INFORMATION
CreateConnection	CRCX	Softswitch→MG/IAD	EndpointID, M, [N, L, Z2, R, B], [Remote SDP]	ReturnCode, I, [Z, Z2, I2], [Local SDP]
ModifyConnection	MDCX	Softswitch → MG/IAD	EndpointID, I, [N, L, M, Remote SDP, R, B]	ReturnCode, [(modified) local SDP]
DeleteConnection	DLCX	1. Softswitch → MG/IAD	1. EndpointID, I, [R, B]	1. ReturnCode, P
		2. MG/IAD → Softswitch	2. C, EndpointID, I, E, P	2. ReturnCode
NotificationRequest	RQNT	Softswitch → MG/IAD	EndpointID, X, [N, R, D, S, Q, T, B]	ReturnCode
Notify	NTFY	MG/IAD → Softswitch	EndpointID, X, O, [N]	ReturnCode
AuditEndpoint	AUEP	Softswitch → MG/IAD	EndpointID, [F]	ReturnCode, EndpointIDList, [R, D, S, X, N, I, T, O, ES, B, RestartReason, RD, E]
AuditConnection	AUCX	Softswitch → MG/IAD	EndpointID, I, F	ReturnCode, [C, N, L, Local SDP, M, Remote SDP, P]
ReStartInProgress	RSIP	MG/IAD → Softswitch	EndpointID, RM, [RD, E]	ReturnCode, [N]
Endpoint Configuration	EPCF	Softswitch → MG/IAD	EndpointID, B	ReturnCode
MoveConnection (Proposed)	MDCX (MOVE)	Softswitch → MG/IAD	EndpointID, I, Z2, [N, L, M, remote SDP, R, B]	ReturnCode, [Z2, I, L]

*   Parameters in [ ] are optional.
†   EndpointID is the *name* of the endpoint.

TABLE 6.2 MGCP Protocol Parameters

INDEX	PARAMETER NAME	CODE	PARAMETER VALUE
1	ResponseAck	K	Indicates the ranges of confirmed transaction IDs to work around potential packet loss and the possibility of the same command being issued to the MG/IAD endpoint by the softswitch more than once.
2	BearerInformation	B	Indicates the line-side coding attribute name and value (e.g., **muLaw** or **Alaw**).
3	CallID	C	Hexadecimal string of, at most, 32 characters long. The value is sent by the softswitch to the MG endpoint and identifies the call, which may involve one or more local connections.
4	ConnectionID	I	This value is selected by the MG endpoint as the result of a CRCX command.
5	NotifiedEntity	N	An identifier in RFC821 formats, as in call_control@softswitch.anynet.com:5625 or *Joe@[128.23.0.4]*. If the actual IP address is used, it must be enclosed in brackets. The entity specified is supposed to receive all notifications for requested events. If this parameter is omitted, the endpoint sends its observed events to the last entity to have sent it a valid command.
6	RequestIdentifier	X	This parameter is selected by the softswitch and sent to the MG whenever an event notification is requested. The MG replies with the same parameter value when the requested event is observed, and a NTFY is sent to the softswitch.
7	LocalConnectionOptions	L	This structure characterizes the encoding method for the media stream, packetization period, bandwidth to be used, type of service, and use of echo cancellation. It is sent by the softswitch to the endpoint, usually in a CRCX command.
8	ConnectionMode	M	Defines the communication channel as fdx, hdx (send or receive only), loopback, inactive, continuity check, or data. Sent by the softswitch to the endpoint.

TABLE 6.2 MGCP Protocol Parameters (continued)

INDEX	PARAMETER NAME	CODE	PARAMETER VALUE
9	RequestedEvents	R	The softswitch sends one or more event codes to be looked for by the MG endpoint with this parameter. Events include on-hook, off-hook, digits collected, etc. Events can be requested to be sent immediately, quarantined for later transmission, or accumulated, as shown in Table 6.9.
10	SignalRequests	S	This parameter is sent by the softwitch to the MG endpoint to request playout of a signal, such as dial tone.
11	DigitMap	D	The digit map is sent by the softswitch to the MG endpoint to facilitate valid digit-string collection according to a numbering plan. It is done so that preliminary digit analysis can be done before a string is passed to the softswitch for further analysis. Strings that do not match the current plan are not transmitted by the MG.
12	ObservedEvents	O	This is sent by the MG to the softswitch when one or more requested events have been observed by the endpoint.
13	ConnectionParameters	P	These are general statistics about the performance of the connection. They are sent by the endpoint when a connection is deleted.
14	ReasonCode	E	A character string optionally sent in DLCX and RSIP messages.
15	SpecificEndPointID	Z	An identifier in RFC821 format, as in *EndPoint@dflx.com:5625, [128.32.0.4]*.
16	SecondEndpointID	Z2	An endpoint ID.
17	SecondConnectionID	I2	A connection ID.
18	Requested Info	F	Contains a list of parameter codes, separated by commas, as in the syntax: F: N,X,R,Q, for requesting the NotifiedEntity, RequestID, RequestedEvents, and QuarantineEvents parameter settings at the endpoint.

TABLE 6.2 MGCP Protocol Parameters (continued)

INDEX	PARAMETER NAME	CODE	PARAMETER VALUE
19	QuarantineHandling	Q	Requested events can occur immediately after a previously detected event caused a NTFY to be generated and before the ACK was received by the softswitch. This is known as the *notification state*. The keyword *process* requests that quarantined, observed events are stored and the keyword *discard* requests that they are discarded by the endpoint.
20	DetectEvents	T	This list of requested events is the minimum that must be detected by the MG endpoint while in the notification state. It is sent by the softswitch to the endpoint.
21	EventStates	ES	This is a list of endpoint states that can be audited and that must be returned to the softswitch in response to an AuditEndpoint command. For example ES: hu means the phone is off-hook.
22	RestartMethod	RM	Supported methods are *graceful*, *forced*, *restart*, or *disconnected*. It is sent by the MG to indicate an endpoint is being taken out of service or being placed back in service.
23	RestartDelay	RD	Sent by the MG/IAD when a RestartInProgess is sent to the softswitch for an endpoint. It specifies the number of seconds after which the endpoint will perform the RestartMethod, except when *forced* is indicated, which is done immediately. If the parameter is missing, the delay is zero.
24	Capabilities	A	The capabilities of the endpoint may be requested by the softswitch via an AuditEndpoint command. Capabilities are the compression algorithm (list of supported codecs), packetization period (range), bandwidth (range), echo cancellation, silence suppression, connection modes, type of service, and event package. An event package is a bundling of signals and events supported by a specific endpoint type—for example, an analog phone.

TABLE 6.3 MGCP Connection Parameters

PARAMETER NAME	CODE	CONNECTION PARAMETER VALUE
Packets Sent	PS	The total number of packets sent in the duration of the connection.
Octets Sent	OS	The total number of octets sent in the duration of the connection.
Packets Received	PR	The total number of packets received in the duration of the connection.
Octets Received	OR	The total number of octets received in the duration of the connection.
Packets Lost	PL	The total number of packets lost in the duration of the connection, as indicated by gaps in the sequence numbers and by packets that arrived too late to be placed in the endpoint playout buffer.
Jitter	JI	An integer expressing the average inter-packet arrival jitter.
Latency	LA	Average latency, in milliseconds, in integer format.

TABLE 6.4 MGCP Return Codes

CODE	MEANING
1xx	*Provisional Responses*
100	Executing transaction; will provide response later.
2xx	*Successful Completion Responses*
200	OK. The requested transaction was executed successfully.
250	OK. Response to DLCX. Connections deleted (sends call statistics).
4xx	*Transient Error Responses*
400	Transaction not executed.
401	Phone is already off-hook.
402	Phone is already on-hook.
5xx	*Permanent Error Indication*
500	Endpoint unavailable.

TABLE 6.4 MGCP Return Codes (continued)

CODE	MEANING
501	Endpoint not ready.
510	Protocol error.
511	Command contained unrecognized extension.
512	Gateway not equipped to detect one of the requested signals.
513	Gateway not equipped to generate one of the requested signals.
514	Gateway could not send the specified announcement.
515	Incorrect connection ID.
516	Unknown call ID.
517	Unsupported or invalid mode.
518	Unsupported or unknown package.
519	Endpoint does not have a digit map.
520	Endpoint is restarting.
521	Endpoint redirected to another MGC/softswitch.
522	No such event or signal.
523	Unknown action or illegal combination of actions.
524	Internal inconsistency in LocalConnectionOptions.
525	Unknown extension in LocalConnectionOptions.
526	Insufficient bandwidth.
527	Missing RemoteConnectionDescriptor.
528	Incompatible protocol version.
529	Internal hardware failure.
530	CAS signaling protocol error.
531	Facility failure.

When the MG/IAD sends a DLCX command to the softswitch, indicating it unilaterally deleted a connection, it includes a reason code, per Table 6.5. Reason codes are also used with the RSIP command to indicate the reason for the restart.

The protocol supports a variety of connection modes, as shown in the annotated Table 6.6. Connection modes with the **M:** protocol parameter override the SDP media attribute **a=** for the currently selected connection mode.

TABLE 6.5 MGCP Reason Codes

CODE	MEANING
000	Normal. Returned if all is OK in response to an AUDIT request.
900	Endpoint Malfunctioning. General hardware or software problems.
901	Endpoint taken out of service.
902	Loss of lower-layer connectivity.

TABLE 6.6 MGCP Connection Modes

CONNECTION MODE	ACTIONS
M:sendonly	The gateway should only send packets.
M:recvonly	The gateway should only receive packets.
M:sendrecv	The gateway should send and receive packets.
M:confrnce	The gateway should place the connection in conference mode.
M:inactive	The gateway should neither send nor receive packets.
M:loopback	The gateway should place the circuit in loopback mode.
M:contest	The gateway should place the circuit in test mode.
M:netwloop	The gateway should place the connection in network loopback mode.
M:netwtest	The gateway should place the connection in network continuity test mode.
M:data	The gateway should use this as a data connection.

6.2 MEDIA GATEWAY INITIALIZATION AND REGISTRATION WITH THE SOFTSWITCH

MGCP endpoints do not have the ability to discover the softswitch serving them, and the underlying assumption is that there will be a preprovisioned softswitch address in the MG/IAD when it is first installed. When it is first booted up, the MG/IAD sends an RSIP command to the default softswitch IP address and waits for an acknowledgment. The MG/IAD must use wildcarding as much as possible to ensure there is no restart message avalanche from all of its endpoints, and at minimum, a single RSIP should be sent (if possible) to indicate the entire box is coming into service.

If no ACK arrives from the preprovisioned softswitch, there is little the MG/IAD can do. If an ACK is received, the restart finishes and the gateway and its endpoints are all placed in service.

In a distributed softswitch platform, it is possible for the entity that receives the initial RSIP, to assign a different signaling agent to service the MG/IAD. In that case, subsequent signaling between the endpoint and the softswitch will be with the newly assigned signaling agent. Furthermore, messages that are sent by the signaling entity to an endpoint may optionally contain a *NotifiedEntity* parameter to steer responses to particular call agents[3] in the softswitch. The combination of these two methods allows the platform to scale to the call capacity level required by the application.

6.3 CALL SETUP AND TERMINATION

In this section we take a look at call flow between an MGCP endpoint and an endpoint in an H.323 domain. The call flow is shown in Figure 6.3 and Figure 6.4. A detailed analysis of Figure 6.3 is given in Table 6.7 and a detailed analysis of Figure 6.4 is given in Table 6.8.

The call can last for as long as the parties want it to, and there is an event in the **Generic Media Package** of the RFC that can be requested by the softswitch running MGCP to signal a repeatable milestone (accumulated one hour). When either party wishes to hang up, a call flow similar to the one in Figure 6.4 is executed. We assume the caller hangs up first.

Before the call termination call flow begins, we see an AUEP or AUCX message sent by the softswitch to the endpoint, to audit itself or the particular connection. This exchange can be initiated by the softswitch at any time—also several times—and returns the optional list of parameters shown in Table 6.1.

---

3.   A call agent may or may not be different than a signaling agent in a softswitch platform. This is an implementation attribute.

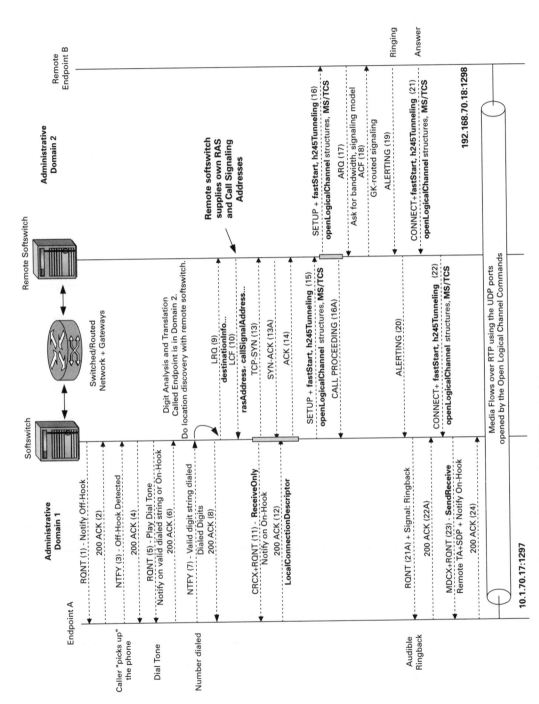

FIGURE 6.3 MGCP call setup with remote H.323 endpoint.

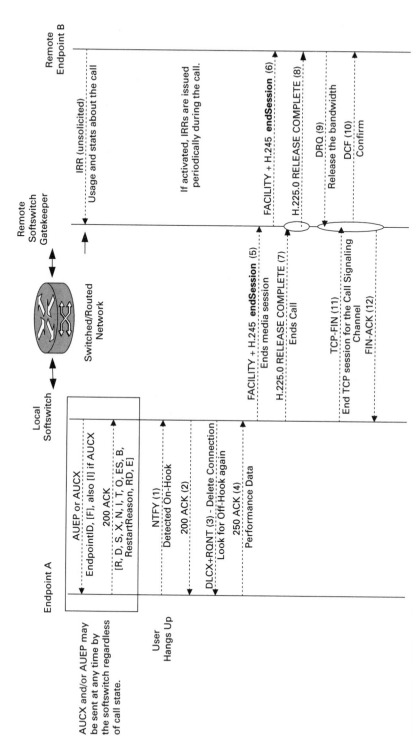

FIGURE 6.4 MGCP call termination with remote H.323 endpoint.

177

TABLE 6.7 MGCP to H.323 Detailed Call Flow

MESSAGE OR COMMAND RESPONSE	PARAMETERS	COMMENTS
(1) RQNT (Softswitch→Endpoint)	56 aaln/1@dflx.com MGCP 1.0	NotificationRequest to the endpoint; TransactionID number is 56, endpoint name, Protocol MGCP version 0.1.
	N:call_control@dflx.com:2427	Send your event notifications to *call_control@dflx.com:2427* (to the default MGCP signaling port). The endpoint must be able to resolve *dflx.com* to an IP address via DNS lookup or other means. Otherwise, an IP address must be supplied.
	X: ABCD56	RequestID is used to correlate an NTFY sent from an endpoint with an RQNT sent by the softswitch.
	R: hd	Notify the MGC upon observing off hook.
(2) ACK (Endpoint→Softswitch)	200 56 OK	The NotificationRequest was accepted by the endpoint.
(3) NTFY (Endpoint→Softswitch)	503 aaln/1@dflx.com MGCP 1.0	Notify, TransactionID 503, endpoint name, Protocol MGCP version 1.0. Observed off-hook at the endpoint.
	N:call_control@dflx.com:2427	The NotifiedEntity is the same as the one received in the previous command received.
	X: ABCD56	RequestID supplied for correlation with the original RQNT.
	O: L/hd	Observed event: off-hook. Reported events are preceded by a package name abbreviation and a forward slash, such as *L/hd* if the endpoint was running the line (L) package.
(4) ACK (Softswitch→Endpoint)	200 503 OK	Notification of the off-hook event accepted by the softswitch.
(5) RQNT (Softswitch→Endpoint)	58 aaln/1@dflx.com MGCP 1.0	Play dial tone, set the digit map, and notify the softswitch when a valid digit string has been dialed. Also look for on-hook again.

TABLE 6.7 MGCP to H.323 Detailed Call Flow (continued)

MESSAGE OR COMMAND RESPONSE	PARAMETERS	COMMENTS
	N:call_control@dflx.com:2427	NotifiedEntity for the events requested in this command. It may be another addressable entity in the softswitch, if load balancing is being implemented.
	X: ABCD57	RequestID for the embedded requested events.
	R: hu, [0–9#*T] (D)	Any digit from 0 to 9 plus the pound sign, on the active digit map. The softswitch asks the endpoint to treat the digit dialing according to the digit map (D).
	D: (0T|00T|[2–9]xxxxxxx|1 1 [2–9]xxxxxxx|011xx.T)	Set this (sample) digit map for the call. A digit map may be preloaded in the IAD and applied to its endpoints for all calls, thus minimizing the overhead of having to send it on a per-call-attempt basis. If the digit map is not supplied when the request to look for a digit string is made, the currently active digit map for the endpoint will be used.
	S: dl	Signal: Play dial tone. In general, dial tone indicates the carrier is present to process the call, and it is recommended not to be provided automatically by the IAD as soon as off-hook is detected.
(6) ACK (Endpoint→Softswitch)	200 58 OK	NotificationRequest accepted by the IAD for its endpoint.
(7) NTFY (Endpoint→Softswitch)	578 aaln/1@dflx.com MGCP 1.0	Notify: TransactionID 578; valid, dialed digit string detected.
	N: call_control@dflx.com:2427	The NTFY is sent to this entity, which had been previously identified in the RQNT as the desired recipient.
	X: ABCD57	RequestID matches the value in the RQNT command.
	O: 1, 7, 0, 3, 5, 5, 5, 1, 2, 1, 2	Observed event: A digit sequence that matches a generic digit map in the dial plan.

TABLE 6.7 MGCP to H.323 Detailed Call Flow (continued)

MESSAGE OR COMMAND RESPONSE	PARAMETERS	COMMENTS
(8) ACK (Softswitch→Endpoint)	200 578 OK	Notification accepted by the softswitch, and it will attempt to route the call.
		At this point, the softswitch needs to translate the telephone number dialed by the caller and convert it to a location identifier (URL), an IP address, or an identifier of the network that hosts the called endpoint. The latter is the context of this example (see Figures 6.3 and 6.4), and after translation of the dialed number, the local softswitch determines the endpoint is served by the remote softswitch in Administrative Domain 2, and that it is an H.323 endpoint. The local softswitch does not have direct access to the H.323 endpoint to initiate call signaling; therefore, we employ location discovery techniques to locate the called user. *If the calling endpoint is capable of placing calls by identifying endpoints as a URL, the resolution of the called URL to an IP address can be done with DNS, or resolution to an E.164 number via DNS can be done with a lookup in a telephone mapping database.**
(9) LRQ (Softswitch→ Remote Softswitch)	RAS command **endpointIdentifier, destinationInfo, sourceInfo, desiredProtocols, desiredTunneledProtocol, etc.**	Locate the endpoint in the **destinationInfo** field.
(10) LCF (Remote Softswitch→ Softswitch)	LCF **rasAddress, callSignalAddress, etc.**	Endpoint located; use **callSignalAddress** for setting up a call (in this case the remote softswitch will act as a GK). GK also supplies its own RAS signaling address and will act as proxy in all signaling with the called endpoint.
(11) CRCX (Softswitch→Endpoint)	62 aaln/1@dflx.com MGCP 1.0	The softswitch may now proceed to create a connection at the called endpoint. Only the LocalConnectionDescriptor is known at this point, and the remote SDP will be sent with an MDCX command later. For now, no SDP is sent for the connection.
	C: ABCD3	Softswitch assigns a call ID.
	L: p:10, a:PCMU	LocalConnectionOptions: packetization period = 10 ms audio type = PCM muLaw The issue of codec negotiation can get pretty complex, but we assume a simple one-pass negotiation.

TABLE 6.7 MGCP to H.323 Detailed Call Flow (Continued)

MESSAGE OR COMMAND RESPONSE	PARAMETERS	COMMENTS
	M: **recvonly**	ConnectionMode is receive only, but could have been set in full duplex mode.
	N: call_control@dflx.com:2427	NotifiedEntity, same as the one used in previous MGCP signaling to the endpoint.
	X: ABCD58	RequestID, for new event requests embedded in this message.
	R: hd	Look for on-hook.
(12) ACK (Endpoint→Softswitch)	200 62 OK I: 01054D	ConnectionID selected by the local called endpoint. The call ID and ConnectionID uniquely identify this session in Administrative Domain 1.
	v=0 c=IN IP4 **10.1.70.17** m=audio **1297** RTP/AVP 0	The local calling endpoint returns its own SDP: its media IP address, UDP port (both fields shown in **bold**), media type, and mode of the connection (payload type 0, 64 Kbps PCM). The ACK response may include more than one SDP.
		The LocalConnectionDescriptor is needed at this time in order to send it to the called endpoint's proxy (remote softswitch).
TCP-SYN SYN-ACK ACK	Establishment of reliable transport channel with remote Softswitch, acting as proxy for the called endpoint in Administrative Domain 2.	Signaling steps 13, 13A, 14.
(15) SETUP (Softswitch→ Remote Softswitch)	**fastStart, h245Tunneling, openLogicalChannel, MS/TCS, parallelH245Control**, etc.	Q.931/H.225.0 command from the local softswitch to the **callsignalAddress** supplied by the remote softswitch during discovery. Asking for fastStart and also sending the forward logical channel parameters, the parallel245control field with the MS/TCS determination structures, and asking for Tunneling of H.245 commands.
(16) Q.931 SETUP (Remote Softswitch→ Called Endpoint)	**fastStart, h245Tunneling, openLogicalChannel, MS/TCS, parallelH245Control**, etc.	The remote softswitch/GK sends the contents of the incoming SETUP to the actual called endpoint.

TABLE 6.7 MGCP to H.323 Detailed Call Flow (continued)

MESSAGE OR COMMAND RESPONSE	PARAMETERS	COMMENTS
(16A) Q.931 CALL PROCEEDING	Optional	This provisional response from the remote softswitch/GK says the call data has been accepted and is in the process of routing the call. The caller is unaware of the methods used inside Administrative Domain 2 to route calls to endpoints.
(17) ARQ (Called Endpoint Remote Softswitch)	Ask for call bandwidth and signaling model.	If during the remote registration procedure (RRQ, RCF), the endpoint had received pregranted ARQ, this exchange would not be necessary.
(18) ACF (Remote Softswitch→ Called Endpoint)	GK replies with Gatekeeper-routed signaling call model (in **destCallSignalAddress**)	
(19) and (20) Q.931 ALERTING	Optional	Indication from the called endpoint that the call has been delivered and the phone is "ringing" (19). This message is passed on to the calling GK (20).
(21A) RQNT (Softswitch → Calling Endpoint)	63 aaln/1@dflx.com MGCP 1.0	Play audible ringback tone to the caller on the current connection. Continue to look for on-hook and supply notification for that event when detected.
	N:call_control@dflx.com:2427	
	X: ABCD58	
	S:G/rt@$	
	R:hd	
(22A) ACK (Calling Endpoint→Softswitch)	200 63 OK	Accepted. Note that audible ringback in the PSTN is generated by the terminating exchange, whereas the MGCP protocol allows for ringback to be generated by the IAD, under command from the call control entity in the softswitch. This is acceptable if the initiation of ringback corresponds to an indication from the remote endpoint that the call has actually been delivered and the phone is ringing.

TABLE 6.7 MGCP to H.323 Detailed Call Flow (continued)

MESSAGE OR COMMAND RESPONSE	PARAMETERS	COMMENTS
		Events 21A and 22A are completely asynchronous to signaling occurring between the remote endpoint and its softswitch/GK.
(21) and (22) Q.931 CONNECT	**fastStart, h245Tunneling, openLogicalChannel, MS/TCS, parallelH245Control,** etc.	Better late than never—when the call is finally answered, the remote endpoint indicates it supports **fastStart** and **h245Tunneling**, and has included the **openLogicalChannel** structures for the reverse channels, as well as MS/TCS structures in the **parallelH245Control** field.
		openLogicalChannel structures can also be sent by the caller requesting bidirectional channels.
		If the endpoint is unable to support tunneling and parallel H.245 control, the GK will have to unbundle H.245 content from tunneled messages coming in from the calling party's GK, establish an H.245 signaling session, and set up the logical channels and all subsequent signaling using explicit H.245 procedures. This will take longer to complete the call setup.
		Message (22) is the same CONNECT message sent by the called endpoint, this time repeated (and possibly modified) by the remote GK to the softswitch/GK in Administrative Domain 1.
(23) MDCX + (embedded) RQNT (Softswitch→ Calling Endpoint)	64 aaln/1@dflx.com MGCP 1.0	The local softswitch now needs to modify the connection at the calling endpoint and finish the setup of the transport addresses. The remote endpoint was aware of the caller's media TA, so we need to set up the calling endpoint with the called party's media TA.
	C: ABCD3	CallID is the same at both ends.
	M: **sendrecv**	ConnectionMode is now full duplex. The remote SDP is available in the message and this can be done.
	X: ABCD60	RequestID.
	R: hu	Look for on-hook.

183

TABLE 6.7 MGCP to H.323 Detailed Call Flow (continued)

MESSAGE OR COMMAND RESPONSE	PARAMETERS	COMMENTS
	v=0 c=IN IP4 **192.168.70.18** m=audio **1298** RTP/AVP 0	This is the SDP of the remote connection. It is shown here as a private IP address, but it can be any public address and does not have to be part of any local addressing schemes or subnets, for either domain. The generated RTP/RTCP packets will be routed to the egress gateway(s) and from there to their ultimate destination. This is a generic operation and applies to both endpoints. It is possible to use firewalls, which implement NAT/PAT on this TA pair. This means that the softswitches themselves will either need to dynamically open and close the ports associated with the public addresses corresponding to the media channels for the duration of the call or employ "smart" firewalls that are capable of understanding the signaling exchanges through the various gateways they protect. Media security (authentication and privacy) can be achieved through encryption, but this does not protect against a denial-of-service attack. Encryption keys, if applicable, are sent via the K parameter of SDP. For simplicity, we show a one-pass acceptance of the codec negotiation.
(24) ACK (Calling Endpoint→ Softswitch	200 64 OK	We are good to go!

At this point media can flow between the calling and called endpoint. However, no attempt was made to ensure the integrity of the physical path between the media transport addresses of the two parties, such as to ensure the cables are plugged in at both ends and that there is end-to-end continuity between the endpoints.

The co1 and co2 continuity mechanisms can be used selectively by the softswitch to establish media continuity prior to completing the call establishment. This would be similar to the way it is done on the PSTN.

TABLE 6.8 MGCP Call Termination

MESSAGE OR COMMAND RESPONSE	PARAMETERS	COMMENTS
(1) NTFY (Calling Endpoint→ Softswitch)	100 aaln/1@dflx.com MGCP 1.0	Notify, TransactionID 3001, endpoint name.
	N: call_control@dflx.com:2427	The NotifiedEntity of the last message that contained the N parameter.
	X: ABCD58	RequestID for the observed event, which matches the last embedded notification request.
	O: L/hu	Observed event: hang-up.
ACK Softswitch→ Calling Endpoint	200 100 OK	Accepted.
(3) DLCX + (embedded) RQNT (Softswitch→ Calling Endpoint)	160 aaln/1@dflx.com MGCP 1.0	Delete the connection and go on the lookout for another off-hook event.
	C: ABCD3	
	I: 01054D	
	R:hd	

185

TABLE 6.8 MGCP Call Termination (continued)

MESSAGE OR COMMAND RESPONSE	PARAMETERS	COMMENTS
(4) ACK (Calling Endpoint→Softswitch)	250 160 OK P: PS=3000, OS=200000, PR=2900, OR=196000, PL=25, JI=22	Returns call statistics in the local connection parameters. The call now needs to be unstitched between the local softswitch/GK and the softswitch/GK of Administrative Domain 2.
(5) and (6) Q.931 FACILITY Domain 1 to Domain 2; Domain 2 then repeats to called endpoint.	**endSession**,...	Terminates the media channels and indicates the session has been terminated locally. The remote GK continues to act as conduit of the Q.931 signaling messages.
(7) and (8) Q.931 RELEASE COMPLETE	Call Identifier, reason, Capacity, etc.	Sent to terminate the signaling channel as well.
H.323 RAS (9) DRQ (10) DCF (Administrative Domain 2)	Disengage from the call and release the bandwidth.	It is not always done.
(11) TCP-FIN (12) FIN-ACK Between Admin Domains	N/A	Remove the reliable transport channel. The call is terminated.

6.4 MGCP-ISUP INTERWORKING

The call flow of Figure 6.5 shows basic MGCP-ISUP interworking, with a call that originated behind a PRI PBX.

The initial SETUP command from the PBX to the local exchange contains the dialed number, which the local exchange analyzes and determines that it belongs to the domain of the softswitch. The Local Exchange (LE) sends a CALL PROCEEDING to the PBX, while it also generates an ISUP-IAM message and sends it through its Signaling Transfer Point (STP) to the softswitch PSTN gateway. The PSTN GW also terminates the TDM voice facilities.

The signaling gateway has been previously sensitized to generate a notification on an incoming call and supply the called number to the softswitch. The softswitch analyzes the number and once the MG/IAD that hosts it has been identified, a CRCX message is sent to both the PSTN GW and the terminating endpoint in the MG/IAD. A RQNT command is sent to the endpoint to commence ringing *(s:rg)* and to be on the lookout for off-hook *(R:oh)*. The final SDP is sent to the GW, along with a signal to play ringback *(s:rb)* to the caller over the TDM circuit, which has already been cut through. The ISUP-ACM is generated at that time and sent to the STP of the local exchange, which the LE translates to a Q.931 ALERTING and sends to the PBX.

When the called party answers the phone, a NTFY with *O:hd* is returned by the endpoint to the softswitch notified entity. The softswitch proceeds to ask the PSTN GW to stop generating the ringback tone (removes the signal in the MDCX command). The ISUP-ANM message is generated by the GW to the LE, which in turn translates it to a Q.931 CONNECT and sends it to the PBX. The softswitch also places the endpoint on the lookout for on-hook when the called party hangs up, and the GW is sensitized to look for an RLC command from the LE.

Either party can initiate call termination. If the caller hangs up first, an ISUP-REL message is received by the GW, which it sends in a NTFY to the softswitch. The softswitch then will delete the connections between the GW and the endpoint and set up the GW up to look for IAM. The GW will send an RLC, and the LE will complete the release of the call with the PBX.

If the called endpoint hangs up first, an "on-hook" is detected and it sends a NTFY with *O:hu*. The softswitch deletes the connection between the endpoint and the GW. The GW is asked to generate an ISUP-REL to the LE, which sends a Q.931 DISCONNECT to the PBX and initiates ISUP-Q.931 call termination procedures between the LE and the PBX.

6.4.1 Handling of Quarantined Events

When an endpoint sends a NTFY message to the softswitch, with the name of an event that was detected, it enters a state during which other events can be

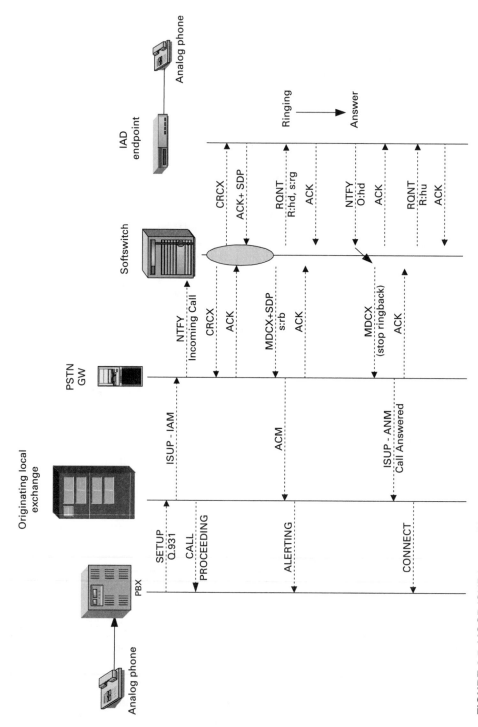

FIGURE 6.5 MGCP ISUP interworking.

detected and placed in a "quarantine" buffer, because additional notifications cannot be sent upstream. The softswitch has the option to tell the endpoint how to handle such quarantined events via the optional QuarantineHandling parameter. The options for handling quarantine events are listed in Table 6.9. Note that if notification of quarantine events has been requested, this may result in multiple notifications as events occur in the quarantine state.

6.4.2 Codec Negotiation and Bandwidth Allocation

In any signaling architecture and topology, the gateways connecting to outside domains will require signaling to "stitch" the legs of the call. For example, RTP PB (RTP Endpoint B) may very well be the egress port for the call we just examined. In cases of intermediate gateways on the path of the call, the issue of codec negotiation comes up as a concern for the quality of the call. Gateways will add some delay and jitter, particularly if the SLA of the party making the call is different than the advertised capabilities outside the domain. For example, we saw a G.711 call end-to-end, but if connectivity with Administrative Domain 2 is via G.729, then transcoding needs to take

TABLE 6.9 Event Actions

ACTION UPON DETECTION OF EVENT	MEANING	CODE
Notify immediately	Send a NTFY immediately, together with all other accumulated events.	N
Accumulate	Do not notify yet, but continue to accumulate events.	A
Treat according to digit map	Accumulate according to the rules of the active digit map.	D
Swap	If the endpoint is handling more than one connection (e.g., call waiting), it is allowed to swap audio streams, when attached to an event like flash-hook.	S
Ignore	Ignore the event. The occurrence of the event is never seen by the softswitch.	I
Keep signal(s) active	All signals that are set remain active during the quarantine period.	K
Embedded notification request	Handle the embedded notification requests for signals that are supposed to start when events on the list occur.	E

place in the egress gateway. Every time we go through such a media format conversion, we degrade the call. Furthermore, the conversion from G.711 to G.729 is irreversible with regard to the original frequency spectrum, and this will always be the case when moving from direct waveform coding methods (e.g., PCM) to a perceptually weighted encoding. In other words, if inside Administrative Domain 2 the process reverses back to G.711 media format, the original voice quality degradation will not be reversed.

The bandwidth considerations for the call are similar to those we saw in Chapter 5 for an H.323 call. In this scenario, there is the additional consideration that the H.323 endpoints may not support a non-ITU codec, which may be indicated in the local SDP of the calling party when it responds to the CRCX command. H.323 allows asymmetric operation—the mandatory G.711 one way and a different format in the reverse direction—but this may be an unlikely scenario for toll calls across carrier and service provider domains.

H.323 specifies support for an extended (non-G-series) media type (non-GSM) in the **openLogicalChannel** structures. It is envisioned that most MG/IAD implementations will support the major codecs of the H.323 suite, such as G.729 and the mandatory G.711, for calls to H.323 endpoints, with the objective to establish the call in a one-pass codec negotiation.

Firewalls, on the other hand, will mess things up if not carefully placed in the topology. The most likely degradation can be jitter, followed by delay. Either of those will decrease the perceptible quality to the parties in the call. Figure 6.6 shows an extended trace of packets captured through a firewall with sightly over 55 Mbps of traffic through it. The jitter variance is low and the distribution forms a bell-shaped curve. The objective of a design is to minimize the width of the curve and thus minimize jitter and the potential for

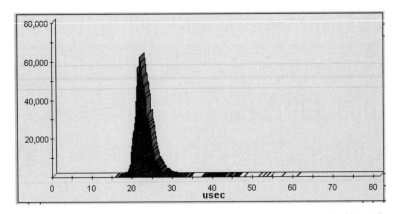

FIGURE 6.6 Firewall jitter, low variance (captured with Adtech AX4000).

increased latency. Firewalls should be load-tested to their specifications, with maximum loading on the links of the deployment configuration.

A serious issue to be addressed with the firewall topology is the potential "shielding" of active calls from failure when a softswitch, gateway or link fails and calls have to be rerouted through another firewall to another softswitch or gateway. If the softswitch relies on a timer expiration tied to RTP stream loss detection, it may take too long to react to failures.

RTP implementations employ heartbeat timers to ensure they are alerted when the RTP stream is lost. They range between 5 and 10 seconds, at the end of which the call is declared lost if no RTP (or RTCP) packets have been received. Whatever actions are taken in case of an intermediate gateway failure, they must be completed and the RTP connectivity reestablished before the heartbeat timers expire. If they do, it is too late and the call will be deleted from the endpoints. This is a critical piece of the network design, and its proper implementation will make the provider offer voice services with the robustness we have enjoyed on the PSTN. Since it is unlikely both legs of a call will be controlled by the same softswitch, and that both legs will be using MGCP signaling, the magnitude of this problem cannot be overstated.

Use of RSVP for VoIP QoS

Use of RSVP on a per-call basis can severely limit the performance of the call processing platform. It is more likely to see RSVP as a means for establishing MPLS tunnels, as we have discussed previously, over which multiple voice calls can be transported. In this case, the use of QoS routing techniques do not affect the performance of the system in any way. Another form of QoS control that may be employed is DiffServ, either by itself or in conjunction with MPLS, which would also not affect signaling and capacity performance in calls per second.

An MPLS tunnel could exist in the core network of each administrative domain. The common interface between gateways may or may not be switched at Layer 2 or Layer 3, but it is expected the call capacity of the links joining the domains to map voice and voiceband traffic to high-priority virtual circuits.

6.4.3 Media Gateway Packages

MGCP specifies endpoint types and the event packages expected to be supported by each type. A package is a list of events and signals required for proper operation of the type of endpoint. Events are reported with NTFY messages, and the event names are composed of an optional package name, separated by a slash (/) from the name of the actual event.

Table 6.10 is a list of the various packages that have been defined for the protocol. If an event can also be signaled by the softswitch, an entry is made in the "signals" column, along with attributes relating to duration and other characteristics.

TABLE 6.10 MGCP Media Packages

PACKAGE NAME	ABBR.	EVENTS	SIGNALS
Generic Media Package	G	mt (modem tone)	rt (ringback tone, TimeOut)
		ft (fax tone)	rbk (###) (ringback on connection tone, TimeOut, 180 seconds)
		ld (long duration call)	cf (confirm tone, Brief)
		pat (###) [pattern ### detected, On/Off]	cg (network congestion tone, TimeOut)
		of (report failure)	it (intercept tone, On/Off)
			pt (preemption tone, On/Off)
DTMF Package	D	0–9 [any digit]	Brief
		A–D [any letter]	Brief
		L (long duration indicator)	2 seconds
		X (wildcard match 0–9)	Not signaled
		T (interdigit timer)	4 seconds
		of (report failure)	Cannot be signaled
MF Package	M	0–9 [any digit]	Brief
		X (wildcard match 0–9)	Not signaled
		T	4 seconds
		K0–K2	Brief
		S0–S3	Brief
		wk (wink)	Brief
		wko (wink off)	Brief
		is (incoming seizure)	On/Off
		rs (return seizure)	On/Off
		us (unseize ckt)	On/Off

TABLE 6.10 MGCP Media Packages (continued)

PACKAGE NAME	ABBR.	EVENTS	SIGNALS
		of (report failure)	
Trunk Package	T	co1	On/Off
		co2	On/Off
			lb (loopback) On/Off
		om (old milliwatt tone)	On/Off
		nm (new milliwatt tone)	On/Off
		t1 (test line)	On/Off
		zz (no circuit)	On/Off
		as (answer supervision)	On/Off
		ro (reorder)	TimeOut
		of (report failure)	--
			bl (blocking) On/Off
Line Package	L	hd (off hook)	adsi display (Brief)
		hu (on hook)	vmwi display (On/Off)
		hf (flashhook)	bz (busy tone)
		aw (answer tone)	ci (ti, nu, na) [caller ID]
		nbz (network busy)	wt (call waiting tone)
		p (prompt tone)	wt1-wt4 (alternate call waiting tones)
		e (error tone)	dl (dial tone)
		oc (report on completion)	mwi (message waiting)
		s (###) [distinctive tone pattern]	ro (reorder tone)
		of (report failure)	rg (ringing tone)
			r0–r7 (distinctive ringing)

TABLE 6.10 MGCP Media Packages (continued)

PACKAGE NAME	ABBR.	EVENTS	SIGNALS
			rs (ringsplash)
			sl (stutter dial tone)
			v (alerting tone)
			y (recorder warning tone)
			sit (SIT tone)
			z (calling card service tone)
			ot (off-hook warning tone)
Handset Package	H	Same as **Line** package, but events can be requested *and* signaled, *except* for **t** and **ot**. Also, no **rs** tone and no **ci** tone.	
RTP Package	R	UC (used codec change)	--
		SR (new sampling rate)	--
		JI (jitter buffer)	--
		PL (packet loss exceeded)	--
		qa (quality alert)	--
		co1	On/Off
		co2	On/Off
		of (report failure)	--
Network Access Server Package	N	pa (packet arrival)	--
		cbk (callback request)	--
		cl (carrier lost)	--
		au (authorization success)	--
		ax (authorization denied)	--
		of (report failure)	--

TABLE 6.10 MGCP Media Packages (continued)

PACKAGE NAME	ABBR.	EVENTS	SIGNALS
Announcement Server Package	A		TimeOut; ann (play an announcement)
		oc (report on completion)	--
		of (report on failure)	--
Script Package	Script		TimeOut; java, pearl, tcl, xml
		oc, of	--

6.5 SPECIAL CALL FLOWS

In carrier environments, there are several call types that require special call flows and equipment to support them. Here is a list of situations that can come up.

- *Connect a media stream to a wiretap device*, as dictated by federal law enforcement requirements. Provide participant information and media content. This is a one-way (**M:recvonly**) single connection into the wiretap device, with no outgoing transmission of RTP or RTCP packets.
- *Continuity testing.* This can be done every few calls to ensure media path connectivity inside the service provider's network and over the external links connecting to other enterprise domains and carriers.
- *Connecting a call to an IVR unit or an application server.* This is a very common feature for Voice over Virtual Private Networks (VoVPN) and calling card services. The IVR will play messages, collect digits, supply the digits to an entity in an application server, receive new instructions, and repeat until the call agent feels the call can proceed, or it will be rejected. IVRs can be independent devices or adjuncts to application servers and softswitches.
- *Connecting a call to a conferencing unit.* Ad hoc conferencing is useful, and the desire to support call migration to a conferencing unit a la H.323 (MCU) may be a requirement regardlen of the endpoint types involved in the call.
- *Routing a call from one endpoint to another.* This is the so-called "hairpin" connection and can manifest itself as routing of a stream between links on the same gateway.

IVRs and announcement servers are slave devices that do not initiate calls. As such, they are recipients of commands to set up connections between themselves and the endpoint in an ingress gateway or the actual calling endpoint in an IAD. They are paced through the steps of the call setup using signals and events from one of the media packages listed in the previous section.

6.6 SDP PROTOCOL REVIEW

SDP is defined in RFC 2327 and IETF draft proposal *<draft-ietf-mmusic-sdp-new-01.txt>*. SDP is rarely used as a protocol by itself in softswitch environments; however, SDP syntax is used by signaling protocols in their message constructs to describe properties of multimedia sessions during call setup and to modify attributes of active sessions in real time. We will see SDP syntax in SIP and Megaco protocol constructs, used much in the same way as we have seen it used under MGCP.

6.6.1 Message Formats

A session description is encoded as an ASCII string, using an abbreviated message format, as shown in Table 6.11. Typical SDP syntax in a packet consists of the parameter abbreviation, followed by the "=" sign and the description. For example,

v=0
c=IN IP4 **192.168.70.18**
m=audio **1298** RTP/AVP 0

Extensions to the standard SDP syntax have been implemented with the use of the character "$", which indicates the recipient of the session description is free to pick the parameter. We will see how it is used in the call flows of the Megaco protocol. An example syntax is m=audio $ RTP/AVP 0, which instructs the endpoint to select the UDP port.

The (-) is used to indicate the parameter value can be omitted, and there are also several extensions to the basic syntax proposed for ATM networks.

As we will see throughout the call flow examples, the designer must keep in mind that firewall openings may need to be modified on the fly, based on the contents of the SDPs for calls in the setup process or for calls that are already active. Therefore, parsing of the SDP may be necessary by a firewall or other signaling proxy (e.g., the softswitch itself) to manage the firewall resources.

TABLE 6.11 SDP Protocol Parameters

PARAMETER	MEANING
v	*Protocol version.* Delineates session descriptions if multiple SDPs are included in a message.
o	Session *owner/creator* and session identifier.
s	Session name.
i	Session information.
e	*Email address* of the sender, if deemed useful.
p	*Phone number* of the sender, if it must be known.
c	*Connection information.* Includes the network type, IP protocol version number, and IP address of an endpoint. The distinction between local and remote endpoints is obtained from the context of the signaling protocol message. The port number of the media connection is supplied with the **m=** parameter.
b	*Bandwidth information.* This parameter is useful, although signaling protocols may employ other means to convey this information to signaling endpoints, and the information may even be derived from the media packetization format and rate.
z	Time zone adjustments.
k	*Encryption key,* which may be required for the session. See Chapter 8, which discusses a method to establish endpoint compliance with required parameters before session establishment can proceed.
a	*Attribute.* An SDP may have one or more attribute lines, but care must be taken not to supply conflicting attributes for the same media stream in the same SDP. SDP allows descriptors that are specific to a particular media format to be exchanged in a manner transparent to the protocol with the **a=fmtp** syntax. Chapter 9 lists extensions to the attribute parameters for support of T.38 real-time fax relay over IP networks.
t	*Time.* Specifies start and stop time in two fields separated by a space. Useful for conference announcement.
m	*Media information,* such as payload type and packetization rate. Also carries the other half of the TA (the port). Note that the packetization rate may also be carried by other means in the same signaling message, so care must be exercised to avoid confusion.

References

1. *IP Telephony: The Integration of Robust VoIP Services,* Bill Douskalis, Prentice Hall PTR, 2000.
2. "PacketCable Network-Based Call Signaling Protocol Specification," PKT-SP-EC-MGCP-I02-991201, December 1, 1999, Cablelabs.
3. RFC 2705: "Media Gateway Control Protocol (MGCP), Version 1.0," M. Arango, et al.
4. RFC 2327: "SDP: Session Description Protocol," M. Handley, et al.
5. The H.323 series of ITU-T specifications listed at the end of Chapter 5 (H.323, H.225.0, H.245).
6. RFC 2916:, "E.164 number and DNS," P. Faltstrom.
7. IETF Draft: *draft-ietf-mmusic-sdp-new-01.txt*, "SDP: Session Description Protocol," M. Handley, et al.
8. IETF Draft: *draft-ietf-mmusic-sdp-atm-05.txt*, "Conventions for the use of the Session Description Protocol (SDP) for ATM Bearer Connections," Rajesh Kumar, et al.

7

H.248: Megaco Protocol

The *spirit* of the MEdia GAteway COntrol Protocol, specified in RFC 3015, is the same as MGCP and is intended to become the ultimate standard for product implementations that require a low-level control, decomposed media gateway from a softswitch or application server. In this chapter we look at the basics of the protocol with a real call flow and decoded packets, and point out the analogies with MGCP in areas where there is strong similarity between the two protocols.

7.1 PROTOCOL OVERVIEW

The ITU-T and the IETF collaborated to create a single signaling specification for media gateway control, acceptable to both standards groups. The result is the H.248/Megaco protocol specification, which uses common text by both organizations. The issue of whether a text-based protocol is a better choice over a binary signaling protocol (or vice versa) was not resolved in this exercise. H.248/Megaco offers both alternatives and recommends that softswitch implementations use both types, whereas IADs can make a declaration of the preferred operation. There is insufficient information at this writing as to which version (binary or text) will prevail by implementation choice. However, since Megaco is intended to replace MGCP implementations, which are text-based, it is expected it will weigh in heavily and that Megaco implementations will manifest themselves inside IADs and more complex Media Access Gateways.

There are many commonalities indeed between MGCP and H.248. We note the similarities to assist in making the transition to Megaco from MGCP. Both protocols operate in master-slave, request-response mode, whereby a softswitch paces an IAD and its endpoints through power-up, event notification requests, setting of signals to be played at the endpoint, and signaling call setup and termination (done by creating and removing logical connections between endpoints).

Some definitions are necessary in order to place this protocol in the proper context with regard to the topology of the implementation. The definitions in Table 7.1 are based on definitions in RFC 3015, but have been enhanced to be adapted to the reference topology for our example call flow, in Figure 7.1.

TABLE 7.1 Megaco Definitions

TERM	DEFINITION
Access Gateway	A type of gateway that provides a user-to-network interface (UNI), such as ISDN. This term is often used to indicate any type of network-to-network access—for example, media gateways between peer networks.
Descriptor	A syntactic element of the protocol that groups related properties. The SDP syntax included in a command to describe the properties of the media stream is such a descriptor. Protocol descriptors are shown in Table 7.3. Descriptors can be present in a command or returned in a response.
Media Gateway	Used synonymously with the term IAD. Formally, the MG/IAD converts media provided in one type of network to the format required in another type of network (i.e., transcoding and transport mechanism type, such as IP and ATM).
	A PSTN-MG could terminate bearer channels from the switched circuit network (for example, a DS0 for a voiceband call) and RTP media streams from the packet network controlled by a softswitch. The IAD may be capable of processing audio, video, and text data for application collaboration, and must be capable of full duplex media handling, especially for voiceband calls. The MG may or may not be capable of playing audio/video messages and performing other IVR functions. IADs support varying degrees of media conferencing.

TABLE 7.1 Megaco Definitions (continued)

TERM	DEFINITION
Media Gateway Controller	The signaling and call processing entity that controls Megaco IADs. In our examples in this text, this capability is included inside a softswitch, which is also capable of other types of call signaling (MGCP, SIP, etc.)
Multipoint Control Unit	Similar in definition to the H.323 MCU. Supports the setting up and coordination of multimedia conferences, either statically or adhoc.
Residential Gateway	Synonymous with IAD in most cases. Capable of offering basic telephony service and seamless support for voiceband calls, such as modem and fax, with other enhanced features, depending on the manufacturer.
PSTN FAS Signaling Gateway	FAS means *facility-associated signaling*. If the signaling channel of a facility traverses the same facility, this is referred to as FAS signaling. The D Channel in ISDN over T1 is an example of FAS.
SCN NFAS Signaling Gateway	NFAS is *nonfacility-associated signaling*. SS7 signaling links terminating in STPs implement NFAS, because the bearer channels appear on other facilities terminating at the SSP.
Trunk	Formally, a communication channel between two switching systems such as a DS0 on a T1 or E1 line. Note that a single DS0 between switching systems is often referred to as a *trunk*, although it carries a single voice call.
Trunking Gateway	A gateway between the PSTN and a packet network controlled by a softswitch.

In spite of the commonalities in the spirit of the two protocols, there is no similarity in the syntax of commands and responses of MGCP and Megaco. There is also no similarity in the coding and abbreviations of events and signals.

The connection model of Megaco makes use of the abstractions *termination* and *context*. We can think of a termination as a logical entity inside an MG/IAD that is capable of sourcing and sinking multimedia streams, much like an MGCP endpoint. A context, on the other hand, is a logical association of terminations—or example, all the terminations that are participating in a conference constitute a single context. So, a context is a higher level abstraction than the MGCP connection and includes in some sense the concept of a "call." As we will see in the residential gateway (MG/IAD) of our call flow example, a termination corresponding to the physical device (e.g., the

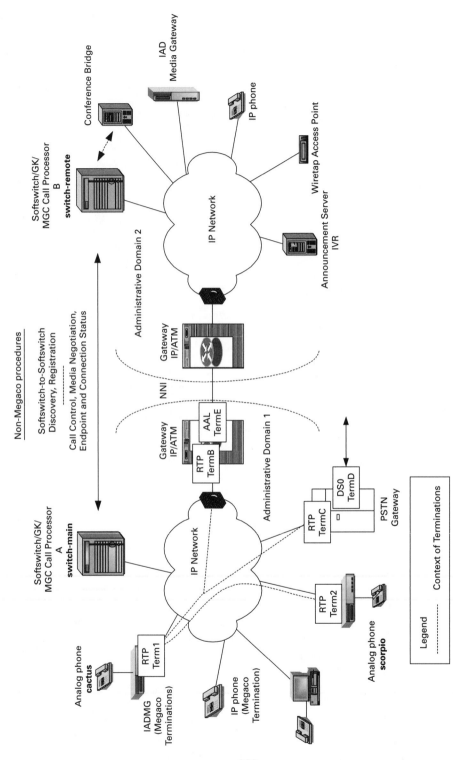

FIGURE 7.1 Megaco signaling topology.

telephone) is placed in the same context as a logical RTP connection to allow full duplex multimedia communication. The context is local to the MG/IAD.

There is a special type of context, the *null* context. It contains by default all the terminations that have no association with any other termination.

The set of messages supported by Megaco is listed in Table 7.2, and the Megaco descriptors are listed in Table 7.3.

TABLE 7.2 Megaco Messages

MESSAGE	PURPOSE
Add	This command is sent by the MGC function of the softswitch, to a termination, and it adds the termination to a context. The Add command sent to the first termination in a context acts in a similar manner to the CRCX command in MGCP and is used to create a new context. A context ID is selected by the termination and returned to the softswitch (analogous to an MGCP endpoint picking the Connection ID as a result of a CRCX command).
Modify	This command is analogous to the command of the same name in MGCP. It is used to modify the properties and events of a termination, as well as to set signals or terminate signals that are being applied to a termination.
Subtract	This command disconnects a termination from its context in a manner similar to the DLCX command in MGCP. The termination then returns the statistics of its participation in the context. A Subtract command to the last termination in a context deletes the context.
Move	The Move command moves the referenced termination to another context. Similar to the proposed command of the same name in MGCP, where an endpoint is moved from its current connection to another one.
AuditValue	The AuditValue command returns the current state of properties, events, signals, and statistics of the referenced terminations.
AuditCapabilities	The combination of AuditValue and AuditCapabilities can be used to obtain the same information as with the AUEP command. This command returns all the possible values for termination properties, events, and signals allowed by the MG/IAD.
Notify	Used in same manner as the command of the same name in MGCP. The Notify command is sent by the MG/IAD to inform the softswitch of the occurrence of requested events in the device.
ServiceChange	Similar to the RSIP command in MGCP, when sent by the MG/IAD. This command allows the MG/IAD to notify the softswitch that a termination or group of terminations (for example, as would be the case in a trunking gateway) is about to be taken out of service or has just been returned to service. ServiceChange is used by the MG/IAD to implicitly announce its availability to the softswitch and to notify the softswitch of an imminent or just completed

TABLE 7.2 Megaco Messages (continued)

MESSAGE	PURPOSE
	restart of the MG/IAD. The softswitch may signal to the MG/IAD that a new element of the softswitch platform (or another softswitch entirely) is in control of this signaling with the MG/IAD by sending it a ServiceChange command. The softswitch may also use this command to signal to the MG/IAD to take a single termination or group of terminations in or out of service (e.g., busy-out a trunk)
Reply	This is the response sent by the receiver of a Megaco message. Responses may be final or provisional. Provisional responses indicate that the message has been received, is syntactically correct, and is being processed. An actual response to the command contents will be provided when known. Provisional responses are signaled with the *TransactionPending* message.
	When a command is sent, call control applications usually set a timer, which is reset when the reply response is received. Recovery procedures from the missing reply to a command are largely implementation-dependent.

Note: Megaco is transport protocol-independent and can be signaled over TCP or UDP. The default signaling port for the text version of the protocol is **2944**. The default port for the binary version is **2945**.

7.2 REGISTRATION WITH THE MGC AND INITIALIZATION

Initialization (power-up or forced reboot) of an IAD results in a Service-Change message being sent to the MGC/softswitch entity that has been provisioned inside the device. The protocol offers no means for softswitch discovery. If the signaling port is known, the ServiceChange command is sent to that TA; otherwise, the default port is used. A simple ServiceChange packet and its reply are shown in Figure 7.2 and Figure 7.3. In this example message exchange, the ServiceChange command (Transaction=1001) indicates the entire box is being taken out of service, as identified by placing ROOT as the termination ID. The version of the protocol is also included at the beginning of the packet (MEGACO/1). Megaco messages contain a transaction ID, which is returned in the response to the command in the Reply for correlation, as shown in the Reply=1001 message. A message can contain multiple transactions in concatenated form and are considered independent of each other.

TABLE 7.3 Megaco Descriptors

DESCRIPTOR	PURPOSE
Modem	Modem type and properties.
Mux	Multiplex multimedia types and properties.
Media	Media descriptions.
TerminationState	Termination properties not associated with media streams.
Stream	List of media descriptors (media types, mode, etc) for a stream. Can be Local, Remote, or LocalControl.
Local, Remote	Contains media properties that the media gateway receives and sends to the remote endpoint, respectively.
LocalControl	Properties to assist the media gateway and softswitch in signaling communication. Also contains the "mode" property, which can be set to send only, receive only, send/receive, local loopback, and inactive.
Events	Sends the events to be detected by the MG/IAD and specifies how to handle notification of the softswitch. Similar in use to embedded notification requests in MGCP.
EventBuffer	Describes handling of events when buffering has been allowed.
Signals	List of signals to be applied to the termination.
Audit	List of items desired as a response to the audit command.
Packages	The types of packages supported by the termination; used in audit commands.
DigitMap	Patterns of acceptable digit strings dialed at the termination, which are reported as a single event when a match occurs. Note that this does not mean a valid number has been dialed. It simply means the digits dialed form a valid sequence according to the loaded map. For example, if the local exchange wishes to see only 10-digit dialing, a digit map that supports 10-digit dialing can be loaded in the MG/IAD. Dialed strings will then be accumulated until all ten digits have been detected and a single event will be reported to the softswitch for the match.
ServiceChange	Service changes affect terminations, groups of terminations (for example, facilities), and entire gateways. Changes can be power-up or power-down, and we will see an example decoded packet in the next section.
ObservedEvents	Used in Notify or AuditValue, its use is similar to the same descriptor in MGCP.
Statistics	Used in Subtract and Audit. Returns the statistics maintained at the termination.

```
------------ MEGACO Header ------------
MEGACO: TPKT Protocol Version = 0x03
MEGACO: TPKT Reserved = 0x00
MEGACO: TPKT Packet Length = 108
MEGACO: Version String = MEGACO/1
MEGACO: Message Identifier = <cactus>
MEGACO:    Transaction=1001{
MEGACO:       Context=-{
MEGACO:             ServiceChange=ROOT{Services{Method=Forced}}
MEGACO:                 }
MEGACO: }
```

FIGURE 7.2 Decoded Megaco packet: ServiceChange command.

```
------------ Header ------------
MEGACO: TPKT Protocol Version = 0x03
MEGACO: TPKT Reserved = 0x00
MEGACO: TPKT Packet Length = 112
MEGACO: Version String = MEGACO/1
MEGACO: Message Identifier = <switch-main>:2944
MEGACO:    Reply = 1001 {
MEGACO:       Context = - {
MEGACO:          ServiceChange = ROOT
MEGACO:             }
MEGACO:
```

FIGURE 7.3 Decoded Megaco packet: ServiceChange reply.

The method of ServiceChange Method is shown as *Forced*. Other acceptable coding choices are

1. *Graceful*, indicating the specified terminations, or the entire box, will be taken out of service after a specified delay.
2. *Restart,* when the box is being placed back in service; usually a cold start.
3. *Disconnected*, when the box had previously lost communication with the softswitch and may require resynchronization.
4. *Handoff*, sent by the softswitch to indicate another signaling entity is taking over.
5. *Failover*, when the primary media gateway is taken out and a secondary (redundant) is replacing it.

The following parameters of the ServiceChange command are optionally filled by the sender as required. A ServiceChange command can be sent by either signaling entity: MG/IAD or softswitch.

- ServiceChangeMethod
- ServiceChangeReason
- ServiceChangeDelay
- ServiceChangeAddress (TA for subsequent signaling)
- ServiceChangeProfile
- ServiceChangeVersion
- ServiceChangeMgcId, (the softswitch ID)
- TimeStamp

The context parameter in both messages is coded with the hyphen (-), which is the symbol of the null context. When a specific context is referenced in a message, the context ID is entered in lieu of the hyphen.

The protocol allows for nesting of commands (piggybacking, as we saw in the MGCP case). Note the use of angle brackets for delineation. Their use will become more evident in the context of our example call flow.

7.2.1 Media Gateway Packages

Megaco defines event and signal packages as groupings of relevant and appropriate events and signals for particular types of gateways and signaling entities. Packages are characterized by a set of properties, events, signals, statistics, and procedures, and they facilitate the interoperability between MG/IAD and softswitch. The concept and types of groupings are analogous to (but not the same as) the packages in MGCP. Not all packages are suitable for all types of media gateways, however, and these groupings indicate the level of compliance with the base protocol specifications, as well as permit the specification of extensions via additional packages and/or new signals and events.

The ITU-T usually handles feature extensions in annexes to the base specification (as in the H.450 series of annexes for telephony features in support of H.323), whereas the IETF handles extensions via RFCs and RFC drafts.

A media package is characterized by

1. The basic package description.
2. Its properties.
3. Supported events.
4. Supported signals.
5. Statistics supplied and supported for interpretation.
6. Any procedures relating to proper support of the package.

The base protocol specification defines 13 packages, whose contents are summarized in Table 7.4.[1]

---

1.   These packages are still in the preliminary phase and the reader is referred to the IETF and ITU specifications for design implementation.

TABLE 7.4 Megaco Package Summary

PACKAGE NAME	FEATURES
Generic Package ID: **g** Example syntax g/	Events cause, (*cause*) 1. NR, normal release 2. UR, unavailable resources 3. FT, temporary failure 4. FP, permanent failure 5. IW, interworking error 6. UN, unsupported Signal Completion (*sc*) 1. TO, specified duration expired 2. EV, interrupted by observed event 3. SD, halted by a new signal descriptor 4. NC, not completed for another reason The generic Package specifies no properties, signals, or statistics.
Base Root Package ID: **root** Example syntax root/	Properties 1. MaxNrOfContexts 2. MaxTerminationsPerContext 3. normalMGExecutionTime 4. normalMGCExecutionTime 5. ProvisionalResponseTimerValue There are no procedures, statistics, signals, or events in the root package. The execution times supplied by the softswitch, are for the typical responses expected to signaling commands and the typical time the softswitch will require to respond to a command. In nonscalable platforms, which cannot guarantee invariance in system responses as a function of the load, these quantities should be set carefully.
Tone Generator Package Package ID: **tonegen** Example syntax: tonegen/	Signals 1. pt (*tl, ind*) indicates Play Tone (tone-list, inter-signal duration) No properties, statistics, procedures, or events are defined.

TABLE 7.4 Megaco Package Summary (continued)

PACKAGE NAME	FEATURES
Tone Detection Package Package ID: **tonedet** Example syntax: tonedet/	Events 1. std (*tl*, *tid*) indicated Start Tone Detected, (tone-list, tone-id) 2. etd (*tl*, *tid*, *dur*) indicated End Tone Detected, (tone-list, tone-id, duration) 3. ltd (*tl*, *tid*, *dur*) indicated Long Tone Detected, (tone-list, tone-id, duration) No properties, signals, statistics, or procedures are defined. The tone detection package is useful for DTMF tone detection as well as machine-generated tones, such as fax and modem.
Basic DTMF Generator Package Package ID: **dg** Example syntax: dg/	Signals Supported: DTMF digits 0–9, *, #, A–D. Coding, respectively: d0–d9, ds, do, da–dd

DTMF detection Package
 	
Package ID: **dd**
 	
Example syntax: dd/
	Digits 0–9, A–F
	
	Coding, respectively
	
	d0–d9, da–df
	
	Events
	
	    Digit Map Completion Event (*ce*)
	
	    Digit String (*ds*)
	
	    Termination Method (*Meth*)
	
	        UM (unambiguous match)
	
	        PM (partial match)
	
	        FM (full match)
	
	No properties, signals, statistics, or procedures.

Call Progress Tones Generator Package Package ID: **cg** Example syntax: cg/	Signals 1. Dial Tone (*dt*) 2. Ring Tone (*rt*) 3. Busy Tone (*bt*) 4. Congestion Tone (*ct*) 5. Special Information Tone (*sit*)

TABLE 7.4 Megaco Package Summary (continued)

PACKAGE NAME	FEATURES
	6. Warning Tone (*wt*) 7. Payphone Recognition Tone (*pt*) 8. Call Waiting Tone (*cw*) 9. Caller Waiting Tone (*cr*) No properties, events, or statistics are defined. For procedures, see ITU-T Recommendation E.180/Q.35.
Call Progress Tones Detection Package Package ID: **cd** Example syntax: cd/	Package **cd** extends the range values of tone-id in the "start tone detected," "end tone detected" and "long tone detected" events. No properties, signals, events, statistics, or procedures.
Analog Line Supervision Package Package ID: **al** Example syntax: al/	Events 1. OnHook (*on*) 2. OffHook (*of*) 3. Flashhook (*fl*) Signals 1. Ring (*ri*) No properties or statistics defined. Procedures govern the initial state of the "hook" (on or off) when requested as an event notification by the softswitch.
Basic Continuity Package Package ID: **ct** Example syntax: ct/	Events 2. Completion (*cmp*) 3. Result (*res*) Signals 1. Continuity Test (*ct*) 2. Respond (*rsp*) No properties or statistics defined. Procedures govern the interaction of the softswitch with the media gateway for establishing the method of continuity testing. **Note:** Turn off all echo cancellation and disable codecs when continuity testing is being performed.
Network Package Package ID: **nt** Example syntax: nt/	Properties Maximum Jitter Buffer (*jit*) Events

TABLE 7.4 Megaco Package Summary (continued)

PACKAGE NAME	FEATURES
	1. Network Failure (netfail)
	2. Cause (*cs*)
	3. Quality Alert (*qualert*)
	Statistics
	1. Duration (*dur*) (of the connection)
	2. Octets Sent (*oc*)
	3. Octets Received (*or*)
	No procedures or signals defined.
RTP Package Package ID: **rtp** Example syntax: rtp/	Events 1. Payload Transition (*pltrans*) Statistics 1. Packets Sent 2. Packets Received 3. Packets Loss Rate 4. Jitter 5. Delay No procedures, signals, or properties defined.
TDM Circuit Package Package ID: **tdmc** Example syntax: tdmc/	Properties 1. Echo Cancellation (*ec*) 2. Gain Control (*gain*) No events, signals, statistics, or procedures defined.

7.3 CALL SETUP

With the basic media packages, it will be easy to examine a Megaco call flow, which we show in the three steps of Figure 7.5, Figure 7.6, and Figure 7.7. Megaco signaling uses RFC1006 (TPKT) to delineate messages when TCP is used as the transport protocol. An example coding is shown in Figure 7.4.

The first step (1) of Figure 7.5 shows a "Restart" service change in the root termination— that is, the entire device. The null context is used for this command in transaction 1001, which is signaled to TCP port 2944 of the softswitch. The softswitch replies by acknowledging the state change in **root**. No

```
------------ MEGACO Header ------------
MEGACO: TPKT Protocol Version = 0x03
MEGACO: TPKT Reserved = 0x00
MEGACO: TPKT Packet Length = 102
MEGACO: Version String = MEGACO/1
MEGACO: Message Identifier = <cactus>
MEGACO: Transaction=1002{
MEGACO: Context=-{
MEGACO: Notify=Termination1{ObservedEvents=1{al/of}}
MEGACO: }
MEGACO: }
```

FIGURE 7.4 Decoded Megaco packet: Notify softswitch of an observed event.

other optional ServiceChange parameters are included in the message, so default addressing will be used by the softswitch.

In transaction 1002, the softswitch modifies Termination 1 to look for off-hook in Termination 1, which is running the Analog Line Package (al/), and this command is acknowledged by the MG/IAD in the next reply message. Both the command and the response refer to the null context.

When off-hook is detected in Termination 1, a Notify is sent in transaction 1003, indicating ObservedEvents al/of. This is also acknowledged by the softswitch, and we are still in the null context.

The softswitch sees the off-hook condition and reacts by sending a command asking the MG/IAD to pick a context ID (the $ sign in context) and add two terminations to this newly generated context. The first one is the analog line termination (Termination 1), which it puts in SendReceive mode, echo cancellation off, and gain set to 0. Note the mode setting for the termination invokes the analog line package (al/).

The second termination is to be selected by the MG/IAD itself, and represents the RTP media source/sink connected to the packet network. By joining them together, a media stream received from the packet network can be played out at the endpoint, and media (voice) can be captured at the endpoint, digitized, and placed in an RTP stream towards another entity in the packet network.

The local media descriptor for the RTP stream is an SDP that calls for PCM (payload type 0) audio, with 10 ms packetization rate. The IP address/port combination (the TA) will be selected by the termination and returned in the reply (the $ entries in the SDP).

Just so as not to forget, a request for notification upon detection of on-hook is also sent with this message, in case the user decides to hang up before completing a dialing sequence.

The reply to transaction 1004 is shown in Figure 7.6. The MG/IAD selects a termination ID (rtpA) and places it in the same context as Termina-

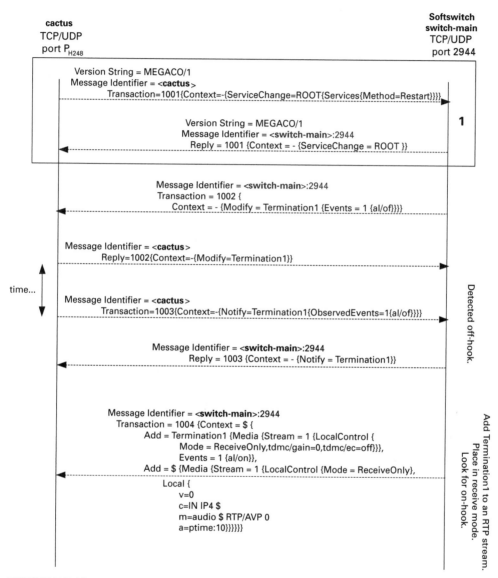

FIGURE 7.5 Megaco power up and initial signaling.

tion 1. The RTP stream (Stream 1) is assigned to transport address <cactus>:2513. Note that <**cactus**> is symbolic notation. A real IP address is returned here (e.g., 192.168.0.1), but we use symbolic addressing in our example so that we can trace the call flow a little easier. Cactus is the "name" of the calling entity.

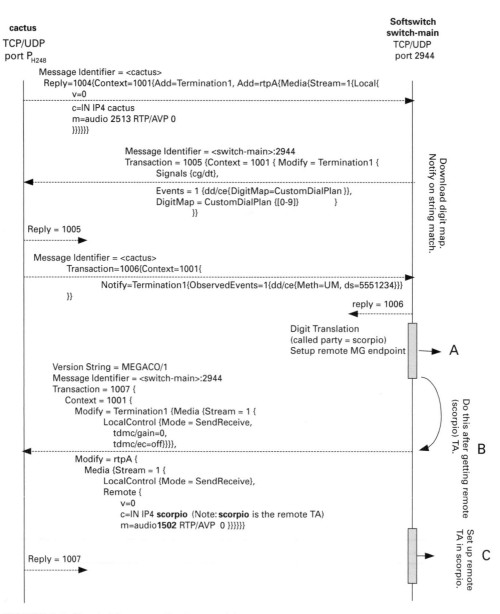

FIGURE 7.6 Simple Megaco call setup, part 1.

Transaction 1005 downloads a digit map from the softswitch and requests a single event to be signaled when there is a string match (dd/ce). See the DTMF detection package for the completion event. This message is also acknowledged, and when a match occurs, it is signaled in the notify command of transaction 1006. The number dialed is 5551234, and the match was unambiguous (UM).

After acknowledging the notification, the softswitch will perform digit analysis to determine how to route the call. In Chapter 8 we will see a complex routing exercise, involving multiple domains, but in this case we will assume the string dialed is the number of a party controlled by the same softswitch (switchmain). Signaling at exit point A begins, and we pick up the call flow in Figure 7.7.

In the block labeled 2, we see a similar initialization process taking place some time earlier at the endpoint of the called party. The number dialed by **cactus** was that of **<scorpio>**. Scorpio is the symbolic notation of the IP address of the called party, obtained by the softswitch after digit translation. At this time, scorpio's analog line termination is idle, with the phone on-hook, and is sensitized to look for an off-hook transition.

The softswitch delivers the call to scorpio in transaction 503 (the numbering scheme for transactions does not obey any rules). This command does several things at once:

- Places the analog line termination in ReceiveOnly mode.
- Turns off echo cancellation (ec=off) and sets the gain to zero.
- Sets the ringing signal (the phone now should be ringing).
- Asks the MG/IAD to pick a context ID and place the analog line and an RTP termination in that context. The termination ID will also be picked by the MG/IAD.
- The local mode of the RTP stream is set to PCM audio, 10 ms packetization rate, ReceiveOnly mode.

The MG/IAD selects the context ID (1001) and returns it in the reply. Termination ID rtpA with symbolic IP address **<scorpio>** is added to the context, on UDP port 1052.

The local information of scorpio is returned to cactus in transaction 1007, as the remote connection parameters. Similarly, cactus's local media stream description is returned to scorpio as the remote descriptor.

Signaling continues with a few additional steps by the softswitch and the media gateways.

1. The softswitch sends a cg/rt (call progress tone package) command to cactus, which will cause the calling party to hear ringback.
2. Scorpio picks up the phone and sends an al/of (analog line/off hook) notification to the softswitch.
3. The softswitch sends a notification request for an al/on event to scorpio and stops ringing by including a void Signals { } descriptor.

At the end of this signaling sequence, we will have an active call between the two parties. At the end of the conversation, when the parties have hung up, the statistics are obtained with audit commands from both parties' RTP terminations, and the softswitch will proceed to subtract terminations from

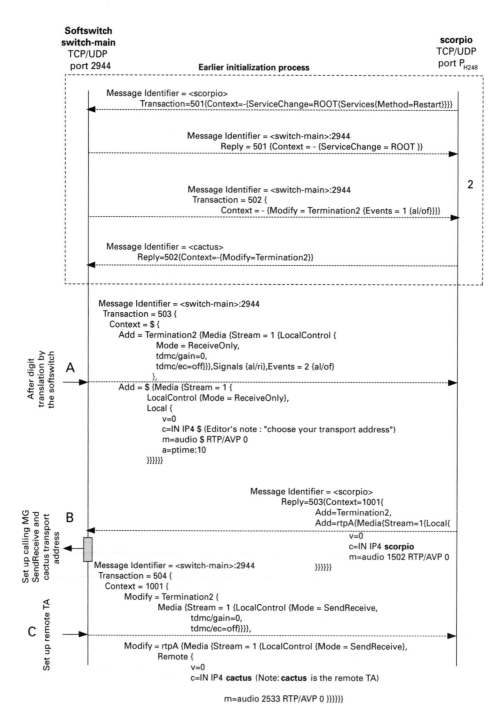

FIGURE 7.7 Simple Megaco call setup, part 2.

the context at each media gateway until each context is deleted (last subtract deletes the context). Both analog line terminations will then be sensitized to look for an off-hook transition again.

7.4 EXTENSIONS AND ENHANCEMENTS TO BASIC MEGACO SIGNALING

Extension packages have already been defined to support voiceband and enhanced services using H.248/Megaco signaling. This section summarizes the extension packages, their basic capabilities, and basic protocol syntax.[2]

1. Annex F covers Fax, Textphone, and Modem tone detection. This is of great interest for the correct engineering of a VoIP network infrastructure, which must support machine-to-machine communication with at least the same quality as the PSTN.

PACKAGE	FEATURE SET
FAX/Textphone/Modem Tones Detection Package Package ID: **ftmd** Example syntax: ftmd/	Offers detection of tones on a fixed telephone line, indicating a possible request to enter some data-related mode, such as fax or modem transmission. **Events:** Same as for the tone detect package, with a new tone id (dtfm): tid=dtfm The tones supported are basic fax tones, such as CNG, V21, V23, V8bis, ANS, ANSAM, etc. No signals, statistics, or procedures are defined.
Call Type Discrimination Package Package ID: **ctyp** Example syntax: ctyp/	Call discrimination determines if a call should be handled as voice, fax, text telephones, or modem data, and performs the initial negotiation of modes, attributes, etc. **Example:** *ctyp/dtone{dtt=cng}* (indicates the signal which has been detected is CNG and qualifies for call discrimination of call type – see Chapter 9 for fax discussion).
Text Telephone Package ID: **txp** Example syntax: txp/	Package for communicating with text phones. **Example:** *txp/convmode=simultaneous* (conversation mode is simultaneous voice and text).

---

2. These extensions are still in preliminary form and teh reader is referred to the IETF and ITU documentation for design implementation.

PACKAGE	FEATURE SET
Fax Package ID **fax** Example syntax: fax/	Basic fax communication package. **Example:** fax/faxstate=prepare
Text Conversation Package ID: txc Example syntax: txc/	Text conversation between terminals in dissimilar networks (text phones are covered with package **txp**). **Example:** txc/bufftime=200 (e.g., buffering time of 200 ms)
IP fax Package ID: ipfax Example syntax: ipfax/	Fax transmission in IP networks using T.38 (real time) or T.37 (store and forward) procedures. **Example:** ipfax/faxstate=negotiating (see Chapter 9 for T.38 fax discussion)

2. Annex G covers user interface elements, such as display and keypads for telephones and other input devices.

3. Annex H specifies operation of H.248 over the SCTP (Stream [or Signaling] Control Transport Protocol, IETF RFC 2960) and tries to protect against multiple deliveries of Megaco messages due to transport difficulties. Most Megaco commands cannot be executed more than once (i.e., they are not idempotent).

4. Annex I covers transmission of signaling over ATM, specifically SSCOP/AAL5 (Service Specific Connection Oriented Protocol).

5. Annex J discusses dynamic definition of tones in a manner that tones can be specified and sent via their characteristics. This maps to the choice of tones versus named events transport in RTP.

6. Annex K specifies a generic announcement package.

There are corresponding RFC draft contributions in the IETF for the same packages.

7.5 CONCLUDING REMARKS

Very sophisticated call flows can be constructed with the Megaco protocol, but it has the same call signaling limitations of MGCP in that it is a master-slave signaling protocol, with no hop-by-hop signaling capabilities. Its nonsupport for topology discovery mandates some preconfigured signaling entity inside the box when it is first plugged in, unless other proprietary discovery techniques can be put in the design, depending on the expected operating environment. However, Megaco IADs are designed to be low cost (as in the MGCP case) so that they will appeal to the public at large for integrated service delivery to the home, including seamless and unqualified basic telephone service. As such, the lack of protocol sophistication in topology discovery may not be an impediment to acceptance, as the expectation will be for the residential MG/IADs to be matched with a particular service provider, who will have all the information preprogrammed in the box at installation time.

If packages are supported in strict compliance to the specification and its approved extensions, even interoperability is possible, as long as vendor proprietary extensions do not find themselves included in the mainstream of basic signaling operations. The last issue may seem benign as we remain entrenched in finding more solutions to more problems in the design and deployment phase of these new packet-based networks. However, we must consider that in the PSTN, all it takes is a phone call to change carriers. Will this consumer luxury continue when we install an MG/IAD in our premise?

In many cases failures will occur not at the signaling or media layer, but at the media transport layer itself. This will manifest itself as loss of signaling connectivity, but troubleshooting a problem of this nature will reduce (more often than not) to troubleshooting a date problem, such as routing topology issues, misconfigured Virtual Circuits (VC) in ATM switches, or QoS issues that result in unacceptable call quality. It is imperative for the designer to keep the overlays and layers in perspective when attempting to understand the origin of failures, but that is not always easy, as even the most sophisticated instrumentation often falls short of understanding all the overlays of all the protocol layers and network overlays at the same time.

References

1. IETF draft, draft-ietf-megaco-h248f-00.txt, H.248 Annex F "(Pre-Decision White Document). Fax Text Conversation and Call Discrimination."
2. IETF drafts, draft-ietf-megaco-h248j00.txt through draft-ietf-megaco-h248k-00.txt.
3. ITU-T Recommendation H.225.0 (1999), "Call signalling protocols and media stream packetization for packet based multimedia communication systems."
4. ITU-T Recommendation H.245 (2000),"Control protocol for multimedia communication."
5. CCITT Recommendation G.711 (1988), "Pulse Code Modulation (PCM) of voice frequencies."
6. CCITT Recommendation G.722 (1988), "7 kHz audio-coding within 64 kbit/s."

7. ITU-T Recommendation G.723.1 (1996), "Speech coders: Dual rate speech coder for multimedia communications transmitting at 5.3 and 6.3 kbit/s."
8. CCITT Recommendation G.728 (1992), "Coding of speech at 16 kbit/s using low-delay code excited linear prediction."
9. ITU-T Recommendation G.729 (1996), "Coding of speech at 8 kbit/s using Conjugate Structure Algebraic-Code-Excited Linear-Prediction (CS-ACELP)."
10. ITU-T Recommendation H.261 (1993), "Video codec for audiovisual services at p x 64 kbit/s."
11. ITU-T Recommendation H.263 (1996), "Video coding for low bit rate communication."
12. ITU-T Recommendation T.120 (1996), "Data protocols for multimedia conferencing."
13. ITU-T Recommendation H.320 (1997), "Narrow-band visual telephone systems and terminal equipment."
14. ITU-T Recommendation H.321 (1996), "Adaptation of H.320 visual telephone terminals to B-ISDN environments."
15. ITU-T Recommendation H.322 (1996), "Visual telephone systems and terminal equipment for local area networks which provide a guaranteed quality of service."
16. ITU-T Recommendation H.324 (1996), "Terminal for low bit rate multimedia communication."
17. ITU-T Recommendation H.310 (1996), "Broadband audiovisual communication systems and terminals."
18. ITU-T Recommendation Q.931 (1998), "ISDN user-network interface layer 3 specification for basic call control."
19. ITU-T Recommendation T.140 (1998) "Text conversation protocol for multimedia application. With Amendment 1 (2000)."
20. ITU-T Recommendation T.30 (07/96) "Procedures for document facsimile transmission in the general switched telephone network."
21. ITU-T Recommendation T.38 (06/98) "Procedures for real-time Group 3 facsimile communication over IP networks."
22. ITU-T Recommendation T.37 (06/98) "Procedures for the transfer of facsimile data via store and forward on the Internet."

8

SIP: The Evolution of the Session Initiation Protocol

SIP continues to evolve with fascinating pace and flexibility to become a premier call signaling protocol with thorough support of the major telephony features, user mobility, and attributes that allow softswitches to act as proxies or redirect servers, as the need arises on a per-call basis. The protocol has certainly received major attention in the IETF and in the industry, where major implementations of SIP are emerging in the mainstream.

We saw the basics of a SIP call flow in my previous book [1], and although it is easy to write an entire text on the attributes and operations of this protocol, no protocol in the packet voice world lives in a vacuum. The best way to describe the capabilities of a protocol is with a call flow that also shows interworking with other major protocols that will probably coexist in a softswitch. Mixed call flows are also mandatory for assessing the performance of a platform, since very few calls in real life will consist of signaling with a single protocol.

8.1 PROTOCOL OVERVIEW

SIP is a text-based protocol, which relies on commands issued by a softswitch and responses to complete fairly contained transactions. The commands are referred to as *methods,* and since the days of the original six commands, three more have found their way into acceptance both inside equipment and in the form of extensions to the basic protocol specification.

At this time, it is not likely the SIP protocol (RFC 2543) will be amended to include all the other popular extensions, but it may happen some day. In any case, "SIP compliance" is a tricky statement and requires an interoperability checklist from the vendors who make it to ensure interoperability when the cables are actually plugged into the equipment.

SIP, with its various extensions, facilitates call establishment, maintenance, user mobility, and sophisticated telephony features during the five major phases of a call. These capabilities are summarized in Table 8.1 SIP can also initiate multiparty conference calls using an MCU and lends itself to interworking with other protocols for call establishment within a domain or across domains.

The current set of major methods in SIP is shown in Table 8.2.

SIP does not depend on a particular transport protocol, but common practice is to use UDP, which makes it easier to account for failover conditions in the servers. Commands are sent to *default port number 5060*. SIP commands can also be sent to any open port in the endpoint or the softswitch, if the port number is known to the sender in advance. SIP may also be implemented over a reliable connection protocol like TCP, but this is not usually practiced. If TCP is used, requests and responses in the same transaction

TABLE 8.1 SIP Major Protocol Capabilities

FEATURE	DESCRIPTION
User location services	Users have the ability to move to other locations and access their telephony features from remote locations via remote registration with a softswitch "visible" to the one serving its home signaling domain. This is analogous to the services provided by RAS in H.323.
User availability	Determination of the willingness of the called party to engage in communications. SIP defines very explicit response codes to provide detailed information about a user's current availability.
Call setup	SIP is self-contained in setting up point-to-point and multipoint conferences, as well as simple calls, in direct endpoint signaling or through proxy server.
User capabilities	Determination of the media and media parameters to be used. SIP uses the SDP protocol format for negotiating media parameters, much like MGCP and Megaco.
Call handling	The major telephony features of the AIN can be supported with SIP and SIP extensions, in addition to newer features (e.g., mobility), but a true A to Z mapping of the AIN origination and termination call model of the PSTN using exclusively SIP signaling is a challenge.

TABLE 8.2 SIP Methods

METHOD	DESCRIPTION
INVITE	This *mandatory* message is the first one sent by the calling party to initiate call signaling. It contains call information in the SIP header, which identifies the calling party, Call-ID, called party, and call sequence number, among other things (see SIP header definition in Table 8.3). It basically indicates a call is being initiated, but can also be sent during a call to modify its operating state (e.g., place a party on hold or retrieve a call that had been placed on hold). Usually the INVITE message contains an SDP description of the call, such as media type and TAS. When a multiple choice of SDP parameters is offered, the ones chosen are returned with the success (200) code in the response message. Final selection of the ones that will be used in the call is made with the ACK method. The original INVITE message should indicate to the called party which optional headers are supported by the caller in the "Supported Headers" field and which methods are allowed in the "Allow" field. This exchange allows the quick identification of the level of signaling interoperability between the endpoints. It has been proposed to allow INVITE commands to be reissued for the purpose of signaling whether a session is still active (see references). If this is supported by the endpoints, it must be explicitly stated in "supported" header field attributes when the session is established, or with the OPTIONS method. If re-INVITE is used for purposes of session information recovery, some state information will need to be kept by the signaling softswitches, for the period specified in the "session-expires" header. A partially decoded INVITE message is shown in Figure 8.5.
ACK	A successful simple SIP session starts with an INVITE message. It is followed by an OK response from the invited party and is confirmed with an ACK sent by the agent that initiated the invitation. The body of the ACK message may contain the SDP description (and usually does, for typical call setup) of the media type capability of the called party. If the success response contained no SDP description, the session description parameters of the initial INVITE message are used for the media connection. An ACK command receives no response, and its support by a SIP-compliant softswitch is *mandatory*.
OPTIONS	This message is sent to query the capabilities of a call agent, as well as to supply the other party with the capabilities of the sender. This is a nice tool for finding out what media types and methods a remote user supports before placing a call. OPTIONS support is *mandatory*. A sample OPTIONS command and its received response are given in Figure 8.2 and Figure 8.3, respectively.
BYE	The client sends this message to the call agent to release the call. The sending endpoint terminates media flow and considers the call terminated, regardless of a response from the far end. A return BYE from the other party is not necessary. A BYE may include the "also" header field, which would contain the contact information of

TABLE 8.2 SIP Methods (continued)

METHOD	DESCRIPTION
	another party. If this is the case, the recipient is supposed to terminate the current call and establish a new call with the new party. This is, in effect, a "transfer" operation, which is also supported with the REFER method. BYE support by a SIP-compliant softswitch is *mandatory*.

CANCEL	This method cancels a request in progress but has no effect on an established call when no requests are in progress. It is sent when requests have been forked in the network and an acknowledgment has been received from one of the legs. The CANCEL method must explicitly identify the call via the Call-ID, Call Sequence (Cseq), and To and From values in the SIP header. Proxy support for OPTIONS is *mandatory*. An example encoding of a CANCEL message is as follows:
	
	`CANCEL sip:bill@dflx.com SIP/2.0`
	`Via: SIP/2.0/UDP dflx.com:5060`
	`From: <sip:george@dflx.com>`
	`To: <sip:bill@dflx.com>`
	`Call-ID: 91757@dflx.com`
	`CSeq: 11101 CANCEL`
	`Supported: sip-cc, timer`
	`Content-Length: 0`

REGISTER	A client uses the REGISTER method to register the address listed in the "To:" header field with a SIP server. A user agent may register with a local server on startup by sending a REGISTER request to the well-known "all SIP servers" multicast address *sip.mcast.net* (224.0.1.75). Registration can be done periodically by the user or by a third party on behalf of the user. This distinction is shown in the "From:" field. The REGISTER method is analogous to the H.323 RAS RRQ command and allows user mobility in generalized SIP domains—domains served by a multiprotocol softswitch that allows mobility for its SIP endpoints.
PRACK	This extension to the basic SIP protocol provides an acknowledgment to provisional responses, such as the 183 Progress response shown in Table 8.4. This method is necessary to ensure reliable delivery of provisional responses to the originating endpoint. Proxies relay PRACK responses instead of regenerating them. In effect, the PRACK is a response to a response, but itself does not command yet another response from the remote endpoint.
INFO	This is another extension of the basic protocol, which allows the transport of ISDN and ISUP signaling to support common telephony features during a call. One such use is the transport of DTMF tones received from the PSTN side of a call, in ASCII format, to the SIP endpoint or server. The INFO method is not supposed to be used to alter the state of a stable call in progress.

TABLE 8.2 SIP Methods (continued)

METHOD	DESCRIPTION
REFER	This SIP extension provides call transfer capabilities in a flexible enough manner to allow for unsupervised call transfer and transfer with consultation. This method supplies a new endpoint to be called by the recipient of the message, who initiates normal call establishment procedures with the INVITE method. Once the new call has been established, a 200 OK is returned to the sender. It is useful for directing a call leg to a device such as a media server, which may need to be interjected in a call temporarily (e.g., to play music). The call can be retrieved at a later time.
COMET	This is a proposed method to allow a party to confirm whether all the preconditions that were set in the SDP of a previously received command are met by the sender. Such preconditions may involve QoS requirements and security for the call, some or all of which may not be optional for the call to be completed successfully. SDP attributes set with the a= parameter can include a "confirm" requirement, in which case the COMET is invoked (if supported) to determine whether the call can proceed given the preconditions. COMET must contain an SDP and follows the same signaling path as the call setup itself. Each precondition in the returned SDP is tagged "success" or "failure." COMET requires a response, which is considered final. Extensions to the SDP protocol required to support COMET are shown in boldface type in the following sample encoding of an SDP. `m=audio 5030 RTP/AVP 0` **`a=qos:mandatory`** `sendrecv` *`confirm`* **`a=secure:optional`** `sendrecv` This encoding will not allow the call to proceed until resources (bandwidth, etc.) for the call have been reserved and confirmed. Security is optional. COMET and PRACK can work synergistically to reserve resources at both ends of a call, based on provisional SDPs provided in a possible 183 response to the initial INVITE message. After the reservation has been made, COMET is used to confirm that the attributes for the call can be met at both ends.

must be carried over the same TCP connection (socket). SIP transport over the newly defined SCTP protocol has also been proposed (see reference). The SCTP protocol is discussed in Chapter 9.

SIP has many flexible and informative headers, but not all of them are mandatory or implemented in major designs. The most commonly used headers of SIP are shown in Table 8.3.

Other complete list of headers can be found in RFC 2543*bis* and associated RFCs and proposed extensions to SIP. In estimating softswitch performance in calls-per-second, care must be exercised in the number and types of

TABLE 8.3 Commonly Used SIP Headers

HEADER	MESSAGE TYPE
Accept	INVITE, OPTIONS, REGISTER, Code 415. Indicates content types acceptable in requests.
Accept-Language	INVITE, OPTIONS, REGISTER, Code 415. Example coding (accept English as the language): `Accept-Language: en`
Allow	INVITE, OPTIONS, REGISTER, Codes 200, 405. Indicates the methods supported by the sender. Example coding: `Allow: OPTIONS, CANCEL, INVITE, ACK, INFO, REFER, BYE` There can be multiple "Allow" headers in a packet.
Authorization	Request Header. Contains user authorization information for the requesting server.
Call-ID	General Header. It is copied from the request message to the response.
Contact	INVITE, OPTIONS, ACK, REGISTER, Response Codes 1xx, 2xx, 3xx, 485. It is usually the URL of the sender where he/she can be contacted, although it can indicate any other party who can be contacted regarding information about this call. Example coding: `Contact: sip:Mark@10.0.0.2`
CSeq	Command Sequence, must be in all requests. Example coding: `Cseq: 9350 INVITE` It is copied from the request message to the response.

Content-Type	Carries the application type of the embedded content in the request message. For example, to embed an SDP description in an INVITE, the SDP would be included in the message, as follows:
	
	`Content-Type: application/sdp`
	`v=0`
	`o=dflx.com IN IP4 <dflx.com>`
	`s=Media Capability Exchange`
	`c=IN IP4 <dflx.com>:20551`
	`t=0 0`
	`m=audio 5066 RTP/AVP 0`
	`a=sendrecv`
	`a=ptime:10`

TABLE 8.3 Commonly Used SIP Headers (continued)

HEADER	MESSAGE TYPE
Content-Length	Specifies the length of the message body (not including the headers). Example coding: `Content-Length: 126`
Date	General Header. The date and time the message was originally sent.
Encryption	General Header. Indicates the packet content has been encrypted.
Expires	For REGISTER and INVITE methods. In REGISTER, it indicates how long the registration is to remain valid. In INVITE messages, it limits the amount of time a URI will remain valid (cached) by the recipient receiver. If not supplied, no caching is provided by the server.
From	Any command. Contains the URI of the originator of the message. It is copied from the request message to the response. Example coding: `From: sip:Mark@208.178.32.21;tag=1c27540` The tag field helps a user identify multiple instances of a called user when a response arrives back at the sender.
Max-Forwards	Request Header. Limits the number of proxies that can forward the request.
Organization	General Header. The originating organization of the request or response.
Proxy-Authenticate	Codes 407 or 401. Must be included in a *Proxy Authentication Required* or *Unauthorized* response.
Proxy-Authorization	Request Header. Contains the necessary authorization information of the sender, which will be examined by the requesting proxy.
Proxy-Require	Request Header. Carries information that must be supported by the proxy.
Priority	Request Header. Common encodings of the priority that should be assigned to this message: `priority : "emergency"	"urgent"	"normal"	"non-urgent"`

Referred-By	Request Header used with the REFER method. It identifies the originator of the call transfer request. Example coding:
	
	`Referred-By= sip:10.0.10.21;tag=16989; sip:10.0.10.40;`
	`Call-ID=call15842734@10.0.10.21`
	
	The Referred-By header includes a copy of the URL placed in the Refer-To header.

TABLE 8.3 Commonly Used SIP Headers (continued)

HEADER	MESSAGE TYPE
Refer-To	Used only with the REFER method, it identifies the party to which this call is being transferred. Example coding: `Refer-To= sip:10.0.10.40;Call-ID=call15842734@10.0.10.21` A sample REFER message is shown in Table 8.13.
Require	Request Header. A list of options the sender is expecting to be supported by the server for proper processing of the message.
Retry-After	Request Header. Return codes 404, 480, 486, 503, 600, 603.
Response-Key	Request Header. Carries the key all responses must be encrypted with.
Record-Route	Request Header. When a proxy adds its SIP URI in this field of a request, all subsequent communication between the endpoints will be routed through this proxy. The header can grow to include all the proxies that want to be in the path of the signaling between endpoints.
Record-Route	Response 2xx. Contains the URIs of the proxies that will be visited in subsequent signaling.
Route	Request Header. Contains the route taken by the request.
Session-Expires	Usually sent with a re-INVITE (an INVITE message used as a refresh) and indicates the approximate length of this session. Since the time someone spends on a call cannot be predicted, it may be necessary to refresh the value conveyed in the header during the call, to ensure no unintended terminations. This header was defined when it was realized SIP stateful proxies do not really know whether a session is still active without the help of a "keep-alive" mechanism. It is defined as part of a SIP session timer proposal. When the INVITE method is used as a periodic session refresh mechanism, it makes SIP sessions stateful, albeit in a "soft" sense. It could also be useful in firewall control signaling entities (either proxy or embedded) to clear the contexts of a session that has expired and for which no proper termination procedures were detected (e.g., a BYE) due to network faults or other reasons. Support of the session timer is indicated in the "Supported: timer" SIP header (below). If the "session-expires" header is present in an INVITE message and is supported by both signaling entities, it indicates the parties will be doing periodic session refreshes.
Server	Response Header. Carries implementation information of the server that will be handling requests.
Subject	Request Header. Contains additional information about the type and nature of the call.

TABLE 8.3 Commonly Used SIP Headers (continued)

HEADER	MESSAGE TYPE
Timestamp	General Header. Indicates the time the message was sent.
To	General Header. Contains the information of the called party. It is copied from the request message to the response. Example coding: `To: <sip:2125551212@10.0.0.2>`
Supported	A list of capabilities supported by the sender of the message. It is recommended that this header appear in all requests and responses, except ACK, and will usually point to supported extensions of the SIP protocol. Example coding: `Supported: sip-cc, sip-cc-02, timer` Indicates support for SIP call control and the session timer (see references).
Unsupported	Response Code 420. List of features unsupported by the server.
User-Agent	Request Header. Contains more information about the client issuing the request. Example encoding: `User-Agent: <company_name> /<release number> (Maker)`
Via	General Header. A list of nodes traversed by the message so far. Example coding: `Via: SIP/2.0/UDP 10.0.20.41`
Warning	Response Header. Carries additional information about the response in text format.

headers beyond the mandatory ones included in SIP messages. Headers will take time to parse and act upon their contents.

8.1.1 SIP Responses

SIP defines six types of responses to the messages we saw in the previous section. Each type of response uses a code from a range, as listed in the response code tables (Tables 8.4 through 8.9). Several of the returned codes require explicit reaction from the servers and endpoints, and several others result in implementation-specific system behavior.

INFORMATIONAL OR PROVISIONAL (1xx)

Provisional responses are issued to indicate the recipient is proceeding with the execution of the request. Valid codes are listed in Table 8.4.

TABLE 8.4 SIP Informational Codes

CODE	MEANING
100	**Trying.** A provisional response analogous to the Q.931 CALL PROCEEDING, and will probably be returned from a proxy server or other intermediate SIP server in the signaling path of a call.
180	**Ringing.** Has similar meaning to Q.931 ALERTING. Means the "virtual" or real phone is ringing.
181	**Call Forwarding.** If a proxy server returns this code, it may also identify where it is forwarding the call in the message body.
182	**Queued for Service.** This is useful for applications that can defer answering the call until they have serviced the calls ahead of them in the queue. Customer service departments of large corporations are major users of this feature.
183	**Session Progress.** A provisional response analogous to the Q.931 CALL PROGRESS. This code is used to provide early media session description information from gateways on the path to the called party, such that an early voice path can be cut through before ringing is applied to the calling endpoint. An example of its use is with SIP-PSTN interworking, whereby a *Session Progress* code with the SDP of the PSTN gateway allows the ringing tone to be supplied by the terminating exchange. Other uses of this response include the playing of a courtesy announcement or music when calling into a domain, prior to the call being established.
189	**Provisional response to a REFER method.** It is useful in providing progress information about the status of the call being transferred, while waiting for the eventual success or failure response from the call leg that is being transferred.

SUCCESS (2xx)
The request was successfully parsed and executed by the called party (Table 8.5).

REDIRECTION (3xx)
The call needs more processing before it can be determined whether it can be completed. The defined codes are listed in Table 8.6.

TABLE 8.5 SIP Success Code

CODE	MEANING
200	Request executed successfully (OK).

TABLE 8.6 SIP Redirection Codes

CODE	MEANING
300	The address in the request resolved into more than one choice. The multiple choices are returned and the caller can pick from the list and redirect the call. This is another way of saying "ambiguous," but ambiguous name resolution results in its own error code.
301	The called user has moved permanently and the calling party should try the new location, which is returned in the response header (in the "contact" field). It is possible to receive a list of possible locations, and the caller can make a choice about the order in which it traverses the list to make the call. If the server cannot find any information about the called party in its store, it returns a NOT FOUND error code.
302	The called user has moved temporarily and can be found at the returned address. This is useful for manual call forwarding, because the server itself is not forwarding the call (offering only redirection). Good for addressing some of the requirements of mobility.
305	The called user cannot be accessed directly, but the call must be handled through a proxy. Only call agents can send this reply.
380	The service requested is not available, but alternative services are possible. This is an unlikely message. SDP parameter mismatches are covered with another code.

CLIENT REQUEST FAILURE (4xx)

The request cannot be parsed by the server or cannot be serviced. The request must be modified before being attempted again. The defined codes are shown in Table 8.7.

TABLE 8.7 SIP Request Failure Codes

CODE	MEANING
400	Bad request, due to syntax error. This means the message text could not be parsed by the far end. Any syntax error should return this code. System behavior is implementation-specific.
401	The user requires authentication before making this request. Special rules apply to message formatting when this error code is received; for example, no SIP compact message format is allowed.
402	The user owes money (for future use). Good feature for telephone companies. Actions not specified, but one could guess.
403	Forbidden request—do not reattempt. The message was parsed, but the request will not be honored. If you attempt to call a number that does not accept calls from your number, you could get this message.

TABLE 8.7 SIP Request Failure Codes (continued)

404	User not found. This message is sent when the user either never existed or the user's records have been purged from this server.
405	The encoded method in the message is not allowed for the called user. It is a good idea to allow all the methods, but this is an implementation decision.
406	The called endpoint will generate responses that will not be understood by the caller (code not acceptable). This response avoids the Tower of Babel syndrome from developing between endpoints if the call process continues.
407	Use Proxy Authentication first, before proceeding.
408	The server cannot produce a response within the time requested by the caller in the request header. Busy network servers could generate this response from time to time. The caller's reaction is implementation-dependent.
409	There is a conflict between the current request and other conditions within the server, possibly due to existing registrations. This response generated if a REGISTER request from a user conflicts with others.
410	The requested user or service is gone from this server and left no forwarding address. "I know that I used to know this person, but I don't know what happened to him or her."
411	The server requires the caller to place the length of the message body in the header. Nitpicking response, but it must be accounted for by the application.
413	The size of the request is too large for the server to handle. Can't imagine what type of SIP message can cause this response, short of a malfunction by the process that creates the messages in the caller agent.
414	The server is having difficulty interpreting the Request URI because of its large size. Keep the URI shorter. There is no other way out of this error.
415	The server cannot accept the request because of its encoding. The server may indicate the proper method to encode the request.
420	The server does not understand the extension of the SIP protocol being attempted by the caller. Upwards compatibility is most likely the problem here, but the probability of running into this issue can be reduced with use of the Allow and Supports header fields.
480	Called party is temporarily unavailable. If the server recognizes the name but does not know where the party is now, it may send this message.
481	The server received a CANCEL for a request that does not exist or a BYE for a nonexistent call. Discarded.

TABLE 8.7 SIP Request Failure Codes (continued)

482	Loop in message routing detected. This is where the Via field is very useful in detecting loops that could be missed by the network and transport protocols. If a server sees itself in a Via field of an incoming message of an as-yet uncompleted call, it is a good guess there is a server loop somewhere in the network. Time to get out the analyzers.
483	The hops required to reach the called party exceed the maximum allowed. This is a good protection against long and unstable routes, especially in the new IP-based public network. Usually means more network engineering work is in order.
484	Address incomplete. Can be used to implement piecemeal sending of user input, as in the case of dialing strings from a phone, which are considered incomplete by the softswitch.
485	Ambiguous address for the called party. The server may wish to offer alternatives to the caller. The usual scenario is multiple choices to be returned to the caller.
486	The called party is either busy or unwilling to take the call. May reply with a better time to call later (depending on the implementation).

SERVER FAILURES (5XX)

The request may have been valid, but the server cannot execute it. See Table 8.8.

TABLE 8.8 SIP Server Failure Codes

CODE	MEANING
500	Server Error. This could be hardware, software, or any internal error.
501	The server cannot service the request because the service is not implemented.
502	Bad response received by the server from a gateway or server on the call path to the endpoint. This could be a typical failure for calls spanning multiple network segments and servers.
503	Service temporarily unavailable, probably due to processing overload or resource exhaustion.
504	The server timed out while accessing a gateway on the call path to the endpoint. The call request is probably still traveling somewhere.
505	SIP protocol version not supported. Upward-compatible designs will probably avoid sending this error. Older servers and call agents may do so when they see a newer version of SIP in the message header.
580	Precondition failure (used with COMET).

GLOBAL FAILURES (6XX)

The user request cannot be serviced by any server. See Table 8.9.

TABLE 8.9 SIP Global Failure Codes

CODE	MEANING
600	The called party is busy. May indicate a better time to call back.
603	The called party declined the call.
604	The called user does not exist anywhere.
606	The user is willing to accept the call, but there are incompatibilities in the requested media, or elsewhere, and thus the user cannot accept the call. For example, if the only choice given to the called agent is for G.728 voice compression, and the called party supports only G.711, it is a good guess that this message will be received. The called party may simply decide not to accept the call.

8.2 BASIC SIGNALING WITH SIP ENDPOINTS

In our analysis, we will consider the topology of Figure 8.1. On the left, we have Administrative Domain 1, which hosts a Megaco endpoint under the signaling auspices of a multiprotocol softswitch (**switch-main**), which also has SIP signaling capability with adjacent domains and endpoints. On the right, we have Administrative Domain 2, with signaling provided by a SIP-compliant softswitch (**switch-remote**), which also has the ability to connect calls to an MGCP-based media server.

We discussed the basics of direct and proxy SIP signaling in my previous book [1], and this call scenario is a little more sophisticated to illustrate the use of SIP procedures in telephony applications. Party **cactus** in Domain 1 initiates a call to **rattler** in Domain 2, using Megaco signaling. Rattler answers the phone and at some time during the conversation, the caller is placed on hold with a redirect to listen to music provided by a media server. Some time later, the call is retrieved by rattler and continues to completion. This call flow will show us the usage of the SIP basic and extended methods, and we will discuss the impact of the firewalls on the signaling path between the two domains.

We begin by showing four captured SIP packets, shown in Figures 8.2 through 8.5. The reference topology for the call flow is shown in Figure 8.1. Figures 8.6 through 8.10 show the detailed call flows, which are explained in Tables 8.10 through 8.12.

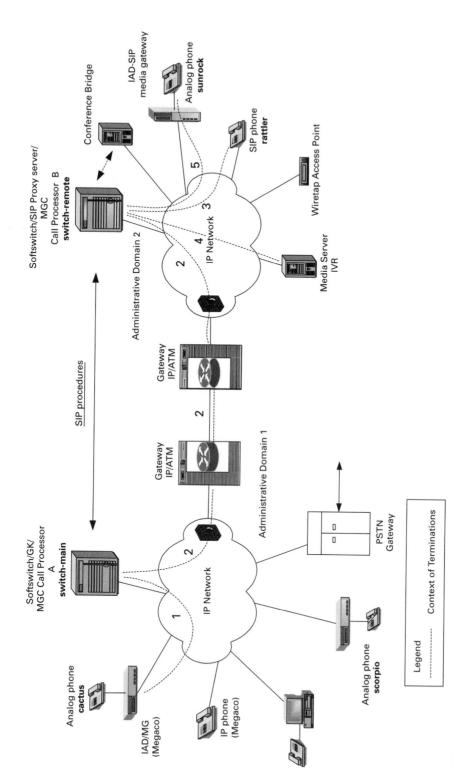

FIGURE 8.1 SIP signaling example topology.

235

```
----------- SIP Header -----------
SIP: Message Type = Request
SIP: Method = OPTIONS
SIP: Request URI = sip:Tony@10.0.10.34
SIP: SIP Version = SIP/2.0
SIP: From = sip:10.0.10.21;tag=16989 (Request Initiator)
SIP: To = sip:Tony@10.0.10.34;tag=1c13179 (Recipient Of Request)
SIP: Call-Id= call-1587679-17@10.0.10.34
SIP: Cseq = 1 OPTIONS (Command Sequence Number)
SIP: Accept =Language: en (Acceptable Media Types)
SIP: Supported= sip-cc, sip-cc-02, timer
SIP: Via = SIP/2.0/UDP 10.0.10.21 (Path Taken By Request Till Now)
SIP: CONTENT-LENGTH= 0
```

FIGURE 8.2 SIP OPTIONS command.

```
----------- SIP Header -----------
SIP: Message Type = Response
SIP: SIP Version = SIP/2.0
SIP: Status Code = Success - OK (200)
SIP: Reason Phrase = OK
SIP: From = sip:10.0.10.21;tag=16989 (Request Initiator)
SIP: To = sip:Tony@10.0.10.34;tag=1c13179 (Recipient Of Request)
SIP: Call-Id= call-1587679-17@10.0.10.34
SIP: Cseq = 1 OPTIONS (Command Sequence Number)
SIP: Via = SIP/2.0/UDP 10.0.10.21 (Path Taken By Request Till Now)
SIP: Contact = sip:Tony@10.0.10.34 (Contact Details)
SIP: Allow = INVITE, ACK, CANCEL, BYE, REFER, OPTIONS (Supported Methods)
SIP: CONTENT-LENGTH= 0
```

FIGURE 8.3 SIP OK response to OPTIONS command.

```
----------- SIP Header -----------
SIP: Message Type = Request
SIP: Method = REFER
SIP: Request URI = sip:Tony@10.0.10.34
SIP: SIP Version = SIP/2.0
SIP: From = sip:10.0.10.21;tag=16989 (Request Initiator)
SIP: To = sip:Tony@10.0.10.34;tag=1c13179 (Recipient Of Request)
SIP: Call-Id= call1158767917@10.0.10.34
SIP: Cseq = 3 REFER (Command Sequence Number)
SIP: Referred-By= sip:10.0.10.21;tag=16989; sip:10.0.10.40;Call-
ID=call15842734@10.0.10.21
SIP: Refer-To= sip:10.0.10.40;Call-ID=call15842734@10.0.10.21
SIP: Accept =Language: en (Acceptable Media Types)
SIP: Supported= sip-cc, sip-cc-02, timer
SIP: Via = SIP/2.0/UDP 10.0.10.21 (Path Taken By Request Till Now)
SIP: CONTENT-LENGTH= 0
```

FIGURE 8.4 SIP REFER method.

```
UDP:
UDP: Source port = 5060 (SIP)
UDP: Destination port = 5060 (SIP)
UDP: Length = 609
UDP: No checksum
UDP: [601 byte(s) of data]
UDP:
SIP:
SIP: INVITE sip:bill@dflx.com SIP/2.0
SIP: Via: SIP/2.0/UDP dflx.com:5060
SIP: From: <sip:george@dflx.com >
SIP: To: <sip:bill@dflx.com>
SIP: Call-ID: 917529_1827179@dflx.com
SIP: CSeq: 12320 INVITE
SIP: Contact: <sip:george@dflx.com:5060>
SIP: Allow: OPTIONS, CANCEL, INVITE, ACK, INFO, REFER, BYE
SIP: Supported: 100rel, sip-cc, timer
SIP: Session-Expires: 120
SIP: Content-Length: 155
SIP: Content-Type: application/sdp
SIP:
SIP: v=0
SIP: o=dflx 3377 11994 IN IP4 10.0.0.2
SIP: s=SIP Initial SDP Exchange
SIP: c=IN IP4 10.0.0.2
SIP: m=audio 5030 RTP/AVP 0
SIP: a=sendrecv
SIP: a=ptime:20
```

FIGURE 8.5 SIP sample INVITE method (partial decoding with Sniffer).

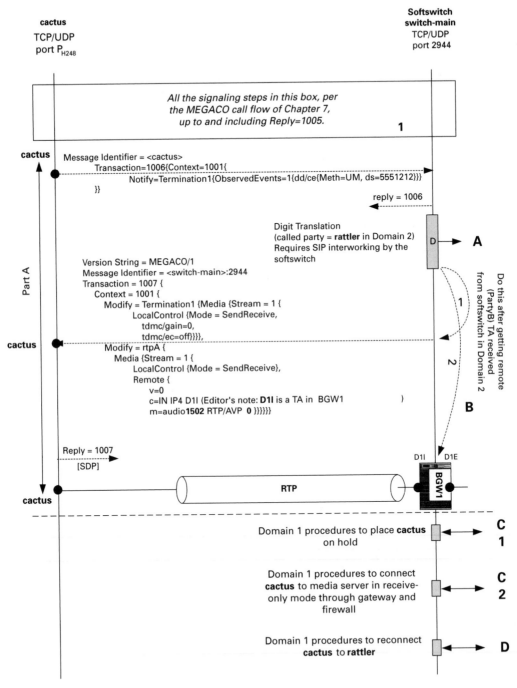

FIGURE 8.6 Domain 1 call setup, **cactus** to **rattler**.

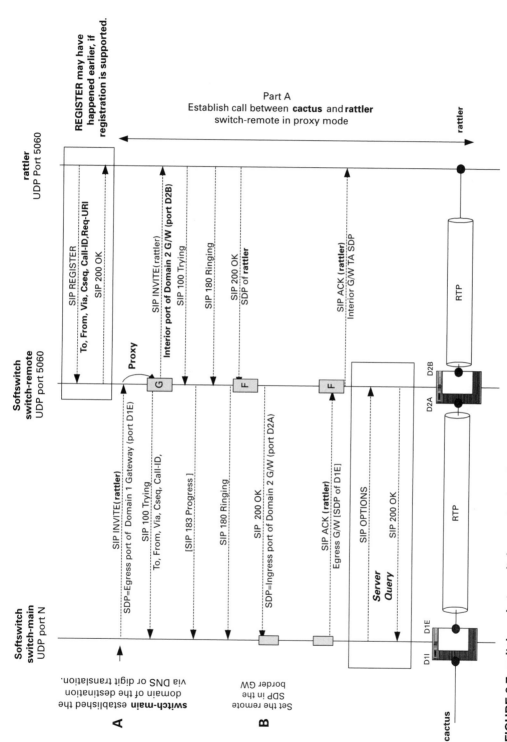

FIGURE 8.7 **switch-main** to **switch-remote** signaling.

239

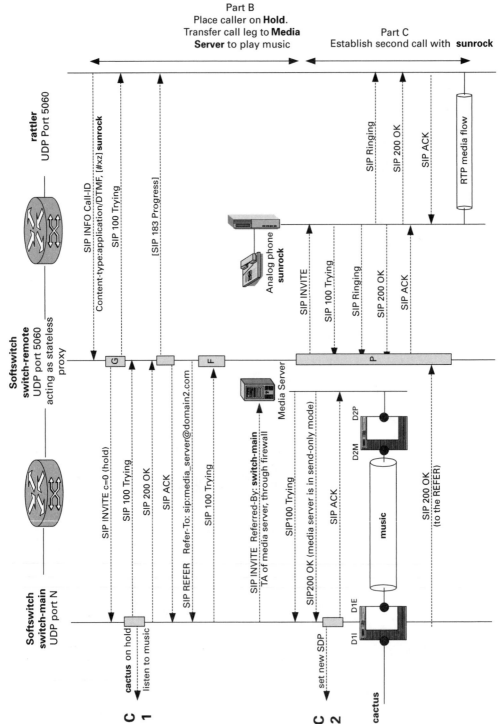

FIGURE 8.8 Call hold-play music.

TABLE 8.10 Telephony Call Flow with SIP Signaling

STEP	CALL SETUP SIGNALING OVERVIEW	COMMENTS
Initialization of IAD hosting the cactus endpoint	In block 1, we have a Megaco call flow, which is identical to the one we saw in Chapter 6, up to and including Reply=1005. Steps 1 and 2 are shown in Figure 8.6.	The IAD powers up and informs the softswitch (switch-main) of its Service Change state, and switch-main creates a termination in the null context, which it sensitizes to look for off-hook (al/of). When the off-hook event is detected (someone wants to make call) it is reported with ObservedEvents. The softswitch then proceeds to create a context and add a media stream, with a TA and context ID to be picked by the device itself. The termination's IP address is cactus (e.g., 192.168.0.5) and is assigned an RTP audio media stream on UDP port 2513 of payload type 0 (PCM). It also selects context ID = 1001 for this call. The final step by switch-main is to modify the termination by downloading a digit map, which simply looks for any digit input and asks to be notified when a valid digit string has been dialed.
Part A Part A is shown in the call flow of Figure 8.7.	In this part, a digit string has been entered by cactus and is reported to switch-main. The softswitch performs digit analysis and determines the call is intended for someone outside Administrative Domain 1. The Part continues up to the point of milestone B, which initiates SIP signaling with a peer softswitch (switch-remote), which has been determined by switch-main as the entry point into Domain 2, following internal call routing procedures.	Megaco Transaction 1006 indicates there was an unambiguous match on the digit string and the number is supplied to switch-main. Once it is determined we need SIP call signaling, we enter the call flow of Figure 8.7. At this point, we do know the media session description of the call originator and we will obtain the same for the called party. Note that even though we will be doing SIP signaling with Domain 2, this does not mean the ultimate destination for the call is a SIP endpoint.

TABLE 8.10 Telephony Call Flow with SIP Signaling (continued)

STEP	CALL SETUP SIGNALING OVERVIEW	COMMENTS
		Also note that the call routing method that determined **switch-remote** is the signaling entry point (if multiple entry points are available) as well as the egress media gateway selection from Domain 1, and requires procedures which are not standardized yet. For more information on the issue of telephony routing over IP, refer to IETF Draft *draft-ief-iptel-trip-04.txt*, "Telephony Routing over IP (TRIP)."
Call Flow Entry Point **A** (switch-main SIP signaling with switch-remote)	The called party is determined to be *rattler@domain2.com*. Resolution of the dialed digits into a URL is not required, as the party could have also been identified as *5551212@domain2.com*. A SIP INVITE is sent to the default signaling address of switch-remote, asking to establish a session with rattler. Switch-remote looks up the destination and determines that it is registered under the signaling auspices of switch-remote. The softswitch decides to act as a proxy server for the call. While the INVITE is being processed, a SIP 100 Trying response is sent to switch-main. A 183 Progress could be issued as well (shown as an optional response) in some cases. If the remote softswitch had determined the call completion would have taken more than a couple of seconds (e.g., the called party had moved somewhere else temporarily), it could have directed the media stream to an announcement server to play something like "Your call is being processed…" until it had found the called party and delivered the INVITE.	Switch-main needs to perform call leg establishment between the Megaco calling party and the egress gateway of Domain 1 (absorbed inside shaded block D of Figure 8.6), before sending the SIP INVITE to switch-remote. This is needed so that the egress SDP from Domain 1 can be supplied in the INVITE message (SDP of port D1E, shown in the RTP path at the bottom of the call flow). These internal gateway signaling procedures can be SIP-based or MGCP/Megaco-based (or proprietary), and in effect consist of establishing an internal connection inside the gateway. The gateway is also asked to perform whatever media transcoding may be required in order to interface with the called party inside Domain 2.

242

TABLE 8.10 Telephony Call Flow with SIP Signaling (continued)

STEP	CALL SETUP SIGNALING OVERVIEW	COMMENTS
Call Flow Part A (switch-remote SIP INVITE to rattler)	The item of interest in this call leg is the SDP supplied to rattler by switch-main. It is the SDP of port D2B, which is the interior port of the gateway (facing inwards in Domain 2). The shaded box labeled G includes all the procedures to activate ports inside the ingress gateway into Domain 2 and select codecs between the two sides (if necessary). We do not have all the information for firewall setup yet.	The softswitch in Domain 2 is acting as a proxy server. Signaling packets from the <switch-main>:5060 will be sent to <switch-remote>:5060, with rattler the ultimate destination. The role of the softswitch as proxy has no impact on the route(s) that will be selected for the media streams in Domain 2.
Call Flow Part A (rattler responds)	Rattler returns its SDP to switch-remote, which in turn completes signaling with port D2B of the border gateway between Domains 1 and 2 and stitches it internally with port D2A. The 200 OK from switch-remote to switch-main contains the SDP of port D2A.	In this segment, we obtain the ensuing ACK from switch-main and the media TA address information to do firewall setup. This process is product-specific and will be done in the shaded boxes labeled F in Figure 8.7.

243

TABLE 8.10 Telephony Call Flow with SIP Signaling (continued)

STEP	CALL SETUP SIGNALING OVERVIEW	COMMENTS
Call Flow Part A Domain 1 call leg completion by switch-main	Point **B** in the call flow is the exit point from the softswitch to softswitch signaling and reentry into Domain 1 (Figure 8.6).	One of two things are possible here. If the RTP media path between cactus and its border gateway has already been established, the only thing switch-main needs to do is modify the internal path between D1I and D1E, with the SDP information it received from switch-remote about port D2A. It may mean media format conversion (as a result of codec negotiation). This is the step indicated by the arrow labeled 2 in Figure 8.6. It is hoped that any necessary port SDP modifications will not propagate all the way back to cactus through the modify termination command (arrow labeled 1).
Call Flow Part A (Optional) Options Exchange	The two softswitches may exchange OPTIONS information in the *Server Query* box.	Most of the supported quirks (i.e., mandatory options) of the protocol can be signaled in the INVITE command and subsequent signaling, but an OPTIONS exchange can be useful to complete the interoperability exchange.
Call Flow Part A Call Setup Completion	A SIP ACK received by switch-remote from switch-main is proxied to rattler and contains final SDP selections from the various ports, and the call is complete.	All this signaling is wonderful indeed, but the designer must keep track of the time required to do it. Disregard for performance for the sake of flexibility is not always a wise choice.

Note: We decided not to use the COMET method in the call setup phase of this example. The call does not have security requirements, and whatever QoS requirements exist have been addressed with preconfigured MPLS, DiffServ tunnels, or both, inside each domain. The media path between the two border media gateways can be network-engineered to allow up to a maximum number of calls with a predetermined QoS per prior agreement between the connected networks.

Additional signaling for resource reservation on a per call basis will reduce call capacity (in cps) by both softswitches and may or may not result in additional scalability shortcomings.

At the end of the signaling exchange, we have established a call between cactus and rattler. In comparison to PSTN signaling with SS7 involving a couple of exchanges, this signaling has more steps, especially since we have to add back-office signaling for billing and accounting (if any), Local Number Portability (LNP) in the case where one domain is a carrier, and so on.

TABLE 8.11 Feature Call Flow: Place Call on Hold, INVITE New Party

STEP	FEATURE SIGNALING OVERVIEW	COMMENTS
Call Flow Part **B**	We create a scenario whereby rattler now wants to place cactus on hold and call another party. This could be the case for special features, such as call transfer, three-way calling, and ad hoc conferencing. The reference call flow for this discussion is shown in Figure 8.8.	We make some assumptions in this call flow about the capabilities of the softswitch and the gateways themselves. First, we require the callers in Domain 2 to dial a feature code (e.g., #xx, where x is any digit) to activate a particular network feature. In this case, a code is require to be entered before the number is dialed so that the softswitch will know to place the existing call on hold with courtesy music and proceed to complete the new call as dialed.
Call Flow Part **B** (Receiving DTMF tones in a live call)	When rattler dials the feature code (#xx) followed by the number for party sunrock, the device serving rattler's phone (or if it is a SIP phone itself) will need a method to transport the detected DTMF tones to the softswitch. Sending the DTMF digits on the media RTP stream with special payload packets will not have an effect in our scenario because there is no media server on the path of the call to detect them and take action on them. So, the DTMF entry must be sent via signaling to the softswitch.	Refer to RFC 2833 for a description of supported methods to transport signals and tones in RTP packets. Different network implementations may allow the ability to distribute tone detection devices (IVRs) that can detect the tones, disrupt the media path, play an announcement, collect more digits, and offer services to the caller based on input. A popular service using these features is a calling card telephony service (e.g., dial an 800 number, enter an access code and PIN, hear an announcement, enter a new number, etc.)
Call Flow Part **B** (place cactus on hold, play music)	The INFO method transports DTMF input to switch-remote, which places cactus on hold with an INVITE message to switch-main and a TA in the c= parameter of the SDP set to IP 0.0.0.0. We reenter Domain 1 at entry point **C1** in Figure 8.6. In the scenario we have constructed, switch-main does not need to do anything with cactus itself, but port D1E of GBW1 is placed on hold in receive-only mode.	After the call-hold signaling exchange is acknowledged, switch-remote sends a REFER method to switch-main, diverting the media stream to a port in the media server of Domain 2, which plays music. **Note:** Firewalls need to be set up all over again for this media diversion, unless the signaling ports and the send-only RTP music ports of media servers are left open (unlikely).

245

TABLE 8.11 Feature Call Flow: Place Call on Hold, INVITE New Party (continued)

STEP	FEATURE SIGNALING OVERVIEW	COMMENTS
		The REFER method causes switch-main to send an INVITE to Media Server (in this example, switch-remote does not want to play proxy) and restitch the media path to D1E with the send-only port of the media server.
		Domain 1 is reentered one more time at point C2, when the SDP of the music port becomes known in the 200 OK response. If the media format setup at port D1E for the original call is consistent with the format of the music, no changes are required. Otherwise, media format conversion will need to be signaled to BGW1 by switch-main.
Call Flow Part **C** (call establishment with new party)	In this part, switch-remote is performing call establishment with sunrock (which was determined to be a user within Domain 2, served by switch-remote). The new call signaling can be performed in parallel while switch-main is trying to connect to the media server to be entertained with music while on hold. This inherent parallelism maximizes performance.	Signaling between rattler and sunrock is basic proxy signaling through the softswitch. There are no border gateways or firewalls involved in this call (the IAD serving sunrock is a hypothetical generic residential device).

At the end of this signaling process, rattler is talking to sunrock and cactus is listening to music, courtesy of the media server of Domain 2.

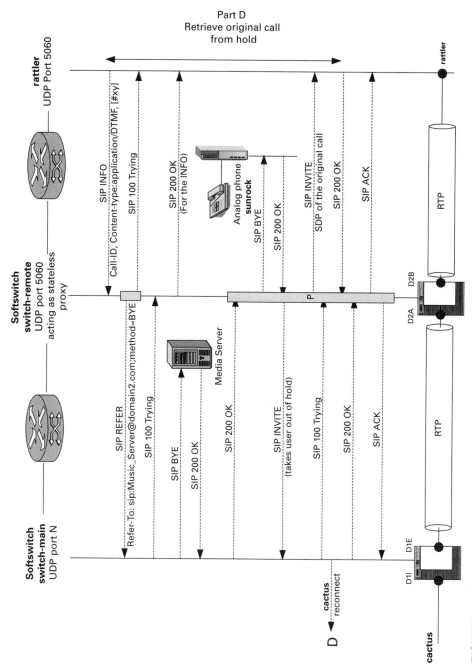

Part D
Retrieve original call
from hold

rattler
UDP Port 5060

**Softswitch
switch-remote**
UDP port 5060
acting as stateless
proxy

**Softswitch
switch-main**
UDP port N

SIP INFO
Call-ID, Content-type:application/DTMF, [#xy]
SIP 100 Trying

SIP 200 OK
(For the INFO)

Analog phone
sunrock
SIP BYE
SIP 200 OK

SIP INVITE
SDP of the original call
SIP 200 OK
SIP ACK

RTP

rattler

D2B

D2A

SIP REFER
Refer-To: sip:Music_Server@domain2.com;method=BYE
SIP 100 Trying

SIP BYE
SIP 200 OK

SIP 200 OK

SIP INVITE
(takes user out of hold)
SIP 100 Trying

SIP 200 OK

SIP ACK

Media Server

P

RTP

D1E

D1I

D

cactus
reconnect

cactus

FIGURE 8.9 Rattler call retrieve.

247

TABLE 8.12 Call Retrieval

STEP	CALL RETRIEVAL OVERVIEW	COMMENTS
Call Flow Part **D** (original call retrieval)	The last part of our scenario involves rattler hanging up with sunrock and retrieving his original call with cactus. Several other options exist in this scenario, with very similar call flows. First, rattler could have elected to bring sunrock into the conversation with cactus (a called-party originated three-way calling). Or rattler could have elected to transfer sunrock to cactus and terminate his own call. Up to this point the call flows we have seen are the same for those follow-up scenarios.	We need to make an assumption in our topology regarding call retrieval. We assume the endpoints are controlled by not very sophisticated devices, and thus a special #xx code is needed to retrieve calls. This code is sent to the softswitch to indicate call retrieval with the INFO method. Note: There may be a need to implement overlap sending of digits in such implementations, particularly if the IAD is not loaded with a digit map (in the sense we saw in the MGCP and Megaco protocols). Overlap sending can be unilateral (the endpoint keeps sending user input as entered) or as a result of the softswitch returning a 484 Status code to the INVITE message. Code 484 will continue to be sent until a string match is made by the softswitch.
Call Flow Part **D** (stopping the music to cactus)	Softswitch switch-remote sends a REFER message to switch-main, asking it to terminate its current session with the media server (method=BYE).	The softswitch switch-remote is not a proxy for courtesy music, so signaling is directly between switch-main and the media server of Domain 2. A SIP BYE is sent to the media server by switch-main, but now there is no media connection at the other end of D1E. However, the port is on hold and is restriched to rattler in the next step.
Call Flow Part **D** (reconnecting the original call)	The reconnection of the original call involves the parallel procedures indicates in shaded box **P** in Figure 8.8.	Softswitch switch-remote sends an INVITE, with the original session parameters for the cactus-rattler call, to switch-main. It also terminates the call between rattler and sunrock with a BYE message.

TABLE 8.12 Call Retrieval (continued)

STEP	CALL RETRIEVAL OVERVIEW	COMMENTS
		We need to reenter Domain 1 through point D and make any session description changes to GBW1. In this case, the same egress port D1E is still in use for the original call, and we modify its far connection to the SDP of port D2A. A different entry port into Domain 2 could have been used, but that would involve gateway setup procedures inside Domain 2 to stitch the new entry port to D2B, which is the one the rattler is still connected to.

At the end of this signaling exchange, rattler is reconnected to cactus and the original conversation resumes.

8.2.1 Call Forward (Always, Busy)

Call forwarding can be to another number or to a voice-mail device, and can be activated always or when the called party is on the phone. The signaling procedures for call forwarding in our call flow scenario are centered around the exchanges in Figure 8.7 and involve a few steps from switch-remote.

When the first INVITE message arrives at switch-remote, activated services are examined, and if call forwarding-always (CFA) or call forwarding-unconditional (CFU, also used as the terminology in H.323) is enabled, switch-remote returns the new number or the identifier of a voice-mail device to switch-main, depending on the details of the activated call forwarding service. This redirection can be done with the REFER method, as we saw in Figure 8.8. If it is a call forward to voice mail, the media server will play the announcement asking the caller to leave a message, and then proceed to record the message. When the caller hangs up (or if special treatment is offered, such as the ability to review the message by the caller, which can be activated with a code, e.g., #1) the media server will keep a log of the call, and the message can be played later when rattler calls his voice-mail number, which connects him to his message box.

Connecting to the message server to retrieve voice mail is a simple SIP call flow between two endpoints—in this example, similar to rattler calling sunrock in the main call flow.

8.2.2 Call Waiting

Call waiting (CW) involves playing a special tone to the party receiving the call and continuing to do so at periodic intervals until one of four things happens.

1. The party never accepts the incoming call, and there is no call forwarding to voice mail due to a no-answer condition. This is known as call forwarding-no answer or call forwarding-no response (CFNA or CFNR).
2. The party never accepts the incoming call and CFNR is activated. From that point on, the call flow continues as in the previous case of CFU.
3. The party never accepts the incoming call, and CFNR is activated to another number (could be an operator or an alternate party that can handle the call).
4. The party decides to accept the new call and places the current call on hold (with or without music).

When a call is delivered to a party with this feature enabled, the caller may or may not hear a distinctive ringback tone, depending on the network providing the service and the gateways providing the telephone service to the parties.

Incoming calls to a party that is already on another call are delivered in a normal INVITE message, just like in the simple call flow example. If the party decides to pick up the new call, the first call is placed on hold (INVITE, c=0) and the new call is accepted with a 200 OK/ACK exchange.

The call waiting tone to the called party can be generated by the IAD or the phone itself.

8.3 SIP-PSTN INTERWORKING

SIP is suitable for signaling calls over the PSTN, through SS7 signaling gateways or ISUP signaling functionality embedded in the softswitches themselves. In such a role, SIP signaling "drives" the SS7 gateway to generate the correct signaling messages and sequences on the PSTN side, and conversely accepts SS7 call initiation signaling and responses and generates appropriate SIP messaging in the softswitch domain.

In the example of this section, we look at Domain 1 signaling a call setup through its SS7 gateway. Cactus dialed rattler at work this time, and the call was determined to need routing to the local exchange for further routing and delivery. The scenario we analyze is shown in Figure 8.10.

The first part of the call consists of cactus making the call in Domain 1, under the Megaco signaling guidance of switch-main. Digit analysis by switch-main determines the call will need a hop on the PSTN and sends an INVITE to the SIP signaling port of its SS7 gateway, with the number of digits sent by cactus when it reported a digit map match.

> *Note:* This example shows a partial dialing string being delivered to switch-main. It is possible for the switch to determine that a call requires PSTN routing from a partial match, and thus initiate SS7 signaling before the entire number has been collected from the calling endpoint.

Signaling to stitch the ports inside BGW1 also takes place because it is using a PSTN media side, which consists of channelized T-carrier facilities. The path cannot yet be stitched because the Circuit ID Code (CIC) of the outbound facility has not been communicated to the softswitch.

The PSTN signaling gateway will send the IAM and will probably wait until a SAM (subsequent address message) arrives with the remaining digits of rattler's phone number. When the digits arrive, the SAM is issued and the local exchange sends back an Aoldnen's Complete Message (ACM), which

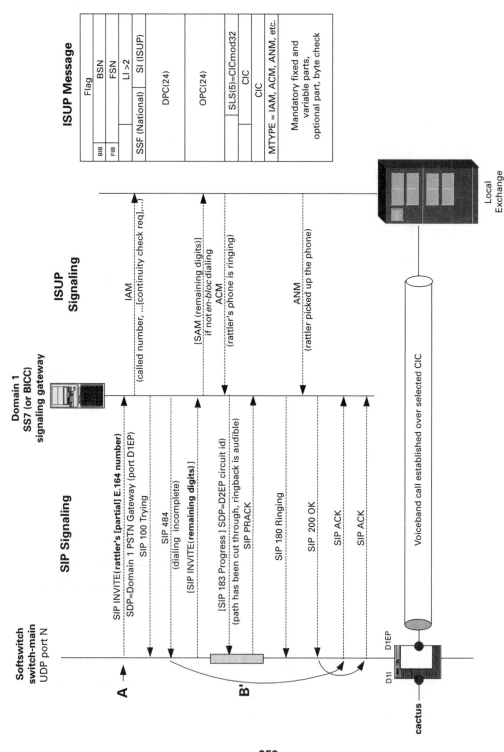

FIGURE 8.10 SIP to PSTN signaling.

indicates the call is delivered. A SIP provisional response from the signaling gateway at this time can include the SDP of the named endpoint D1EP, which is a DS0 on a trunk (the setup can be done in the shaded block at point B in Figure 8.6). This information is used by switch-main to stitch the path inside BGW1 and thus the audible ringback[1] can be heard by cactus. At this point, the call has been delivered, and when rattler picks up the phone at work, the Answer Message (ANM) is returned by the local exchange to the signaling gateway, which causes the SIP from the softswitch to be sent.

The signaling between cactus and switch-main in this scenario did not change, because of the presence of the BGW1 media gateway and the PSTN signaling gateway.

There can be many permutations of this type of SIP-SS7 signaling, and with proper use of response codes, mapping requirements for basic telephony service can be handled.

8.4 COMPLIANCE AND FAILURE SCENARIOS

In the course of a design, the design engineer (who has the ultimate knowledge of how things really work) needs to account for the possibility of failures. In the context of call flows, it is best to deal with "missing arrows" and "bad arrows" in the ping-pong diagrams we have been discussing in this text. Generally speaking, hardware and software failures will ultimately manifest themselves as malformed signaling exchanges, lost media streams, or both. It is then up to the network operator to determine where things went wrong. In the meantime, depending on the robustness of the design, the network may or may not be able to maintain all established calls and may in fact drop a few or all of them until the system has routed around failed links or equipment.

Communications protocols do not get too deeply into system behavior in the presence of failures, but some of them get into ways to failover in a seamless manner so that established calls do not get dropped. A quick survey of the suite of VoIP signaling protocols immediately brings out the different schools of thought as to what error codes the system when things go wrong. The more sophisticated the error code suite, the more information is obtained about the failure and the easier it is for the softswitch (if it is still alive in

---

1.   There is a draft proposal to define a new SIP header (ringback) which would convey the characteristics of the ringback tone to be played at the origination endpoint. For PSTN interworking, however, it is more likely to encounter a requirement to make the far-generated ringback audible to the caller, just like it works now in the PSTN.

some form of reduced capacity) to recover and plod along until the error conditions are removed.

A first observation of the topologies of VoIP networks is that there are a lot of network elements that are *invisible* at the signaling layer. For example, all the routers between an IAD and the softswitch in the signaling path are nonexistent from the perspective of the signaling protocol (H.323, SIP, MGCP, Megaco, etc.). So, what do we do when a failure occurs in an invisible element? How quickly and accurately does the signaling intelligence of the softswitch find out about it? And how quickly can it be circumvented so that the system can continue operating? These are the questions that the signaling protocols for call establishment have not overly concerned themselves with, and there are schools of thought in the industry as to whether this lack of concern was a good idea. We can draw some comparisons between the MTP layer capabilities for rerouting traffic in the public network and any of the packet-based signaling protocol capabilities we discussed in this text so far. Indeed, even in the much-maligned PSTN, there are "invisible" elements in the path of SS7 signaling (e.g., digital cross-connect systems have no point codes and are not addressable elements; therefore a similar analogy exists). However, SS7 offers the ability (at the MTP layers, with which call signaling is integrated) to detect failures and reroute traffic accordingly. If we draw the analogy with TCP/UDP, which are below the signaling protocols, we can see the loose integration (i.e., no integration) between signaling protocols and the network and link layers.

Another issue the design engineer needs to be concerned with is compliance with standards. Even with strict and disciplined specifications (H.323), it is often unknown the extent to which the protocol has been implemented, and a compliance statement is necessary. However, conformance test suites are few and far between, and the issue becomes how well the design has accounted for feature implementation to the letter of the specification. Beta-testing protocols in a live environment are as good as useless in my experience, because the same things will be exercised over and over again, with no guarantee that a spanning test will be performed, unless all the implementation software has been invoked in all the permutations and feature invocations in a thoroughly constructed test environment.

Then, we must consider the issue of compliance testing in the presence of load conditions. For example, any system that claims to support 911 dialing probably does, but how does it do it when it is operating at maximum call capacity? Some federal regulations dictate system availability. Suffice it to say that one of the most misquoted numbers in the industry is the 99.999% reliability. That's not the reliability of any particular box; it is the reliability of the telephone service. So, how do we plan to quantify the impact of software "features" (i.e., a euphemism for bugs that take longer to get out of the system) in the service execution environment on this reliability number?

It is difficult enough to try to establish compliance with a strict specification, so we can only imagine the challenge when trying to design with features and behavior descriptions that are not fully specified and may lend themselves to loose interpretations.

A major source of "pain" in the design process comes from connecting protocol stacks to get a true multiprotocol switch. No protocol lives in a vacuum, and a fully working stack in a homogeneous signaling environment (e.g., SIP only or H.323 only) may work just fine, but when integration times comes around, the sum of the two stacks is a product that does not quite "work." This particular issue is completely implementation-dependent, but it highlights the need for a thorough second-tier test suite in system integration. Once again, this kind of a test suite is left as an exercise for the designer and the engineering management, but that's where we find out how things really work, especially when dealing with a mixed development, such as the integration of a commercially available protocol stack with something that was developed internally.

Along comes media testing, and we have spoken several times about the perils of excessive transcoding. The step from G.711 PCM voice to any form of low-bit rate codec compression is irreversible with respect to retrieval of the original voice quality. We saw in my previous book [1] that perceptual weighting of the audio spectrum results in a distortion (warping and masking) of the frequency spectrum, and original frequency content is discarded and never makes it to the other end. The codec simply decides which frequency content would have been imperceptible and filters it to achieve higher bit compression. Going from G.711 to G.731.1 and then back to G.711 will not restore voice quality.

Last, but not least, is the performance issue. How do we determine the performance of a softswitch in calls-per-second? This is a tough question. H.323 has several modes of operation and call-routing models. SIP signaling can make the softswitch act as a proxy or redirect server. MGCP requires hand-holding through the call setup, and so does Megaco. So, when we put all of these protocols in the same box and call it "softswitch," what is its anticipated performance? This question cannot be answered very reliably unless a complete test suite has been executed under the various call mixes that are permitted in the system. We could possibly plot a curve from extrapolations based on each individual protocol's performance, but then along come firewalls!

It took longer than I had expected for the groups that develop protocol specifications to come to grips with the specter of firewalls in the VoIP environment. There are already efforts underway to create "decomposed" views of a typical firewall (similar to the method used in the MGCPs), but one of the real problems with firewalls is handling failure scenarios. Some ports open and close dynamically (for example, when we diverted music to a media server in our example, it was done dynamically), and information about those ports is contained inside signaling messages. Either the firewall itself or some controlling entity must parse signaling messages to manage the dynamic opening and closing of ports in the firewall. Or some other signaling stimulus must be provided to the signaling entity responsible for control of all the firewall devices through other means. The next step (and maybe the toughest) is to account for failover scenarios that involve traffic through firewalls and to try to keep traffic flowing without losing the established calls. It makes for an interesting exercise in network design, particularly if a requirement exists to seamlessly salvage entire conferences and maintain the voice quality (no additional jitter and latency) for the new media paths. And when all this is specified, we should not forget to create a realistic test topology and try it out with whatever QoS routing mechanism is intended to be in the final deployment (MPLS, DiffServ, or the latter over the former).

In Chapter 9, we will revisit the subject of performance estimation to reassure those less intimately familiar with the innards of packet voice technology that we have not exceeded the limits of comfort in their understanding of complexity in packet-based telephony.

SIP References

1. *IP Telephony: The Integration of Robust VoIP Services*, Bill Douskalis, Prentice Hall PTR.
2. RFC 2543bis: "SIP: Session Initiation Protocol," Handley, et al.
3. RFC 2976: "The SIP INFO method," S. Donovan.
4. RFC 2848: "The PINT Service Protocol: Extensions to SIP and SDP for IP access to telephone call services," Petrack, et. al.
5. RFC 2327: "SDP: Session Description Protocol," M. Handley, V. Jacobson.
6. IETF drafts are works in progress but it may be appropriate to use them as references in this context because several of them in the SIP area have found their way into equipment implementations, as application-specific extensions to the protocol.
7. IETF Draft: "Reliability of provisional responses in SIP," *draft-ietf-sip-100rel-02.txt*, J. Rosenberg, et. al. (defines the PRACK method).
8. IETF Draft: "SIP call control—Transfer," *draft-ietf-sip-cc-transfer-02.txt*, R. Sparks (defines the REFER method).
9. IETF Draft: "ISUP to SIP mapping," *draft-ietf-sip-isup-00.txt*, G. Camarillo, A. Roach.
10. IETF Draft: "SIP extensions for caller identity and privacy," *draft-ietf-sip-privacy-00.txt*, W. Marshall, et. al.
11. IETF Draft: "A SIP extension: Informational responses to the REFER method," *draft-mahy-sip-189-00.txt*, R. Mahy.

12. IETF Draft: "MIME media types for ISUP and QSIG objects," *draft-ietf-sip-isup-mime-06.txt,* Zimmerer, et. al.

13. IETF Draft: "The SIP session timer," *draft-ietf-sip-session-timer-04.txt,* S. Donovan, J. Rosenberg (defines use of re-INVITE as a refresh method).

14. IETF Draft: "SIP telephony call flow examples," *draft-ietf-sip-call-flows-02,* Johnston, et. al. (SIP-PSTN call flows and other useful telephony info).

15. IETF Draft: "SCTP as a transport for SIP," *draft-rosenberg-sip-sctp-00.txt,* Rosenberg, et. al.

16. IETF Draft: "Telephony Routing over IP (TRIP)," *draft-ietf-iptel-trip-04.txt,* Rosenberg, et. al. (TRIP model after BGP-4).

17. IETF Draft: "Architectural considerations for providing carrier class telephony services utilizing SIP-based distributed call control mechanisms," *draft-dcsgroup-sip-arch-02.txt,* Marshall, et. al.

18. IETF Draft: "Best current practice for ISUP to SIP mapping," *draft-camarillo-sip-isup-bcp-00.txt,* G. Camarillo, A. Roach.

19. IETF Draft: "Integration of resource management and SIP," *draft-manyfolks-sip-resource-01.txt,* Marshall, et. al. (describes the COMET method).

20. IETF Draft: "Ringback tones in SIP-based telephony," *draft-roach-voip-ringtone-00.txt,* A. Roach.

21. IETF SIP WG drafts and other proposed SIP extension drafts outside the formal SIP working group, as they become available and/or find implementation acceptance.

9

PSTN Signaling Adaptation and Transport

The wealth of capabilities of the new signaling protocols aside, there is a serious need to transport information present in messages of the PSTN signaling protocols (e.g., SS7 and Q.931) to endpoints and gateway controllers (softswitches). One reason is simply that there is no exact one-to-one mapping of message parameters between any two protocols, and functions of the AIN call model will still need to be supported well after we have replaced the Time Division Multiplex (TDM) infrastructure with a packet-based network. A second reason may be the desire to reuse existing software to accelerate development and minimize risk. It is a relatively simple exercise to construct the signaling flow for a toll call under any of the IP-based protocols of the previous sections, and to look at implementation issues like Global Title Translation (GTT), toll free calls, calling card calls, collect calls, operator-assisted calls, emergency calls, operator-assisted busy line verification, and billing and accounting, to realize that the old is not about to be obsoleted by the new in its entirety, at least in the short term.

In this chapter we look at a couple of things that weigh heavily in the minds of network designers. The first is signaling adaptation of the PSTN protocols in a manner that is useful, complete, and simple to implement. The second is the need for a transport mechanism for message-oriented, IP-based call signaling that will overcome some of the limitations of TCP, while offering reliability similar to TCP.

9.1 PSTN PROTOCOLS OVER IP

Signaling on the PSTN (which we discussed in my previous book) is easy, relatively uniform, and robust. The major digital signaling protocols (ISDN/Q.931 and SS7/ISUP [ISDN Usert Part] offer call-establishment and session-management capabilities with orthogonal and mostly symmetric procedures, albeit with spartan extensibility. The hop-by-hop nature of call establishment between exchanges uses one of the two protocols (mostly ISUP) with procedures that are strictly governed by exact specifications regarding the structure of protocol messages and the information parameters they convey to signaling entities. There is a certain degree of uniformity in the handling of adversity, such as congestion in facilities and exchanges, failed trunks, and signaling rerouting in the presence of link or STP failure. Failover is commonly addressed via equipment redundancy, and active calls can stay "up" when signaling between exchanges fails, although the failover capabilities of the PSTN signaling protocols themselves are rudimentary at best. Although their capabilities are limited, the PSTN signaling protocols have been tailored to work with the equipment of the PSTN, and as such, at least some signaling parameters must be made known to the signaling entities in the packet domains if seamless interoperability is desired.

Adaptation of ISUP/Q.931 with SIP and H.323 signaling is possible, using the tunneling capabilities of H.323 and the SIP INFO method, as well as MIME-encapsulation of included information elements in other messages. However, we run into the issue that lower level SS7 information cannot be mapped or tunneled easily, as in the way the MTP layers and their exchanges affect proper operation of signaling links and bearer facilities. In some applications, lower layer signaling behavior must be known and thus adapted and transported to the softswitch.

A couple of definitions[1] are needed at this point to set the context for *signaling transport* and a related concept known as *signaling backhaul*.

1. **Signaling Transport:** SIG (the name of the IETF working group doing signaling transport) refers to a *protocol stack*[2] for transport of PSTN signaling protocols over an IP network. The stack implementation offers primitives to interface with PSTN signaling application above, and

---

1. Definitions adapted from RFC 2719. Purists would argue that signaling transport encapsulates and transmits the application unmodified, as is stated in the RFC. However, real life may often dictate otherwise.

2. The term "protocol stack" here means "hierarchical ordering of software modules in layers, each offering distinct services to the layer directly above it in the hierarchy, and using the services of the layer directly below it."

supplements a standard IP transport protocol below with functionality designed to meet transport requirements for PSTN signaling. Signaling transport may occur after termination of PSTN signaling at the adaptation point and may transport the entire original application unmodified.

2. **Backhaul:** Backhaul refers to the transport of signaling from the point of interface for the associated signaling stream (i.e., a signaling function in a gateway for PRI PBX) back to the point of call processing (i.e., the softswitch), if call processing is not done locally by the gateway. Backhaul does not require termination of the protocol being transported at the gateway.

Let's take a quick look at a reference topology for this chapter, shown in Figure 9.1.

9.2 SCTP

The IETF is proposing a protocol significantly different than TCP—the Stream Control Transmission Protocol—to transport user-adapted SS7 signaling and possibly other applications. SCTP is intended to replace TCP as a reliable transport mechanism for applications that do not require the entire suite of capabilities of TCP, but still prefer a stateful connection-oriented transport layer protocol. SCTP is like TCP in spirit, but it streamlines data transfer operations, states maintenance operations, and states update operations to only those actions that are necessary to transport message streams between endpoints in a reliable and robust manner. TCP is viewed as suffering from some significant shortcomings when it is placed in the role of supporting signaling transport (as adapted from the motivation discussion for the SCTP protocol).

1. TCP provides both reliable data transfer and strict order-of-transmission delivery of data. Some applications need reliable transfer without sequence maintenance, while others would be satisfied with partial ordering of the data. In both cases, the head-of-line blocking offered by TCP causes unnecessary delay.

2. TCP keeps track of bytes sent and acknowledges bytes received. This stream-oriented, byte-centered nature of TCP is often an inconvenience when an application sends and wants to keep track of entire messages. Applications must add their own record marking to delineate their messages, and must make explicit use of the TCP **push** facility to ensure that a complete message is transferred in a reasonable time.

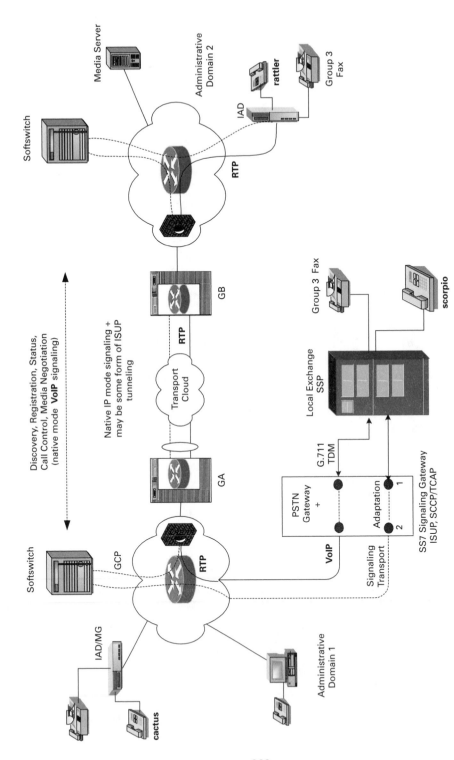

FIGURE 9.1 Sigtran topology in a mixed network.

Media Server

Softswitch

Administrative Domain 2

rattler

IAD

Group 3 Fax

RTP

GB

RTP

Transport Cloud

Native IP mode signaling + may be some form of ISUP tunneling

Discovery, Registration, Status, Call Control, Media Negotiation (native mode **VoIP** signaling)

GA

Group 3 Fax

scorpio

Local Exchange SSP

G.711 TDM

PSTN Gateway +

Adaptation

1

2

VoIP

Signaling Transport

SS7 Signaling Gateway ISUP, SCCP/TCAP

Softswitch

GCP

RTP

IAD/MG

cactus

Administrative Domain 1

3. The limited scope of TCP sockets complicates the task of providing highly available data transfer capability using multihomed hosts. TCP sockets are also "expensive" resources on most platforms, a fact that has influenced protocols to streamline signaling (e.g., H.323).
4. A lesser issue with TCP is its vulnerability to *denial-of-service* attacks, such as SYN attacks (SYN attacks can clog the network and make legitimate access close to impossible). A TCP-SYN attach is one whereby a malicious entity constantly attempts to open TCP connections with the entity under attack, for the purpose of exhausting its resources. Although *denial-of-service* is hard to eliminate entirely as a risk, methods can be instituted to limit the effectiveness of such attacks.

With these issues in mind, its replacement, SCTP, can be thought of as providing the following services:

1. Acknowledged, validated, error-free, and nonduplicated transfer of user data, in **message streams**. A mode is provided whereby strict sequencing of messages is circumvented and messages are forwarded to the upper layer as soon as they are received.
2. Data segmentation to accommodate the MTU size of the discovered end-to-end path. This is a must in the IP world. Message reassembly is performed at the far end.
3. Optional multiplexing of user messages into SCTP datagrams (bundling), and network-level fault tolerance through support of multihoming at either or both ends of an association. The latter is very important, and the need for the former is obvious when we try to streamline signaling steps to improve performance.
4. SCTP supports congestion avoidance and resists flooding and masquerade attacks.
5. The protocol offers path management capabilities, such that destination reachability is determined in real time through heartbeat messages, and if the currently active TA is unreachable, another one is selected from the list of possible destination TAs.
6. Inherent fault-tolerance capabilities through multihoming at either or both ends of an endpoint association is a particularly useful attribute in VoIP networks with redundancy requirements.

Although SCTP is connection-oriented in the sense that the endpoints establish an "association" prior to dava transfer taking place, it is somewhat simpler in comparison to TCP in some areas (and not so in others), yet does not compromise the robustness of the transport layer in areas it simplifies. It also takes advantage of some of the same algorithms that have been developed over the years and of the lessons learned in bandwidth usage to assist in maximizing the TCP throughput over the WAN and high-speed LANs.

SCTP is IP Protocol Number 132.
The terminology of the SCTP protocol is summarized in Table 9.1.

TABLE 9.1 Key SCTP Terminology

TERMINOLOGY	MEANING
Active destination transport address	The TA on a peer endpoint that the transmitting endpoint is using for receiving user messages. To maintain the connection state when the active TA cannot be reached, other TAs from a list of available ones on the far endpoint are attempted.
Bundling	An optional multiplexing operation whereby more than one user message may be carried in the same SCTP packet. Each user message occupies its own DATA chunk.
Chunk	A unit of information within an SCTP packet, consisting of a chunk header and application-specific content.
Congestion window (cwnd)	An SCTP variable that limits the data, in number of bytes, a sender can send to a particular destination TA before receiving an acknowledgment. This is similar to the variable of the same name in TCP.
Cumulative TSN ACK point	The TSN (Transmission Sequence Number) of the last DATA chunk acknowledged via the Cumulative TSN ACK field of a SACK (Selective Acknowledgment).
Idle destination address	An address that has not had user messages sent to it within some length of time, normally one heartbeat interval or greater.
Inactive destination transport address	An address that is considered inactive due to errors and unavailability to transport user messages.
Message = user message	Data submitted to SCTP by the Upper Layer Protocol (ULP).
Message Authentication Code (MAC)	An integrity-check mechanism based on cryptographic hash functions using a secret key. Typically, message authentication codes are used between two parties that share a secret key in order to validate information transmitted between these parties. In SCTP it is used by an endpoint to validate the state cookie information that is returned from the peer in the COOKIE ECHO chunk (see SCTP call flow to establish context of term usage in this table). The term MAC has different meanings in different contexts. SCTP uses this term with the same meaning as in [RFC 2104].
Network byte order	Most significant byte first, known as Big Endian.

TABLE 9.1 Key SCTP Terminology (continued)

TERMINOLOGY	MEANING
Ordered message	A user message that is delivered in order with respect to all previous user messages sent within the stream the message was sent on.
Outstanding TSN (in the transmit direction of an SCTP endpoint)	A TSN (and the associated DATA chunk) that has been sent by the endpoint but for which it has not yet received an acknowledgment.
Path	The route taken by the SCTP packets sent by one SCTP endpoint to a specific destination TA of its peer SCTP endpoint. Sending to different destination TAs does not necessarily guarantee getting separate paths. The latter point is significant, as the protocol does not do dynamic engineering of paths. This is left for network engineering of tunnels (label switched or differentiated services).
Primary path	The primary path is the destination and source address that will be put into a packet outbound to the peer endpoint by default. The definition includes the source address, since an implementation may wish to specify both destination and source address to better control the return path taken by reply chunks and on which interface the packet is transmitted when the data sender is multihomed. Again, the sending endpoint may not be completely path-agnostic as to which route the messages actually traverse end-to-end.
Receiver window (rwnd)	An SCTP variable used by a data sender to store the most recently calculated receiver window of its peer, in number of bytes. TCP implementations do similarly. This gives the sender an indication of the space available in the receiver's inbound buffer.
SCTP association	A protocol relationship between SCTP endpoints, composed of the two SCTP endpoints and protocol state information, including verification tags and the currently active set of TSNs. An SCTP association can be uniquely identified by the TAs used by the signaling endpoints. Two SCTP endpoints must not have more than one SCTP association between them at any given time.
SCTP endpoint	The logical sender/receiver of SCTP packets. On a multihomed host, an SCTP endpoint is represented to its peers as a combination of a set of eligible destination TAs to which SCTP packets can be sent and a set of eligible source TAs from which SCTP packets can be received. All TAs used by an SCTP endpoint must use the same port number, but can use multiple IP addresses. A TA used by an SCTP endpoint must not be used by another SCTP endpoint. In other words, a TA is unique to an SCTP endpoint.

TABLE 9.1 Key SCTP Terminology (continued)

TERMINOLOGY	MEANING
SCTP packet	The unit of data delivery across the interface between SCTP and the connectionless packet network (e.g., IP). An SCTP packet includes the common SCTP header, possible SCTP control chunks, and user data encapsulated within SCTP DATA chunks.
SCTP user application (SCTP user)	The logical higher layer application entity that uses the services of SCTP, also called the ULP.
Slow-Start threshold (ssthresh)	An SCTP variable, similar in spirit to the TCP slow-start threshold. This is the watermark which the endpoint will use to determine whether to perform slow-start or congestion avoidance on a particular destination transport address. *Ssthresh* is expressed in number of bytes.
Stream	A unidirectional logical channel established from one SCTP endpoint to its associated one. All user messages in a stream are delivered in sequence except for those submitted to the unordered delivery service. The RFC states, *The relationship between stream numbers in opposite directions is strictly a matter of how the applications use them. It is the responsibility of the SCTP user to create and manage these correlations if they are so desired.*
Stream Sequence Number	A 16-bit sequence number used internally by SCTP to assure sequenced delivery of the user messages within a given stream. One stream sequence number is attached to each user message.
Tie-tags	Verification tags from a previous association. These *tags* are used within a state cookie so that the newly restarting association can be linked to the original association within the endpoint that did not restart.
Transmission Control Block (TCB)	An internal data structure created by an SCTP endpoint for each of its existing SCTP associations. TCB contains all the status and operational information for the endpoint to maintain and manage the corresponding association.
Transmission Sequence Number	A 32-bit sequence number used internally by SCTP. One TSN is attached to each chunk containing user data to permit the receiving SCTP endpoint to acknowledge its receipt and detect duplicate deliveries.

TABLE 9.1 Key SCTP Terminology (continued)

TERMINOLOGY	MEANING
Transport address	A TA is traditionally defined by network layer address, transport layer protocol and transport layer port number. In the case of SCTP running over IP, a TA is defined by the combination of an IP address and an *SCTP port number* (where SCTP is the transport protocol).
Unacknowledged TSN (in the receive direction of an SCTP endpoint)	A TSN (and the associated DATA chunk) that has been received by the endpoint but for which an acknowledgment has not yet been sent, or in the opposite case, for a packet that has been sent but no acknowledgment has been received.
Unordered Message	Messages presented in the order of their arrival, rather than in their logical or time-ordered association with respect to other messages in the same stream. This may result in both unordered as well as ordered messages being linearly queued and delivered to the upper layer protocol. When the unordered message delivery service is used, no ordering is guaranteed.
User message	The unit of data payload across the interface between SCTP and its user.
Verification Tag	A 32-bit unsigned integer that is randomly generated. The verification tag provides a key that allows a receiver to verify that the SCTP packet belongs to the current association and is not an old or stale packet from a previous association.

SCTP defines a suite of messages used in basic association setup and termination procedures, as well as in data transmission, acknowledgments, and error conditions. The structure of an SCTP packet is shown in Figure 9.2. The key construct of the SCTP protocol is the *chunk*, which is a unit of information transported between endpoints. A chunk carries either control or data information, and chunks can be bundled in the same message, with a few exceptions.

The chunk types of SCTP are summarized in Table 9.2[3].

3.   This description of SCTP summarizes key elements and features to assist in understanding the operation of signaling transport over SCTP. Refer to the RFC for a complete listing of the parameters for each chunk and specification of procedures.

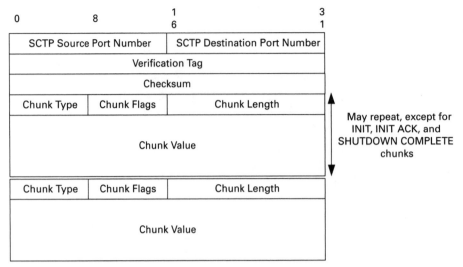

FIGURE 9.2 Generic SCTP packet.

TABLE 9.2 SCTP Chunks

CHUNK NAME (TYPE)	USAGE SUMMARY
DATA (0)	Data chunks flow between endpoints once an association between them has been established. For early data transmision, DATA chunks can be bundled with COOKIE-ECHO and COOKIE-ACK control chunks, as long as the control chunks are placed first in the message. Messages may end up fragmented as a result of path MTU size. If so, a flag on the chunk indicates the beginning and end fragment of the original message. DATA chunks can be delivered as received (which could be out of order), or the original complete message may be reassembled before it is presented to the upper layer protocol. The type of service requested by the stream is indicated with a flag on the chunk.
INIT (1)	This is the first chunk sent to initiate association establishment between two endpoints. It conveys parameters such as the TA of the association (may be more than one and may be IPv4 or IPv6 or a combination), the number of inbound streams that can be supported by the sender, and the number of outbound streams the sender would like to support over this association. At this time, the resource allocation by the sender (size of the input buffer in bytes) is also advertised to the far endpoint. An INIT chunk may not be bundled with other chunks.

TABLE 9.2 SCTP Chunks

CHUNK NAME (TYPE)	USAGE SUMMARY
INIT ACK (2)	Sent in acknowledgment of the INIT chunk and contains the state cookie variable. It may also identify unrecognized paramaters in the INIT message, and just like INIT, it specifies the number of outbound and inbound streams for the association with this endpoint and the TAs that can be used in this association.
SACK (3)	The SACK chunk is sent to acknowledge DATA chunks or to inform there is a sequence gap between received DATA chunks.
HEARTBEAT REQUEST (4)	Sent periodically to confirm reachability of the destination endpoint.
HEARTBEAT ACK (5)	This is the acknowledgment to the HEARTBEAT REQUEST. Must be sent to the source IP address of the sender of the HEARTBEAT REQUEST chunk.
ABORT (6)	This chunk closes an association immediately and may contain parameters that specify the cause. Cannot be bundled with DATA chunks.
SHUTDOWN (7)	Sent to initiate graceful closing of an association.
SHUTDOWN ACK (8)	The recipient of the SHUTDOWN chunk sends this ACK as an acknowledgment.
ERROR (9)	Sent to identify various error conditions at the endpoint. Errors can be internal (out of resources) or protocol errors, such as invalid parameters in control or data chunks.
COOKIE ECHO (10)	Used only during the association establishment phase, and completes the establishment process at the sender (see call flow in this section for chunk usage). Can be bundled with a data chunk, but it must be the first chunk in the bundle.
COOKIE-ACK (11)	Acknowledges receipt of COOKIE-ECHO during the association setup process. Can be bundled with a data chunk, but it must be the first chunk in the bundle.
ECNE (12) and CWR (13)	Explicit congestion notification and congestion window reduced are reserved for future use.
SHUTDOWN COMPLETE (14)	Sent to acknowledge receipt of the SHUTDOWN ACK chunk.

The basic structure of the DATA chunk is shown in Figure 9.3. There are no delimiters between bundled chunks, and the beginning of the next chunk is derived from the *chunk length* parameter. Control chunks vary in construction, depending on chunk type and control parameters.

The basic protocol state diagram for association establishment is shown in Figure 9.4. The exchange begins when an endpoint sends an INIT chunk to the TA of a far endpoint, thus initiating association establishment. The sender starts a timer and enters the cookie-wait state.

The far endpoint that receives the INIT chunk formats an INIT-ACK chunk and returns it to the IP address of the sender of the INIT. The INIT-ACK contains the state variable cookie, and as soon it is received, the sender of the INIT chunk stops the timer and sends a COOKIE-ECHO chunk. A new timer is started and the sender's state is cookie-wait.

When the far end receives the COOKIE-WAIT and returns a COOKIE-ACK chunk, both endpoints are in the *established* state. At the end of the established state, data chunks for the established streams can be transmitted in bundles with data from the same or other streams. For those in a hurry, the COOKIE-ECHO and COOKIE-ACK messages can accept DATA chunks as well, as long as the control chunks are the first ones in the message.

DATA chunks are acknowledged with SACK chunks, which are also used to indicate gaps in the stream data sequence.

HEARTBEAT chunks are exchanged periodically to maintain reachability between endpoints on the currently active paths (i.e., routes between the TAs). The HEARTBEAT/HEARTBEAT-ACK chunk pair is useful for estab-

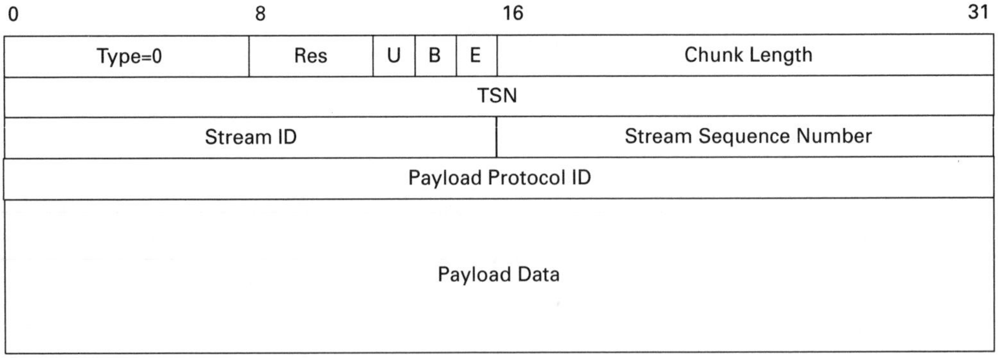

0		8				16	31
Type=0		Res	U	B	E		Chunk Length
TSN							
Stream ID						Stream Sequence Number	
Payload Protocol ID							
Payload Data							

Legend:
U: Unordered service (if =1, no stream sequence is maintained)
B: Beginning of message fragment
E: End of message fragment

FIGURE 9.3 SCTP DATA chunk.

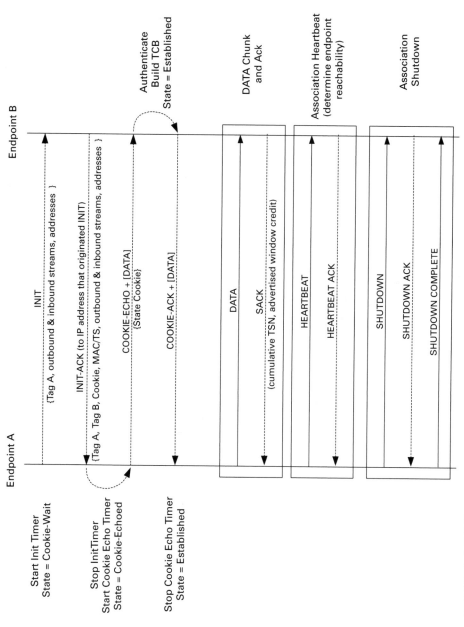

FIGURE 9.4 SCTP state diagram.

Endpoint A

Endpoint B

INIT
{Tag A, outbound & inbound streams, addresses }

Start Init Timer
State = Cookie-Wait

INIT-ACK (to IP address that originated INIT)
{Tag A, Tag B, Cookie, MAC/TS, outbound & inbound streams, addresses }

Stop InitTimer
Start Cookie Echo Timer
State = Cookie-Echoed

COOKIE-ECHO + [DATA]
{State Cookie}

Authenticate
Build TCB
State = Established

COOKIE-ACK + [DATA]

Stop Cookie Echo Timer
State = Established

DATA

DATA Chunk
and Ack

SACK
(cumulative TSN, advertised window credit)

HEARTBEAT

Association Heartbeat
(determine endpoint
reachability)

HEARTBEAT ACK

SHUTDOWN

Association
Shutdown

SHUTDOWN ACK

SHUTDOWN COMPLETE

271

lishing the RTT between endpoints, which in turn is used to calculate transmission window sizes. Multiple failed attempts to reach an endpoint with this chunk type (or timer expirations waiting for SACK in response to DATA chunks) can declare the current TA as unreachable.

Associations can be terminated abruptly due to errors with an ABORT chunk, or gracefully with the SHUTDOWN/SHUTDOWN-ACK/SHUTDOWN COMPLETE signaling procedure, as shown in the call flow.

> Note that unlike TCP, SCTP does not support the half-open state, whereby one side can continue sending data while the other side is closed.

SCTP has two early customers—two signaling transfer protocols intended for use of SCTP services—both of which are still in draft proposal form.

9.3 M2UA

The need to transport SS7 signaling between endpoints was not immediately obvious when work on VoIP networks first started. After it became apparent that new VoIP signaling was not covering all the bases quickly enough for access to the PSTN, focus shifted towards using major pieces of the SS7 protocol, but replacing either MTP3 or MTP2 with an IP-based transport mechanism. Thus was born M2UA and M3UA, along with other notable attempts to solve the same problem, such as Tekelec's TALI.[4]

Both M2UA and M3UA accommodate signaling transport of SS7 signaling. M2UA has equivalent functionality to the MTP2 layer of SS7, and transports everything above (and including) MTP3 signaling units (MSU). It defines an adaptation method to send link-layer messages and a method defined to send upper layer signaling data.

M3UA operates in the third layer of the protocol stack, as a replacement of MTP3, and provides for both adaptation and transport of messages generated by the users of MTP3, such as ISUP and SCCP. It is obvious that both adaptation methods can send ISUP and SCCP messages, and their use preference is an implementation issue based on other attributes that differentiate the two methods.

---

4. The Transport Adapter Layer Interface (which is implemented and deployed) is described in detail later in this chapter.

The relative position of M2UA and M3UA with respect to each other and to the IP protocol is shown in Figure 9.5, which also positions M2UA architecturally with respect to services it provides to its upper protocol layers. The M2UA message suite is shown in Table 9.3.

The intent is to use SCTP as the transport protocol, whereby the combination of the inherent SS7 recovery procedures, coupled with the inherent fault tolerance of SCTP, will match the signaling robustness of the PSTN.

Two definitions in the context of M2UA are necessary in order to avoid confusion with the terminology used elsewhere in VoIP.[5]

1. *Application server (AS).* A logical entity serving a specific application instance. An example of an application server is a softswitch or softswitch adjunct, handling the MTP Level 3 and call processing for SS7 links terminated by the signaling gateways (SGs). Practically speaking, an application server is modeled at the SG as an ordered list of one or more related application server processes. The softswitch adjunct can be the host of other generic applications.

2. *Application server process (ASP).* A process instance of an application server. Examples of ASPs are primary or backup softswitch instances or instances of distributed softswitch adjuncts.

M2UA takes advantage of the robustness and its own failover capabilities as well as those of SCTP to allow the design of very reliable SS7 signaling transport between an SG and the softswitch that controls the gateway along with its signaling links. The M2UA failover model is *1+N,* whereby *1* ASP is handling the signaling and there are *N* ASPs available to take over in signaling failover.

M2UA messages consist of a common header and variable-length parameters. There is also a message-specific header, which is used with MTP2 user adaptation messages. The M2UA protocol element structure is shown in Figure 9.6.

The ASP state machine in a M2UA signaling point is shown in Figure 9.7. M2UA messages are sent in DATA chunks over SCTP associations.

9.4 M3UA

M3UA signaling adaptation provides MTP 3 layer services to higher protocol layers, which may in fact be SS7 signaling user parts, such as ISUP, and SCCP (for support of Transition Capabilities Application Part [TCAP] and

---

5. Adapted from the draft proposals listed in the references.

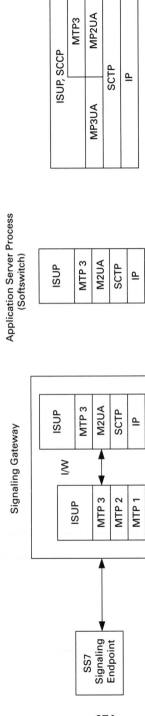

FIGURE 9.5 SCTP/M3UA/M2UA protocol stack.

274

TABLE 9.3 M2UA Message Summary

MTP2 USER ADAPTATION MESSAGES	COMMENTS
Data Establish Request, Confirm Release Request, Confirm, Indication State Request, Confirm, Indication Congestion Indication Retrieval Request, Confirm Retrieval Complete Indication	The Data message contains an SS7 MTP2-User Protocol Data Unit (PDU). This can be an MTP3 PDU, which may also contain ISUP or SCCP data. Establish, Release, and State messages are related to the SS7 signaling link itself. Retrieval messages are used in MTP3 changeover conditions to request pending PDUs and to flush the PDU queue. Congestion indication messages carry the level of congestion (1 to 3) on the signaling links.
APPLICATION SERVER PROCESS MESSAGES	**COMMENTS**
ASP Up (ASPUP) ASP Down (ASPDN) ASP Active (ASPAC) ASP Inactive (ASPIA)	The ASP messages are state indications of the Application server process inside the softswitch or softswitch adjunct device. See state transition diagram for usage explanation.
LAYER MANAGEMENT MESSAGES	**COMMENTS**
Error (ERR) Notify (NTFY)	The ERR message is sent when an invalid value is found in an incoming message or the message was not expected in the current ASP state. Notify is used for autonomous notification of events to the softswitch.

other telephony applications). It is also recommended for transport over SCTP and its operation is consistent with all the procedures defined in the SCTP protocol. M2UA messages are sent in DATA chunks over SCTP associations. In an SG, M3UA protocol interworking with the SS7 protocol stack would be as shown in Figure 9.8.

M3UA signaling adaptation provides the following features and services.[6]

---

6.   Adapted from the references, with extensions. This is work in progress.

M2UA Message Structure

0	8	16	31
Version	Spare	Message Class	Message Type
Message Length			
Parameter Tag		Parameter Length	
Parameter Value			

M2UA Message Structure

MTP2 User Adaptation Message Headers

0	8	16	31
Version	Spare	Message Class	Message Type
Message Length			
Tag		Length	
Interface Identifier (may be text or integer, depending on Tag)			

MTP2 User Adaptation Message Headers

Message Classes in M2UA

0   Management (MGMT) Message
      [IUA/M2UA/M3UA/SUA]
1   Transfer Messages
      [M3UA]
2   SS7 Signaling Network Management (SSNM) Messages
      [M3UA/SUA]
3   ASP State Maintenance (ASPSM) Messages
      [IUA/M2UA/M3UA/SUA]
4   ASP Traffic Maintenance (ASPTM) Messages
      [IUA/M2UA/M3UA/SUA]
5   Q.921/Q.931 Boundary Primitives Transport (QPTM) Messages
      [IUA]
6   MTP2 User Adaptation (MAUP) Messages
      [M2UA]
7   Connectionless Messages
      [SUA]
8   Connection-Oriented Messages
      [SUA]

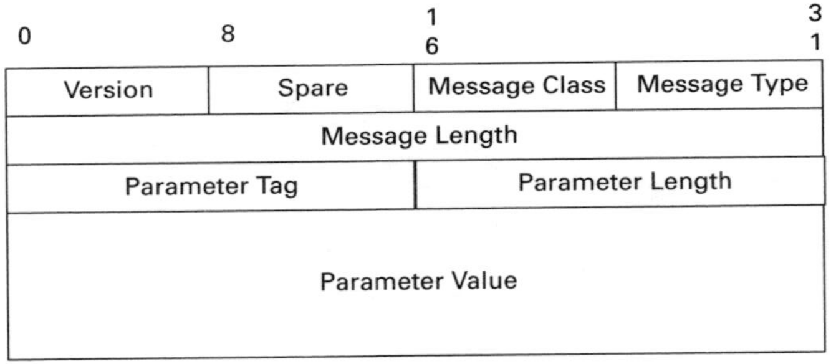

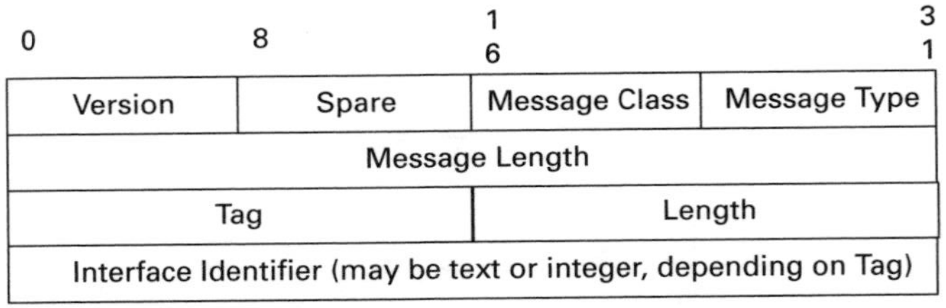

FIGURE 9.6 MPUA packet structure.

276

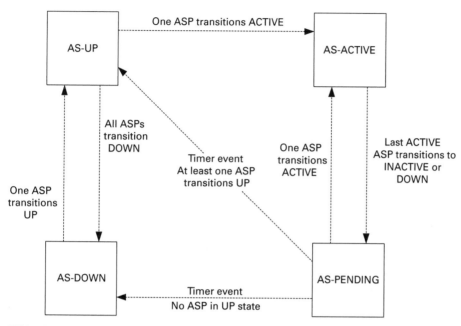

FIGURE 9.7 M2UA and M3UA state machine.

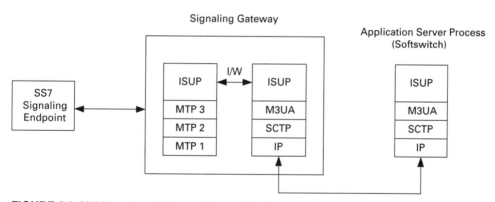

FIGURE 9.8 M3UA protocol interworking architecture.

1. Support for the transfer of all SS7 MTP3-user part messages (e.g., ISUP, SCCP, Telephone User Part [TUP], etc.). This implicitly includes TCAP.
2. Support for the seamless operation of MTP3-user protocol peers. Adaptation of the MTP3 layer in SGs does not alter the message content of the MTP3-user peers.

3. Support for the management of SCTP transport associations and traffic between an SG and one or more softswitches, softswitch adjunct application servers, or switching control points.
4. Support for softswitch or switching control point process failover and load-sharing.
5. Support for the asynchronous reporting of status changes to the management layer.

M3UA interworks with the MTP3 layer in an SG and provides indications to MTP layer 3 users at a softswitch for the following conditions:

1. A remote destination in the SS7 network is not reachable.
2. A remote destination in the SS7 network has now become reachable.
3. Messages to a remote MTP3-user peer in the SS7 network are experiencing SS7 congestion.
4. The routes to a remote MTP3-user peer in the SS7 network are restricted.
5. A remote MTP3-user peer is unavailable (e.g., ISUP, SCCP).

The terminology of M2UA with respect to context-specific application server and ASP is used in the M3UA context as well. Key M3UA messages used to perform its adaptation functions and services are summarized in Table 9.4.

TABLE 9.4 M3UA Message Summary[*]

M3UA MESSAGE	COMMENTS
Data	Sends MTP3 user data (e.g., ISUP or SCCP).
Destination Unavailable (DUNA)	The MTP3-User at the ASP is expected to stop traffic to the affected destination through the SG initiating the DUNA (per MTP3-User procedures).
Destination Available (DAVA)	The ASP MTP3-user protocol is expected to resume traffic to the affected destination through the SG initiating the DUNA.
Destination State Audit (DAUD)	Sent by the softswitch ASP to the SG to audit the availability and status of an SS7 signaling endpoint.
SS7 Network Congestion State (SCON)	Sent by the SG to indicate congestion to an SS7 signaling endpoint, with the following severity levels. Value Description 00 No Congestion or Undefined 01 Congestion Level 1 02 Congestion Level 2 03 Congestion Level 3

TABLE 9.4 M3UA Message Summary* (continued)

M3UA MESSAGE	COMMENTS
	The congestion levels are as defined in the national congestion method in the ITU MTP recommendation or in the ANSI MTP standard. For MTP congestion methods that do not employ congestion levels (e.g., the ITU international method), the parameter is always Undefined.
Destination User Part Unavailable (DUPU)	Sent by the SG to the softswitch to indicate that a peer MTP3-user part at a signaling endpoint is unavailable. The possible indications are Value Description 00 Unknown 01 Unequipped Remote User 02 Inaccessible Remote User User Identities Value Description 00–02 Reserved 03 SCCP 04 TUP 05 ISUP 06–08 Reserved 09 Broadband ISUP 10 Satellite ISUP
Destination Restricted (DRST)	Sent by the SG to indicate a destination is now restricted.
ASP Up ASP Ask (Response)	The ASP UP (ASPUP) message is used to indicate to a remote M3UA peer that the adaptation layer is ready to receive traffic or maintenance messages. The ASP needs to acknowledge this message with ASP ACK.
ASP Down ASP Down ACK (Response)	The ASP Down (ASPDN) message is used to indicate to a remote M3UA peer that the adaptation layer is not ready to receive traffic or maintenance messages. The ASP needs to acknowledge this message.
Heartbeat	The Heartbeat message is optionally used to ensure that the M3UA peers are still available to each other. It is recommended for use when the M3UA runs over a transport layer other than the SCTP, which has its own heartbeat.
Registration Request (REG REQ) Registration Response (REG RSP)	Sent by the ASP function to the SG to register one or more routing keys.* The recipient needs to acknowledge this message.

TABLE 9.4 M3UA Message Summary[*] (continued)

M3UA MESSAGE	COMMENTS
De-Registration Request (DREG REQ) De-Registration Response (DREG RSP)	Sent by the ASP to revoke a previous routing key registration. The recipient needs to acknowledge this message.
ASP Active (ASPAC) and ASP Active Ack	The ASPAC message is sent by an ASP to indicate to an SG that it is active and ready to be used. The recipient acknowledges it.
ASP Inactive (ASPIA) and ASP Inactive Ack	The ASPIA message is sent by an ASP to indicate to an SG that it is no longer an active ASP to be used from within a list of ASPs. The SG will respond with an ASP Inactive ACK.
Error (ERR)	The ERR message is sent when an invalid value is found in an incoming message (general protocol error).
Notify (NTFY)	The Notify message is used to provide an autonomous indication of M3UA events to an M3UA peer.

[*]   A routing key is a set of parameters used to filter SS7 messages. Parameters in the routing key must be within a single SS7 DPC, and the keys must be unique. Example routing keys are the DPC, and the DPC/OPC/CIC combination.

The application server transition diagram for M3UA is similar to the one for M2UA, as one might expect. The protocol element construction of M3UA is similar to that of M2UA as well.

Other signaling adaptation work in progress includes SCCP User Adaptation (SUA), for the transport of TCAP and support of connection-oriented and connectionless SCCP services, and the V5.2-User Adaptation layer (V5UA), for signaling transport of the V5.2 protocol. The ISDN Q.921 User Adaptation Layer is described in RFC 3057. The ITU is also proceeding with the definition of the Bearer-Independent Call Control Protocol (BICCP, Q.1901), which is being written as a series of exceptions to the ISUP signaling specification.[7] An immediate observation is that the Circuit ID of TDM facilities (CIC) has no direct equivalent in the packet world, and needs to be replaced with a different identifier in ISUP over packet, among other changes that are necessary to adapt the signaling.

Next in this chapter, we will see the use of user adaptation signaling in the context of a composite call flow, which involves voice and fax.

---

7.   This is work in progress.

9.5 TRANSPORT ADAPTER LAYER INTERFACE (TALI)

Tekelec's TALI specification describes an alternative implementation of SS7 signaling adaptation and is defined in RFC 3094, albeit with a disclaimer.[8] However, it is a deployed and commercially available implementation of signaling adaptation, encapsulation, and transport in IP-based signaling endpoints and signaling gateways operating in hybrid TDM/VoIP telephony networks.

Architecturally, the TALI protocol stack looks very similar to M2UA, but there are major differences in the adaptation approach. TALI runs over TCP and offers signaling adaptation services to hybrid networks terminating the traditional 56Kbps (DS–0, V.35, etc.) dedicated SS7 signaling using all three MTP layers. It runs over AAL5 in topologies using SS7 signaling over ATM virtual circuits and high-speed facilities, such as T1. As Figure 9.9 shows, in the traditional case, TALI replaces the MTP2 layer and adapts signaling from the SS7 network layer (MTP3) and above. It is thus capable of adapting MTP3, ISUP, and SCCP signaling, the latter of which includes TCAP services—for example, those used in toll-free number translation with the use of an SCP. Therefore, other application parts in the SS7 protocol stack are also supported. In an ATM environment, TALI is located under the Signaling ATM Adaptation Layer (SAAL), which provides services similar to MTP2 for this application.

> TALI is defined to work over TCP. It's operation over SCTP, however is not precluded in future implementations.

The protocol definition makes it suitable for adapted SS7 signaling transport between any two nodes that wish to exchange such signaling over IP. For example, any two IP-based signaling gateways can be connected over an IP network using TALI internally and terminating dedicated SS7 signaling links towards the PSTN. Also, any IP-based signaling gateway, policy server, and so on, can exchange SS7 signaling with a softswitch and an IP-based SCP. It thus offers a bridge from the TDM signaling world to VoIP domains in a seamless manner, with enhanced management capabilities.

---

8.   The contents of RFC 3094 originally appeared in the TALI protocol specification from the vendor (Tekelec).

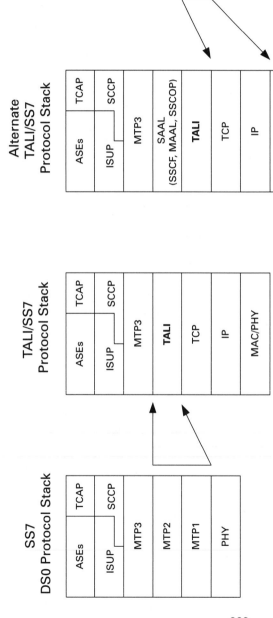

SS7
ATM Protocol Stack

ASEs	TCAP
ISUP	SCCP
MTP3	
SAAL (SSCF, MAAL, SSCOP)	
ATM AAL5	
ATM PHY	

GR-2878-CORE

Alternate
TALI/SS7
Protocol Stack

ASEs	TCAP
ISUP	SCCP
MTP3	
SAAL (SSCF, MAAL, SSCOP)	
TALI	
TCP	
IP	
MAC/PHY	

TALI/SS7
Protocol Stack

ASEs	TCAP
ISUP	SCCP
MTP3	
TALI	
TCP	
IP	
MAC/PHY	

SS7
DS0 Protocol Stack

ASEs	TCAP
ISUP	SCCP
MTP3	
MTP2	
MTP1	
PHY	

SAAL : Signaling ATM Adaptation Layer

Components

SSCF : Service Specific Coordination Function
MAAL : Management Adaptation ATM Layer
SSCOP: Service Specific Connection-Oriented Protocol

Note : SCTP can be used instead of TCP as the transport protocol.

FIGURE 9.9 TALI protocol stack, TDM and ATM versions.

282

A major feature of TALI is the ability to dynamically register circuits and offer call routing based on the location of a circuit. This attribute allows network design flexibility over call routing based strictly on DPC only.

The TALI message structure is shown in Figure 9.10. Messages begin with the four bytes of the SYNC field, which set to 'TALI' in ASCII. This is followed by an opcode field, which is also ASCII and basically identifies the type of message. The length field is a 16-bit integer, sent with the Least Significant Bit (LSB) first, for the length of the flexible payload data field. The numbers in parentheses in Figure 9.10 indicate the allowable data range for each type of message. The payload data field carries SS7 upper layer messages, as shown in Figure 9.11 and Figure 9.12.

TALI is currently in version 2.0, but there are few differences between versions 1.0 and 2.0. Three new messages have appeared in version 2.0, and some of the payload data fields have modified length ranges.

In the detailed look at the TALI message definition below, we see that the protocol supports both peer-to-peer messages at the TALI layer (messages 1

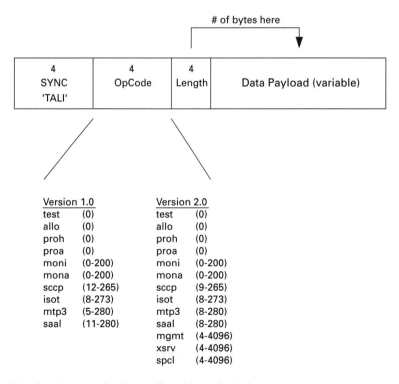

Numbers in parenthesis are allowable payload size.

FIGURE 9.10 TALI message structure.

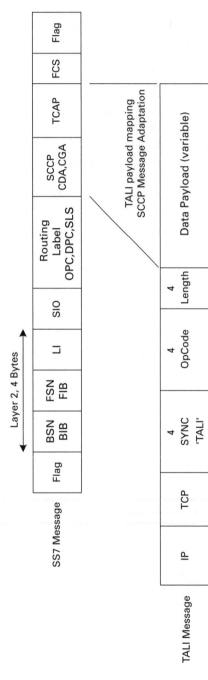

FIGURE 9.11 SCCP/TCP signaling adaptation in TALI.

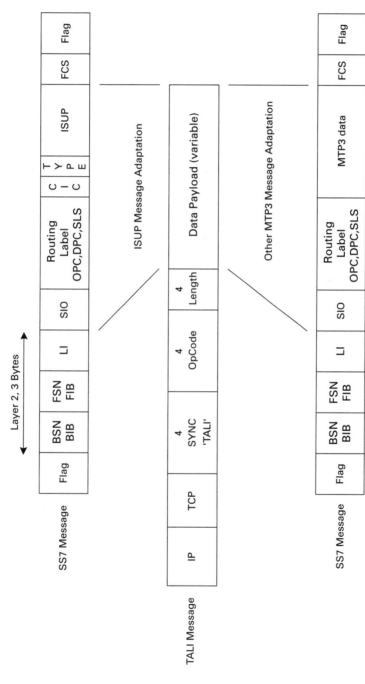

FIGURE 9.12 ISUP and general MTP message adaptation in TALI.

through 6 for version 1.0 and 10 through 12 for version 2.0) and adaptation service for the layers above.

1. **'test'**:This message is a simple query of the far end to determine if it is ready to accept SS7 data. It is sent periodically to ensure the remote application is running (the connection integrity is at the TCP layer), and when seen by the remote end, it must reply with either **'allo'** or **'proh'**.

2. **'allo'** (Allow) and **'proh'** (Prohibit): One of two possible responses to the **'test'** message. In order for SS7 data to be transported between signaling endpoints, neither endpoint should be in the **'proh'** state.

3. **'proa'** (Prohibit Acknowledgment): Sent as a response to the receiving **'proh'**. Only the prohibit response to a **'test'** message has a formal acknowledgment from the receiving signaling endpoint.

4. **'moni'** (Monitor): This message offers a generic Echo capability to the protocol. In version 2.0 of TALI, it is used to establish that the endpoints support the correct protocol version (there is no other mechanism to do so, but the two versions are otherwise backwards compatible). It is used also to measure round trip message transfer time (which includes queuing and processing of the message at the remote end). The receiving node responds with **'mona'** (Monitor Acknowledge). The data payload portion in the **'moni'** message is reflected in the **'mona'** response. Version 2.0 of TALI defines a 12-byte area at the beginning of the data field to send a string identifying the version of the protocol, encoded as *'vers xxx.yyy'*, whereby x and y encode the major and minor versions of the protocol, right justified, as in *'vers 002.001'*. If the far end sends a **'moni'** without such an encoding of protocol version, it is assumed to be running version 1.0.

5. **'mona'** (Monitor Acknowledge): A mandatory response to a **'moni'** message, which also returns the contents of the data payload field.

6. **'sccp'** (SCCP Service): Used to send SS7 MSUs with the Service Indicator (SI) field in the Service Information Octet (SIO) equal to 3 (SCCP). Version 1.0 supports Class 0 and Class 1 SCCP messages, specifically Unitdata (UDT), Extended Unitdata (XUDT), Unitdata Service (UDTS) and Extended Unitdata Service (XUDTS). SCCP messages must contain a Point Code in the calling party and called party fields in order to be transferred. Message construction is shown in Figure 9.11.

7. **'isup'** (ISUP service): Used to send SSCP MSUs with the SI field in the SIO equal to 5 (ISUP). The payload data is the raw field of the original ISUP message, beginning with the SIO.

8. **'mtp3'** (MTP Service): Used to send SSCP MSUs with the SI field in the SIO set to anything other the 0–2, 4, and 6–15. **'mtp3'** is only meaningful in non-SAAL implementations.

9. **'saal'** (Signaling ATM Adaptation Layer Service): The **'saal'** opcode is used to deliver SS7 MSUs with any SI over a TALI connection. This opcode is only used on TALI protocol stacks that are implemented with SAAL.

10. **'mgmt'** (Management Data, version 2.0 only): The structure of the **'mgmt'** message is shown in Figure 9.13. This opcode is used to pass network management and configuration data as well as formatting instructions for the data. The data payload field begins with a 4-byte ASCII encoding of a primitive. The following primitives are defined, and the data field encoding is dependent on the type of primitive used.

   a. *'rkrp' (Routing Key Registration Primitive)*: Allows signaling nodes to identify the SS7 streams they want configured for transport over each open socket. **'rkrp'** supports keys for ISUP, SCCP, TUP, QBICC, and other MTP traffic.

      The allowable **'rkrp'** operations are ENTER (create association between a socket and a specific application routing key), DELETE (delete association between a socket and a specific application routing key), SPLIT (convert the original application routing key into two routing keys, which together cover the same SS7 traffic stream as the original one), and RESIZE (modify the CIC range for a single application routing key).

      The **'rkrp'** messages also include a request/reply common field (2 bytes, integer) and a success/failure common field (2 bytes, integer).

   b. **'mtpp'** (MTP Primitives): Passes information regarding the availability and congestion state of SS7 signaling links.

   The valid Operations are

       Point Code Unavailable
       Point Code Available
       Request for Point Code Status
       Cluster Unavailable
       Cluster Available
       Request for Cluster Status
       Congested Destination (SS7 Point Code)
       Request for Congestion Status (of an SS7 Point Code)
       User Part Unavailable

   The coding of the operations field is shown in Figure 9.13.

   c. **'sorp'** (*Socket Options Registration Primitives*): Socket options may be independently enabled or disabled for each signaling device. The currently defined operations for this primitive are

      Set SORP Flags: Used to set the flags bit field. The receiver of this message should store the bit settings indicated in the SORP Flag field.

Request Current SORP Flags Settings: Poll for the status of the flags bit field. The receiver of this message should send a reply with the current SORP flag settings.

Reply with current SORP Flag Settings: Reply to a poll with the current bit field settings.

11. **'xsrv'** (Extended Service opcodes, version 2.0 only): Allows TALI to grow beyond the SCCP, ISUP, and MTP message support to possibly other types of data.

12. **'spcl'** (Special Services, version 2.0 only): Allows vendor-specific services to be implemented using the TALI protocol, which are applicable between endpoints implementing the same services. Only four primitives are defined for this code:

'smns': Special Messages Not Supported
'qury': Query
'rply': Reply
'usim': UnSolicited Information Message

> **Note:** Messages 'mgmt,' 'xsrv,' and 'spcl' will cause a protocol violation if sent to a version 1.0-compliant signaling endpoint, and the TCP connection will be closed.

TALI uses four timers (T1–T4) with the following usage:

1. The T1 timer represents the time interval between originations of a **'test'** message. The TALI implementation should send a **'test'** upon expiration of T1.

2. The T2 timer represents the amount of time that the peer has to return an **'allo'** or a **'proh'** in response to a **'test'**. T2 expiration without receiving **'allo'** or **'proh'** is a protocol violation. Note the requirement for T2 < T1 in order for these timers to work properly.

3. The T3 timer controls how long this signaling endpoint should continue to process service data that is received from the far end after a Management Prohibit Traffic Event has occurred locally. This timer is used when a transition from *Near End Allowed–Far End Allowed* (i.e., both ends allowed to send service data) to *Near End Prohibited–Far End Allowed* (only far end willing to send service data) occurs. On such a transition, it is expected that the far end needs some time to adjust its TALI state machine and divert service data traffic away from this connection. The T3 timer controls the amount of time the far end has to divert traffic, following the state transition.

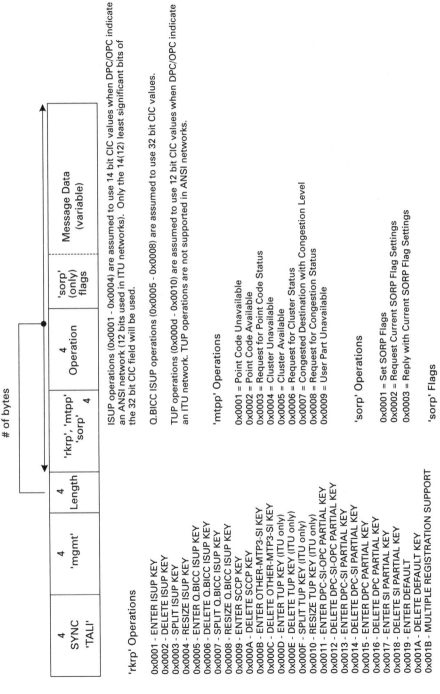

# of bytes

4 SYNC 'TALI'	4 'mgmt'	4 Length	'rkrp', 'mtpp' 'sorp' 4	4 Operation	'sorp' (only) flags	Message Data (variable)

'rkrp' Operations

0x0001 - ENTER ISUP KEY
0x0002 - DELETE ISUP KEY
0x0003 - SPLIT ISUP KEY
0x0004 - RESIZE ISUP KEY
0x0005 - ENTER Q.BICC ISUP KEY
0x0006 - DELETE Q.BICC ISUP KEY
0x0007 - SPLIT Q.BICC ISUP KEY
0x0008 - RESIZE Q.BICC ISUP KEY
0x0009 - ENTER SCCP KEY
0x000A - DELETE SCCP KEY
0x000B - ENTER OTHER-MTP3-SI KEY
0x000C - DELETE OTHER-MTP3-SI KEY
0x000D - ENTER TUP KEY (ITU only)
0x000E - DELETE TUP KEY (ITU only)
0x000F - SPLIT TUP KEY (ITU only)
0x0010 - RESIZE TUP KEY (ITU only)
0x0011 - ENTER DPC-SI-OPC PARTIAL KEY
0x0012 - DELETE DPC-SI-OPC PARTIAL KEY
0x0013 - ENTER DPC-SI PARTIAL KEY
0x0014 - DELETE DPC-SI PARTIAL KEY
0x0015 - ENTER DPC PARTIAL KEY
0x0016 - DELETE DPC PARTIAL KEY
0x0017 - ENTER SI PARTIAL KEY
0x0018 - DELETE SI PARTIAL KEY
0x0019 - ENTER DEFAULT
0x001A - DELETE DEFAULT KEY
0x001B - MULTIPLE REGISTRATION SUPPORT

ISUP operations (0x0001 - 0x0004) are assumed to use 14 bit CIC values when DPC/OPC indicate an ANSI network (12 bits used in ITU networks). Only the 14(12) least significant bits of the 32 bit CIC field will be used.

Q.BICC ISUP operations (0x0005 - 0x0008) are assumed to use 32 bit CIC values.

TUP operations (0x000d - 0x0010) are assumed to use 12 bit CIC values when DPC/OPC indicate an ITU network. TUP operations are not supported in ANSI networks.

'mtpp' Operations

0x0001 = Point Code Unavailable
0x0002 = Point Code Available
0x0003 = Request for Point Code Status
0x0004 = Cluster Unavailable
0x0005 = Cluster Available
0x0006 = Request for Cluster Status
0x0007 = Congested Destination with Congestion Level
0x0008 = Request for Congestion Status
0x0009 = User Part Unavailable

'sorp' Operations

0x0001 = Set SORP Flags
0x0002 = Request Current SORP Flag Settings
0x0003 = Reply with Current SORP Flag Settings

'sorp' Flags

Bit 0 = Broadcast Phase MTPP Primitives
Bit 1 = Response Method MTPP Primitives
Bit 2 = Normalized SCCP
Bit 3 = Normalized ISUP
....

FIGURE 9.13 TALI 'mgmt' message structure.

4. The T4 timer is set to the time interval between originations of the **'moni'** message. When T4 expires, the TALI implementation should send **'moni'** and expect **'mona'**.

Refer to the vendor documentation for the specification of the TALI state machine and further information on the protocol implementation.

9.6 FAX RELAY IN IP NETWORKS

No discussion of signaling transport is complete without accommodating seamless support for Group 3 fax. Fax in the PSTN is using the same bearer circuit as a voice call, and machine-generated tones are coded in G.711 format, just like the human voice. But there is a catch. When a call is initially set up and the phone at the far end is ringing, there is no advance warning that the call will be voiceband, and not a simple human conversation. Therefore, the ends will pick their default codecs, which may use compressed voice. Codecs perform their compression magic by tossing frequency content and even implementing perceptual weighting of the audible spectrum, which may distort the tones to the point they are unusable by the machines. Therefore, fax over compressed voice circuits is not supported, and a couple of means have been pursued by the industry to address the problem. The first is a real-time upspeed of the coding format to G.711, such that all the perceptual weighting will be removed and the machines will be able to complete negotiation and transmit the fax. This requires speedy recognition of the fax tone from the remote end and notification of the internal circuits to forego compression and use the PCM voice format. The far endpoint must be notified to accept the G.711 format, and the softswitch will need to be made aware that bandwidth utilization for the call has scaled upwards. This may not sound like much for a few calls, but for a switch serving a part of a metropolitan area, the scalability issue may prove prohibitive.

We discussed fax relay procedures in my previous book [1], and we revisit the subject in this text in the context of a call flow. The basic Group 3 fax protocol is specified in Recommendation T.30 and governs the signaling and image transfer between fax terminals across the PSTN. It is an end-to-end protocol; that is, there may be several exchanges in the path of a fax call, but they are transparent to the signaling and image transfer. Fax signaling tones traverse the PSTN in-band over the voice bearer channel and have no impact on the signaling of the call itself in the Class 4 and Class 5 systems being traversed by the circuit. The challenge in the packet networks is to accommodate the T.30 protocol between the endpoint fax terminals and their local exchange, while transporting signaling and the image across the network with packet methods, in a manner that is transparent to the terminals.

Two ITU recommendations offer a choice between real-time and store-and-forward (delayed) fax transport.

Recommendation T.37 defines procedures for store-and-forward fax transmission over the Internet or over carrier IP environments with controlled QoS. The functionality provided through this specification is facsimile transmission with *non-real-time* requirements. Simply stated, the fax begins and ends with a local device emulating Group 3 facsimile operation, and the actual transmission of the image to the intended final destination fax machine occurs in a second step, after the entire image has been transmitted from the originating fax endpoint to the local exchange, which acts as a fax gateway and is transparent to the caller. ITU Recommendation T.38, on the other hand, defines real-time procedures for fax support over IP networks. The fax terminal endpoints cannot distinguish the presence of a packet network in the path of the call and in an ideal implementation the QoS of the PSTN for fax is achieved with an IP infrastructure. Both standards address commercial needs, but T.38 operation is desirable when seamless fax integration is a requirement. This is indeed the method recommended by H.323 for enterprise and wide area networks (H.323 Annex D).

Either approach may be implemented for fax support in the reference network and call flow between **cactus** and **scorpio** in this section.

For easy reference in our discussion, the fax signals of the T.30 protocol are summarized in Table 9.5.

TABLE 9.5 T.30 Fax Signals

SIGNAL	NAME	NOTES
CIG	Calling subscriber identification	Sent by a terminal wishing to receive a fax to a remote terminal capable of transmitting.
CRP	Command repeat	Asks for the previous command to be resent.
CSI	Called subscriber identification	Sent by the called fax terminal immediately after the CED tone to identify itself by its telephone number.
DCN	Disconnect	Initiates Phase E—call termination.
DCS	Digital command signal	The transmitting terminal sends this signal, after receiving DIS, to place the called terminal in a state ready to receive.
DIS	Digital identification signal	Identifies the capabilities of the called fax terminal.
DTC	Digital transmit command	Sent by a calling terminal that wishes to receive from the called end, after DIS.

TABLE 9.5 T.30 Fax Signals (continued)

SIGNAL	NAME	NOTES
FCD	Facsimile coded data	This message contains the actual fax image data.
FCF	Facsimile control field	The HDLC frame containing the signal information is divided into the FCF and FIF parts. Signals are sent by encoding of the FCF field in the HDLC frame.
FIF	Facsimile information field	This field provides optional clarification of the signal being sent.
MCF	Message Confirmation	This is a positive acknowledgment to the PPS signals and indicates that additional signaling messages can now be sent.
NSC	Nonstandard facilities command	This is the response to the NSF command.
NSF	Nonstandard Facilities	NSF indicates there are attributes to the operation of the fax station not specified by ITU recommendations. The attributes are coded in the Facilities Information Field, and the coding is not specified.
NSS	Nonstandard setup	See NSF.
PID	Procedure interrupt disconnect	This signal indicates the previous messages were received fine, but further transmissions are undesirable at this time, and the calling station should enter Phase E—call termination.
PPR	Partial page request	The previous pages had frames received in error and should be retransmitted. The frames in error are coded in the FIF field of the HDLC frame.
PPS-EOM	Partial page signal	End of message. (The PPS signals are used when optional error correction mode is in effect.)
PPS-EOP	Partial page signal	End of procedure.
PPS-MPS	Partial page signal	Multipage signal.
PPS-NULL	Partial page signal	NULL.
PWD	Password	Optional field to carry a password when polling mode is used and the calling terminal is the receiver of the fax.

TABLE 9.5 T.30 Fax Signals (continued)

SIGNAL	NAME	NOTES
RCP	Return to control for partial page	
RNR	Receiver not ready	
SUB	Subaddress	This optional field carries a subaddress, in the form of a digit string, to help with routing towards the called terminal, inside the terminal's domain.
TCF	Training check	Offers a first indication of the suitability of the channel to handle the selected data rate.
TSI	Transmitting subscriber identification	Indicates that the FIF field in the HDLC frame of this signal encodes the calling terminal identification.
XID	Exchange identification procedure	Used during Phase A and indicates the called station has Group 3C attributes.

9.6.1 Store-and-Forward Fax over IP: T.37

Recommendation T.37 defines two modes for non-real-time fax. Simple mode supports plain transmission of data, but capabilities negotiation between terminals may not take place and is undefined in the specification. All fax terminals must support simple mode. Image data is sent in Tag Image File Format (TIFF) per the specification of RFC 2301, Profile S, with Modified Huffman Compression. It supports Group 3 standard and fine image resolutions. The fundamental element for T.37 fax operation is the fax gateway (FG), which emulates Group 3 operation towards the fax terminal and has a direct connection to a packet network acting as a host or router. The FG can be a standalone gateway or can be part of the PSTN gateway implementation in the reference topology of this chapter. In the latter type of operation, the gateway is a terminating endpoint of the incoming fax call. In other words, when a call is established between the PSTN gateway and the local exchange and is determined to be T.30 fax, the PSTN gateway performs the necessary T.30 signaling with the calling fax terminal through the local exchange (e.g., **cactus**) and acquires the fax image. Once the fax call is completed, the image is sent as email content to the destination identified by the sender. No confirmation is supplied in simple mode. Any Internet mail transport protocol can be used in full mode to carry the image data.

T.37 full mode adds the requirement to confirm that the fax was received properly, and the requirement to negotiate the capabilities of the fax terminals.

Delivery confirmations are sent to the sender as MIME-encoded *Delivery Status Notifications* (DSNs) for gateways, as described in RFC 1894. Message Disposition Notifications (MDN) are also used, per RFC 2298.

9.6.2 ITU Recommendation T.38: Real Time Fax Relay

> The requirement for robust, real-time fax transmission can be stated in simple terms as the ability to send an *arbitrarily long fax* anywhere in the world, with connection establishment between fax terminals *on the first try* and in a *single session,* with *confirmation.*

The alternative to non-real-time fax over IP networks is described in Recommendation T.38 and specifies procedures to "emulate" the PSTN through a packet network, such that the Group 3 fax terminals are not made aware of the presence of different signaling and bearer transports. The idea is simple, but there can be implementation obstacles when one tries to emulate the speed of wire-speed signaling with packet-based procedures. T.38 gives the "look and feel" of real-time facsimile by emulating the handshake activities of the T.30 protocol on the packet network side. The protocol defines two messages.[9]

1. **T30_INDICATOR** packets for fax signaling tones. *Indicator* packets carry signaling information to the far terminal, such as the presence of a CNG/CED tone, modem modulation training, or preamble flags, each time the line is turned around.
2. **T_DATA** packets carry image data, delineated in HDLC frames.

These messages are specified as part of the Internet Fax Protocol (IFP) of the ITU recommendation. Group 3 fax equipment attaches to T.38-compliant gateways and executes the T.30 protocol in real time, without modifications. Adherence to strict timing requirements is thus very critical in the handshake exchanges between end terminals. A T.38 gateway can be a standalone gateway or can represent embedded functionality inside PSTN and packet network access gateways. The IFP allows either TCP or UDP to be used as the transport protocol over IP. In the case of TCP use, the IP payload is simply the TCP header and the concatenated indicator or data packet.

---

9.   The T.38 specification has been amended to incorporate additional procedures for real time Group 3 fax over IP networks.

When UDP is used, its payload consists of a new protocol layer header UDP Transport Layer Protocol (UDPTL), followed by the *indicator* or *data* packet. The UDPTL header adds a packet sequence number to the standard UDP header to account for packets arriving via different paths and out of order. Although it is possible to route T.38 packets randomly over an IP network, it is not recommended. T.38 implementations will likely use QoS paths engineered with MPLS, DiffServ, or both. The UDPTL payload also contains an optional Forward Error Correction (FEC) field to recover from bit errors. Also optionally, redundant messages can be included in a single UDPTL packet to increase the robustness of the transport infrastructure.

Flag sequences are required for every line turnaround and are transmitted as indicator (*T30_INDICATOR*) packets. Training is sent as an indicator packet, with the V-type modulation used by the sending terminal. This is used to adjust the speed of the terminal, for instance, to switch from V.17 modulation for sending image data to V.21 modulation for control sequences.

The same type of training is generated by the receiving gateway at the far end towards the remote fax terminal. Modulation training sequences have timing requirements, which must be carefully adhered to in an end-to-end transmission for the presence of the IP network between the gateways to be completely transparent to the fax application. This imposes stricter delay requirements on the packet infrastructure for fax support than the values that have been stated as "acceptable delay" for simple human conversations.

> Error correction could recover a missed portion of an image sent with T.38 procedures due to packet loss, *if the packet loss occurred during the image transmission.* Modem training and line turnaround are not as forgiving to packet loss.

Training Check Field (TCF) can be used in one of two ways in T.38-compliant networks. For connection-oriented, TCP-based implementations, the TCF is generated by the far end gateway. When UDP is used, the TCF needs to be sent across the packet network (see Table 6 of ITU Recommendation T.38). Note that the intended handling of TCF in H.323 calls is indicated in the **T38FaxRateManagement** field during the capability exchange phase of the call setup.

The major fax modulation methods and data rates are shown in Table 9.6.

Let's look at the basic protocol operation in a scenario where **scorpio** sends a fax to **cactus** from a machine attached to a POTS line. Scorpio's machine is a Group 3 facsimile device, and as such, it executes the T.30

TABLE 9.6 Major Fax Modulation Schemes and Data Rates

MODULATION TYPE	BIT RATES	NOTES
V.17	14400 12000 9600 7200	Half-duplex, synchronous. Uses V.21 modulation for handshaking. Considered more reliable than V.29 at the same speeds.
V.29	9600 7200	Half-duplex, synchronous. Uses V.21 modulation for handshaking.
V.27ter	7200 4800 2400	Half-duplex, synchronous. Uses V.21 for handshaking, and Differential Phase Shift Keying for image transfer. It is a very robust modulation scheme. Also supports the lowest speed that is common to all fax modulation schemes.
V.34	33600 21600	Uses 1200 bps or 2400 full duplex, phase/amplitude modulation for handshake messages (V.8). Half-duplex phase/amplitude modulation for image data transfer. Uses line probing during startup sequence to probe line.
V.21	2 x 300 bps secondary channels Channel 1 – Sender TX Channel 2 – Receiver TX	Used for all handshake messages between sending and receiving fax stations to negotiate data rate, image resolution, compression scheme, etc. Not used in V.34 fax.

protocol. Cactus's fax machine is attached to an MG/IAD, which does not support T.38. Cactus's fax machine is also a Group 3 fax device, which means the T.30 protocol messages will need to be executed between the fax terminal and the MG/IAD. The call flows of Figure 9.14 and Figure 9.15 are used.

T.38 procedures are invoked by our hypothetical PSTN Gateway+ connected to scorpio's local exchange and terminated at the T.38 MG/IAD in Administrative Domain 1, where cactus's fax terminal is located. After the initial call between cactus and scorpio fax terminals has been established, the T.30 protocol executes between scorpio's fax terminal and the local exchange. The first part of the call between any two fax terminals on the

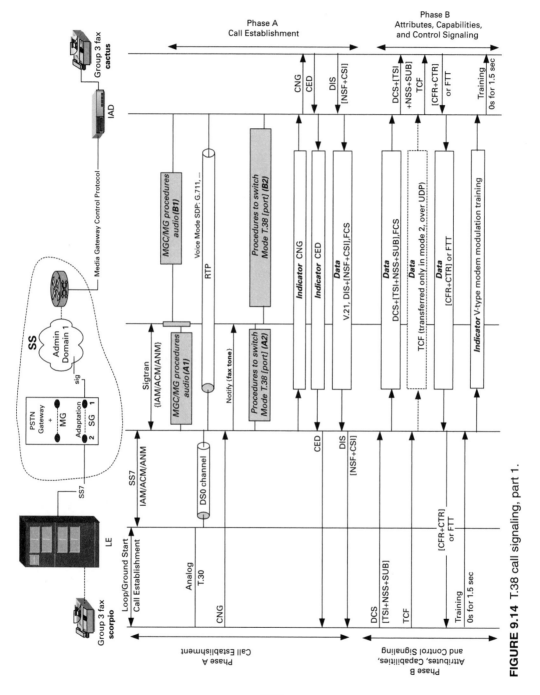

FIGURE 9.14 T.38 call signaling, part 1.

297

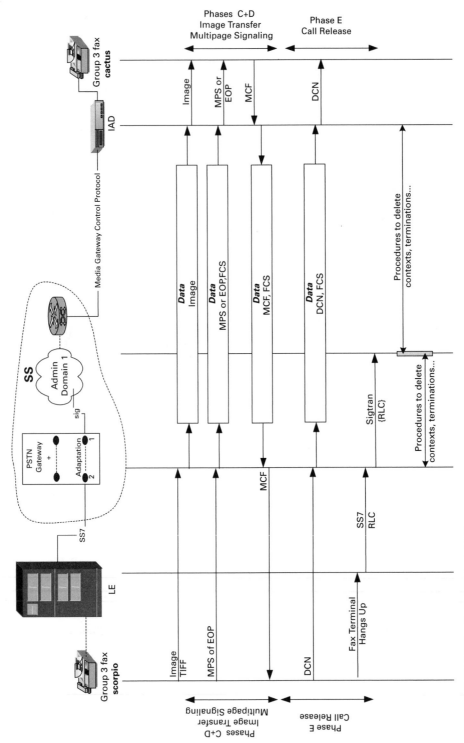

FIGURE 9.15 T.38 call signaling, part 2.

PSTN proceeds like any other voice call, but after the call is completed the equipment at both ends realize this is a fax voiceband call and proceed with T.30 signaling. The way they realize it is via tones on the bearer channel—there is no subsequent SS7-type signaling activity for fax communication.

The case of an IP network between scorpio and cactus is a little different. Call setup between scorpio's terminal and the local exchange will proceed as before, and the local exchange may be connected to cactus' domain via a media gateway, which transports SS7 signaling via M3UA or M2UA. Media Gateway Control functionality between the softswitch, the PSTN Gateway, and cactus's IAD for call and bearer path control can be based on MGCP, Megaco/H.245, SIP, or H.323. In this example, we will consider a Media Gateway Control Protocol (MGCP or Megaco) between the softswitch and the two gateways, and will discuss general aspects of alternative procedures when using peer protocol signaling. The enumeration of steps in the call setup and fax connection establishment are as follows:

1. SS7 call setup signaling from the local exchange will reach the SG, which will make the appropriate adaptation and inform the softswitch in Domain 1. The ISUP IAM message will reach the SG on the PSTN side, signaling adaptation will take place in the SG with M2UA, M3UA, or TALI and the ASP will be informed (it is running in the softswitch or an adjunct device in the softswitch domain). The softswitch will return an adapted ACM to the SG, once it has determined it can terminate the call locally, and the SG will form an SS7 message with ACM and send it to the local exchange.

   The SS/AS-SG signaling communication occurs over the arrow labeled "Sigtran" in the call flow. The SS/AS in Domain 1 delivers the call to cactus's IAD, addressed to the port hosting the fax terminal and the terminal is alerted of the incoming call. This is shown in the box labeled "MGC/MG procedures – audio (**B1**)" and is similar to the procedures for call establishment we already discussed in MGCP and H.248.

   The SS/AS also creates the appropriate context and media connections inside the gateway, again through procedures we discussed in MGCP and Megaco/H.248. The procedures are included in the box labeled "MGC/MG procedures audio (**A1**)."

   Note that it is possible in practice to have mixed signaling protocol topologies, for example, the IAD may be MGCP based whereas the gateway may be H.248. Protocol interworking is supposed to be handled by the softswitch. If either endpoint uses a peer protocol such as SIP or H.323, then the softswitch will have to proxy the other endpoint running master-slave signaling.

2. Once cactus's fax machine answers, the RTP bearer path is set up
    between the media gateway[10] and cactus' MG/IAD by the Media
    Gateway Control Protocol signaling to each endpoint in turn. The
    attribute is set to audio. This completes the bearer path setup process
    end-to-end, because the bearer path on the other side of the SG had
    already been cut through with the SS7 signaling procedures, when ACM
    was returned by the SG to the local exchange. At the end of the call setup
    phase, there is a G.711 path between the LE and the PSTN gateway on a
    DS0 identified by a CIC (SS7 Circuit Identification Code), which is
    "stitched" internally to connect with an RTP stream to the endpoint
    hosting the fax terminal in cactus's IAD. The media compression format
    in the RTP stream can be any type.

3. Our composite PSTN gateway now detects CNG on the bearer path and
    realizes it needs to invoke T.38 procedures with the IAD. That's because
    voice compression may be in use, or via configuration selection.
    At this point it is important to remember to disable echo cancellation on
    the end-to-end bearer path. It is now also important to decide whether to
    cut through to T.38 procedures while the CNG tone is active, or to signal
    to the gateway with additional attributes regarding this fax session before
    the media stream is cut through with T.38 packets. The first choice
    involves fewer signaling steps and in effect change the transport address
    (TA) for the media stream to direct it to the TA which supports T.38, and
    fax mode is selected. This is shown in the box labeled "Procedures to
    switch Mode T.38 [port] (**A2**)" and (**A1**). An *Indicator* packet is sent to
    cactus's fax terminal first with the CNG indication and procedures to
    send the image are initiated between the PSTN gateway and the IAD.
    Indicator packets are sent over IP like any other packet traffic (although
    perhaps with different QoS mapping at the IP and / or link level), and
    also carry idle flags sent by either fax terminal (not shown on the call
    flow).
    The first alternative, that is, performing additional signaling steps with
    additional attributes involves use of a fax or ipfax package (like the one
    we discussed in H.248), and requesting additional features that may be
    applicable to the gateway and the IAD. For example, the gateway may be
    able to offer transcoding services from one compressed image type to
    another. The additional detailed signaling capability allows invocation of

---

10.   There is no architectural restriction from the perspective of the call signaling protocols and
signaling adaptation methods as to the construction of the gateways in a VoIP network. Signaling
and media could be handled by the same device, or separate devices. This is a matter of the
desired scalability (including cost) of the final design, among other factors.

features at intermediate gateways, which would otherwise would not be accessible in fax media pass-through mode. See Table 9.7 for the current list of attributes for T.38 real-time fax relay.

4. The indicator packet will be processed by cactus's IAD, and the CNG will be played in analog form to the fax terminal. It will in turn respond with CED, which will be wrapped in an *Indicator* message, placed over IP, and returned to the SG. The SG will reverse the action and play CED to the local exchange over the DS0 for the call, which in turn will play the analog signal over the wire to scorpio's fax terminal.

5. This process will continue with *Data* packets carrying the DIS signal, and at that time, Phase A of the fax transmission setup is complete.

6. In Phase B the connected terminals exchange attributes, capabilities, and control signaling with *Data* packets. The selected modulation will be used to determine the line's ability to handle the selected data rate. This is one place where QoS is extremely important. Lost packets in the TCF sequence (if TCF is transported across the two networks) could be seen as line drop-outs by the fax terminal and the negotiation will not succeed. If TCF is generated locally, it is the responsibility of the IAD for cactus and the gateway for the local exchange to ensure proper TCF. However, note that the training sequence is transported end-to-end in all cases.

7. Assuming the network is good enough to pass the Phase B test, we enter Phase C, during which the actual image is being sent one page at a time. At the end of each page, an MPS signal is sent, except for the last page, when the EOP indicates all the pages are sent. In this phase, error recovery procedures can happen both in correcting bit errors in packets carrying the image, with ECM activated, and in packet retransmission, if packets are dropped and the timing of the T.30 specification can be guaranteed.

8. Once the last page has been sent, the sending fax terminal transmits DCN and the call is terminated, from the perspective of the fax terminals. However, SS7 procedures will take over to clear the call with Release Complete (RLC), which will be adapted and sent to the softswich in Domain1, and which in turn will send a SIP BYE to the IAD.

9.6.3 Extensions to SDP for support of T.38 fax

The following values (Table 9.7) can be sent in SDP "a="attributes to select the proper operating mode for T.38 fax communication.

Notes: 1. The registered protocol choices for T.38 are: UDPTL | TCP.
           2. The registered MIME media type is: *image/t38*.

TABLE 9.7 SDP attribute selection for T.38 fax mode

SDP "ATTRIBUTE"	VALUES	EXAMPLE-COMMENTS
T38FaxVersion	Single Digit 1*DIGIT	0
T38maxBitRate	Digit String 1*(DIGIT)	9600
T38FaxFillBitRemoval	Boolean	0
T38FaxTranscodingMMR	Boolean	0 This is the Modified-Modified Read, two-dimensional coding used in ITU-T Recommendation T.6 for efficient image compression.
T38FaxTranscodingJBIG (The Joint Bi-level Image experts Group (JBIG) standard)	Boolean	0 This standard offers a way for progressive and lossless compressed encoding of black-and-white (bi-level) images. A progressive encoding system transmits a compressed image by first sending compressed data with reduced-resolution and then enhancing the image as needed by transmitting additional compressed information, which builds on the image already transmitted.[*]
T38FaxRateManagement	localTCF | transferredTCF	localTCF (selects whether TCF is generated locally or transported across the network)
T38FaxMaxBuffer	optional - 1*(DIGIT)	70 (in bytes)
T38FaxMaxDatagram	optional - 1*(DIGIT)	Size depends on redundancy; 316 (in bytes)
T38FaxUdpEC	t38UDPFEC t38UDPRedundancy	T38UDPRedundancy

[*] ITU-T specification T.82, *Information Technology — Coded representation of picture and audio information—progressive bi-level image compression,* 3/93.

Example SDP syntax for selecting the desired T.38 fax mode:

m=image 3233 udptl t38 (media is image, protocol carrying t.38 is UDPTL)
a= T38FaxRateManagement : local TCF
a= T38FaxUdpEC : t38UDPFEC

These attributes can be included in session descriptions of signaling protocols using SDP, for example, MGCP, SIP, Megaco/H.248.

In H.323 these attributes can be set in **T38FaxProfile**, **T38FaxRateManagement**, **T38FaxUdpOptions**, and **T38FaxTcpOptions** during the capabilities exchange phase of call setup. Note that when **maxBitRate** is included in the **genericDataCapability**, its value must be set the same as the value of **maxBitRate** in the **DataApplicationCapability** structure.

9.7 GENERAL OBSERVATIONS ON TESTING ISSUES

Given the complexity of the material we have discussed in this text, one might wonder how long it really takes to fully test a deployment and how quickly a network engineer can identify problems and institute a remedy in real time. A real system might very well have all of the protocols we have discussed so far, interworking with one another in some fashion, while traffic engineering of the bearer paths may be using DiffServ, MPLS, or the former over the latter, with either LDP or RSVP providing the label distribution. Connecting to LECs and IXCs may (i.e., most likely will) involve SS7 signaling, which may or may not have international variants. There are no easy answers, and there are no universally accepted automated test suites, as of this writing, to establish conformance, because in many cases it is protocol interworking, rather then native mode protocol operation, that causes failures. In other words, the signaling parts of a system may each work fine, but not so when we sum them up. To aggravate the problem, the geographical separation of network elements may prove an intimidating factor when faced with a real-time problem situation.

So, how do we proceed to get a degree of confidence in a topology design? *Simulation* is fine and has been tried with some success, but it is still a 3,000-feet level view of the "works," which is still high enough to cause serious injury if landing abruptly, that is, if faced with a real-time issue. *Duplication* seems to be a more reliable alternative. This may sound prohibitively expensive, but when the critical elements of a topology are duplicated, with a simulation of the actual distances between them, the real picture of product reliability will begin to emerge.

Testing "the works" is much fun if done right, or it can result in grief if shortcuts are taken. *Beta test* is a very popular term in the industry, which many experts (i.e., the engineers who designed the system and know how it really works) often view with suspicion, for a simple reason. Beta testing is not guaranteed to be a thorough test. The only thorough test is the one that tests all the decision trees in the code and exercises all the branches.

Where do we begin? This may sound like an old-fashioned and simplistic view, but more and more engineers are reverting to unit test followed by system integration, in two steps. Unit test covers all the functionality that does not require the presence of other modules (e.g., software features). When this phase is successfully completed, *incremental integration test* is performed in the next step. Integration test must be incremental and proceed to build up the system one piece at a time, such that all the interdependencies among modules can be ironed out before a new module is introduced. We all know the kind of finger-pointing that can happen during integration, especially for large and sophisticated systems. After the system has been built from the ground up, element by element, a thorough beta test will uncover such hidden "treasures" as feature interdependence, and so on. In other words, if during the beta test the system cannot complete a basic call, the testing approach itself needs immediate review.

Accounting for failures in system integration must be done carefully and thoroughly. It is all an accounting process. The failures that have been accounted for and tested will be handled as expected. Other failures could very well crash the system when they occur—and when telephony systems crash, it is a serious problem.

System behavior under heavy load can only be established when the heavy load itself is pushed through the system. This may be a tough task, given that even moderate-sized systems can have thousands of calls active at any given time, and time-of-day issues are simply hard to duplicate in the lab after the fact. This situation coupled with failover scenarios (rerouting signaling and data traffic to other elements in a seamless manner) is reason enough to design the test suite for realistic, but also complete, coverage of failure modes.

Clearly, there is no "best" way of testing that is applicable to every system, and situations might arise that cannot be adequately addressed even with the latest test tools. The only defense engineers can put in place early on in the design phase is strict clarity and discipline in the specification of the system attributes and its performance and of the signaling protocols in use, plus a set of test plans that adhere to a couple of rules of thumb:

1. Coverage of the system-level and application software.
2. Allocation of enough time to execute the test plans.

The software development preferences of an organization's culture (a waterfall process versus a spiral convergence or other method) is important, and any reasonable development process can be used effectively to produce good designs. If the design is of high quality, the quality of the product itself will be a function of the thoroughness of the test plan and its careful execution.

9.8 KEEPING TRACK OF THE OBJECTIVE

The promise of VoIP has been to allow carriers to decompose the Class systems to manageable and modular components, which is expected to reduce costs (per port and total) and allow for expedient service creation and delivery to customers. What does the consumer get from this technology? At first, the consumer gets basic telephone service done differently, but it is also bundled up front with Internet access and data capabilities, which may or may not be of importance to the public at large, depending on the recurring cost. Once the first phase has been completed, integrated video and interactive services will be introduced on the same infrastructure and to the same consumers. To those coming from the data world, voice has proven to be a trickier subject to tackle than expected. Aside from the uncompromising real-time requirements for packet delivery, latency, and jitter, there is also the issue of telephony feature development, which must match the look and feel of features being offered over the PSTN. With a little bit of trial and error over the last few years, most signaling protocols now seem to support the basic capabilities required to offer feature-rich telephony service.

This brings up the issue of voice quality, which we discussed at length in my previous book [1]. The public has two fundamental measures of quality of telephone service: service availability and voice quality. Service availability is indeed taken for granted on the PSTN, and in cases of emergency, it is vital. A system that processes an enormous number of calls per second, yet throws away emergency 911 calls when it reaches its capacity, is of little use to the service providers, and could even get them in trouble if they deployed service with such oversights. The only reliable way to test such load-dependent features, as we said, is to load the system to capacity and observe its behavior when additional load is presented.

Voice quality is purely objective in the PSTN, as the G.711 coding format provides minimum compression, but transports the analog waveform in digital form such that its frequency content is largely undistorted in the voice-band range of 300 to 3400 Hz. Such is not the case with codecs implementing perceptual weighting of the frequency content, and sending what is in effect lesser information to the far end. When an analog waveform is reproduced by the receiver, its frequency content is such that the excitation of the brain results in the perception of pretty good voice quality, but the spectrum is different in weight and content from the original one at the sending end. A few things come to mind immediately:

1. Network designs need to minimize transcodings—conversions of the encoded voice from one format to another within a network or across network boundaries. This causes quality degradation, which may be irreversible, even if we return to G.711 some time later. In other words, it is desirable to keep the same digital voice format end-to-end, if possible. A good test of this issue is to make a wireless call from one carrier to another wireless customer of another carrier, with a hop on the PSTN and a packet network. Objective quality measurement techniques such as PSQM and PAMS can be used at different points in the path of the call to characterize the impact of each network technology on voice quality.[11]

2. Delay is a problem and it has cumulative effects on gateways that connect a packet domain to a TDM network. The issue is that the packet stream needs to be de-jittered before TDM samples can be placed on the facility. Each such hop causes delay equal to the packetization rate times the number of packets that need to be kept in the jitter buffer. The last jitter buffer is at the MG/IAD port of the receiving party.

3. Jitter adds to the problem if it is in the same order of magnitude as end-to-end delay. For properly engineered networks (this does not include the Internet), jitter can be a manageable quantity and minimized as a function of traffic load and priorities assigned to stream types.

The question of whether mean opinion scores (MOS) is a better measure for voice quality than objective measurement techniques such as PSQM and PAMS, will probably remain an unanswered question in the short term, until a universally accepted, objective voice quality measurement technique is developed. The ideal solution would allow probing of a network at select points to map voice quality degradation to individual parts of the topology and thus sectionalize the problem. It would then offer an objective measure that adheres to a basic rule of measurements; that is, given the same stimulus into a black box, the result is *repeatable*. This does not mean the result is identical, but that the measurement results are consistent. Objective measurements of voice quality tend to offer a better convergence to a single value after many test iterations, given the same stimulus and topology, than subjective tests using derived opinions. In addition, they offer the exact places in the time domain where distortions occurred, which is valuable information when trying to map voice quality degradation to precise packet loss, delay, or jitter.

---

11. And the emerging PESQ method from the ITU.

9.9 DIRECTION IN LAN EQUIPMENT INFRASTRUCTURE

I have often said in jest that bandwidth obeys the *law of horizontal flat surfaces*. Just like horizontal flat surfaces accumulate junk, more bandwidth will always accumulate more traffic. With the demand for broadband services, and to accommodate increased supervisory (signaling and control) traffic, the equipment infrastructure of the next-generation nevtworks is primed for an upgrade, both in flexibility and speed. For those who originally thought that 100-Base-T Ethernet would be sufficient, it was proven inadequate before the argument had even started. Then along came Gigabit Ethernet, which itself is not quite enough for large deployments of converged networks.

Switch manufacturers are now preparing to introduce standards-compliant 10 Gigabit Ethernet switches, while looking to address such issues as how to bring better QoS to Ethernet, which has traditionally been accepted as a "best effort" technology. Work on the 10 Gigabit Ethernet standard has already begun. The 10 Gigabit Ethernet Alliance *(www.10gea.org)* includes more than 80 companies, from components and systems vendors to telephone companies, and is established to accelerate standards for 10 Gigabit Ethernet, educate early adopters about migration issues, and establish a neutral third party to do interoperability testing of different vendors' 10 Gigabit Ethernet equipment. The alliance isn't a standards body, but rather works to create consensus on standards relating to 10 Gigabit Ethernet and shares that information with the Institute of Electrical and Electronics Engineers (IEEE, *www.ieee.org*) 802.3ae task force.

The actual standard isn't expected to be finalized by the IEEE until March 2002, but vendors are expected to be bringing "somewhat" standard-compliant[12] 10 Gigabit Ethernet products to market between March and September 2001. The group is now working on defining new physical layer specifications so 10 Gigabit Ethernet can run over different media types (i.e., single-mode and multimode fiber). The alliance has come to a consensus on specifications that would allow 10 Gigabit Ethernet to run at 2, 10, and 40 kilometers over single-mode fiber. The group is still working to achieve consensus on the particulars of how to do 10 Gigabit Ethernet at 100 meters on FDDI-grade multimode fiber and at 300 meters over new "laser-grade" multimode fiber.

In addition to this standards work, vendors and their customers are also considering how to standardize quality and class of service mechanisms for all speeds of Ethernet. The IEEE's 802.1d is one of the most popular LAN quality/class of service standards. Carrier-grade routers, meanwhile, already support

---

12. Often a euphemism for "noncompliant."

DiffServ QoS routing, while MPLS is making inroads in acceptance. There is also industry activity to establish mapping between 802.1d and DiffServ. Still, the view is that in spite of the effort to bring ATM-type QoS to the Ethernet environment, there will always be something lacking, due to the different nature of the transport technologies and the standards that govern them.

Industry data shows that 80 percent to 85 percent of LAN connections are Ethernet based, so network administrators are usually familiar with the technology. Newer Metropolitan Area Networks (MANs) are being built based on IP Ethernet technology replacing SONET. According to some viewpoints, Ethernet—at whatever speed—also presents the potential for end-to-end connectivity over a single technology, which would further reduce the cost and complexity of managing a network. This would translate to fewer protocol conversions and potentially increase the performance of end-to-end applications.

References

1. *IP Telephony: The Integration of Robust VoIP Service*, Bill Douskalis, Prentice Hall PTR, 2000.
2. RFC 2719: "Framework architecture for signaling transport," L. Ong et. al.
3. RFC 2960: "Stream Control Transmission Protocol," R. Stewart, et. al.
4. RFC 3057: "ISDN Q.921-User adaptation layer," K. Morneault, et. al.
5. IETF Draft: "SS7 MTP2-User adaptation layer," *draft-ietf-sigtran-m2ua-07.txt*, K. Morneault, et. al.
6. IETF Draft: "SS7 MTP3-User adaptation layer (M3UA)," *draft-ietf-sigtran-m3ua-06.txt*, G. Sidebottom editor, G. Mousseau, et. al.
7. IETF Draft: "V5.2-User adaption layer (V5UA)," *draft-ietf-sigtran-v5ua-00.txt*, E. Weilandt, et. al.
8. IETF Draft: "SS7 SCCP-User adaptation layer (SUA)," *draft-ietf-sigtran-sua-05.txt*, J. Loughney, et. al.
9. IETF Draft: "SCTP dynamic addition of IP addresses," *draft-ietf-sigtran-addip-sctp-01.txt*, R.R. Stewart et. al.
10. IETF Draft: "SCTP unreliable data mode extension," *draft-ietf-sigtran-usctp-01.txt*, Q. Xie, et. al.
11. IETF Draft: "Generic method for transmitting reliable SCTP control chunks," *draft-ietf-sigtran-relreq-sctp-01.txt*, Q. Xie, et. al.
12. IETF Draft: "SIP T.38 call flow examples and best current practice," *draft-mule-sip-t38callflows-00.txt*, Mule, et. al.
13. RFC 2880: "Internet Fax T.30 feature mapping," L. McIntyre, et. al.
14. ITU-T Recommendations Q.701–Q.705: "Signalling System No. 7 (SS7) Message Transfer Part (MTP)"
15. ANSI T1.111: "Signaling System Number 7—Message Transfer Part"
16. ITU-T Recommendation Q.764: "Specifications of Signalling System No. 7—ISDN user part."

17. ITU-T Recommendation T.4: "Standardization of Group 3 facsimile terminals for document transmission."
18. ITU-T Recommendation T.6: "Facsimile Coding Schemes and Coding Control Functions for Group 4 Facsimile Apparatus.
19. ITU-T Recommendation T.38: *"Procedures for real time Group 3 Facsimile over IP networks* (including Amendment)."
20. ITU-T Recommendation T.80: *"Common Components for Image Compression and Communication–Basic Principles."*
21. ITU-T Recommendation T.82: *"Information technology–coded representation of picture and audio information–progressive bi-level image compression."*
22. ITU-T Recommendation T.85: *"Application profile for recommendation T.82—progressive bi-level image compression (JBIG encoding scheme) for facsimile apparatus."*

Appendix A

Call Capacity Considerations

Communications networks have traditionally been modeled with analytical techniques through methods derived from queuing theory. Heuristic methods have also been employed whereby "fitting" of partial experimentally derived data on top of analytical approximations is used, whenever applicable, to refine the model and increase its accuracy. Especially in the case of the TDM network, two queuing formulas have played a major role in estimating circuit capacity between exchanges and switches: the Erlang B (also extended Erlang B) and Erlang C formulas. To better understand the differences between these formulas, consider the following:

1. The Erlang B formula is the most commonly used traffic model in telephony, and is used to predict the number of circuits required if the offered load during the busiest hour is known. The model assumes that all blocked calls are immediately cleared (e.g., the caller gets a *fast busy* or an announcement about all circuits being busy).

2. The extended Erlang B model is similar to Erlang B, but takes into account that a percentage of the blocked calls are immediately represented to the system, instead of being discarded. The retry percentage can be specified as a system parameter.

3. The Erlang C formula assumes that all blocked calls stay in the system and enter a queue until they can be handled.

The Erlang C formula takes as variables the number of "servers," *m* (could be the number of trunks connecting two exchanges), and incoming traffic intensity, *u*, from which it computes the probability that new arriving customer (request for a bearer circuit) will find all the servers busy and thus have to wait until one of them is freed up.

The traffic intensity is given by the following formula:

$$u = \lambda \times Ts$$

whereby λ is the rate of arrival of call setup attempts (e.g. 50 calls per second) and Ts is the average time a server (voice circuit) stays on the call (i.e., the duration of the call). The system utilization is then expressed by

$$\rho = u/m$$

The Erlang C formula can be expressed in many forms, but for purposes of this discussion, we want to tie it to the Erlang B formula, and the expression becomes

$$Ec(m,u) = Eb(m,u) / [1 - \rho[1 - Eb(m,u)]]$$

whereby Eb(m,u) is the Erlang B formula. The B formula is of more interest in telephony, because it computes the probability that given a number of trunks, traffic intensity, and an average call holding time, an arriving call will find all trunks busy and it will be dropped (the caller will get fast busy or an announcement like "All circuits are busy now." In any case, the call is lost from the system.

The Erlang B formula, also known as the Erlang loss model, has the form:

$$Eb(m,u) = (u^m/m!) / [\Sigma(u^k/k!)]$$

where the sum in the denominator is computed for k=0 .. m.

Although it is easy to state the formula and possibly compute it for a few points, it is not as easy to compute it for reasonable size parameters, because the presence of factorials in the numerator and denominator would cause operand overflows in conventional computer systems. One numerical algorithm in use for decomposition and computation of the Erlang B formula is Ham's Algorithm, which we use in a MathCAD application to solve for the probabilities.

As an example, let's look at the following problem statement:

We want to model a local calling area consisting of N users, each of which makes n calls per hour during BHBD (busy hour of the busy day). In our case, there are m_{max} = 4096 voice circuits to the local exchange, each call during BHBD lasts about 3 minutes (180 seconds), and each subscriber makes on the average n = $calls_{user}$ = 1.4 calls during the busy hour.

For this example, we set N=100000 (a small city). From the data, we see each user offers α = $calls_{user}$ x (Ts/ 3600) = 0.07 Erlang load to the system. Therefore the maximum load offered to the system by this population is a_{max} = 7,000 Erlangs. Given there are only 4,096 voice circuits, we really need to know the probability that an arriving call request will be bounced. Solving the Erlang B formula, we obtain the graph of Figure A.1.

The server (circuit) utilization for this example is shown in Figure A.2.

This result tells us that when the entire subscriber population places this kind of load on the system, the probability of the system operating in full capacity when a new call comes in is over 40 percent. If this number is too high, we can solve for the number of circuits required to serve the entire population. It is apparent from the figure that 4,096 circuits cannot handle more than 60,000 subscribers who offer 1.4 calls per hour each during the BHBD.

In comparison, the Erlang C formula, also known as the wait model, gives us the curve shown in Figure A.3, which means the number of calls queued for service in the BHBD would exceed the call buffer, and the system

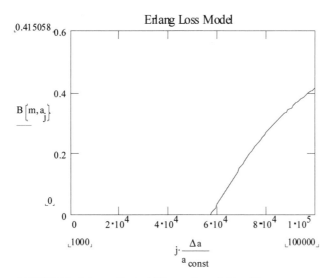

FIGURE A.1 Loss Probability vs. Population Size.

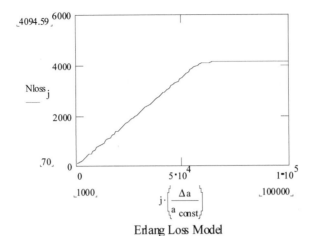

Erlang Loss Model

FIGURE A.2 Server Utilization versus Population Size.

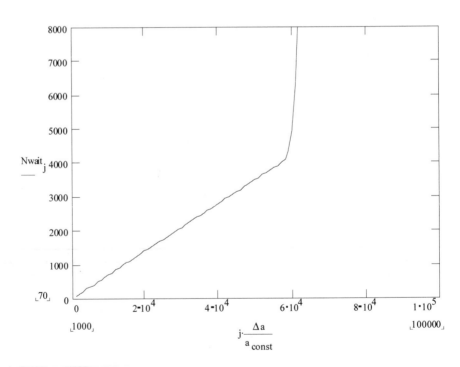

FIGURE A.3 Queue Size versus Population Wait Model.

would be unstable. The knees of both models occur at the same place, but the loss model continues operating at capacity by discarding incoming calls, while the wait model queues them for service when a circuit becomes available. A raw implementation of the wait model could make post-dial delay entirely unpredictable, since calls would be queued until resources could be found to complete the signaling for call setup.

This kind of analysis is simple enough, and we can relate to it rather easily because we are calculating integer quantities required to support a call load (i.e. the number of DS0s connecting two exchanges). The problem in the packet world does not have a widely acceptable and uniform solution yet as to how much bandwidth is required between two domains or between a domain and its subscriber base, if the expected call load can be predicted from the demographics.

One of the first decisions that must be made is whether to allow oversubscription of voice virtual facilities (i.e., plain old virtual paths, MPLS tunnels, etc.) with voice traffic. There may be a tendency to do so, if we look at the benefits gained from silence suppression and voice compression. If we assume this is not allowed, and voice virtual facilities are never oversubscribed, then the virtual facility can be treated as a virtual TDM facility by dividing the total bandwidth of the facility by the bandwidth of each call and thus obtaining the usable number of virtual circuits that connect the domains. Analysis would then proceed as in the TDM model, and the Call Admission algorithm would do little more than compute the comfort zone for system capacity and operate in that range.

As an example, let's consider the same serving area and offered load per subscriber, but now we connect to the local exchange with an ATM link, over which we have carved out a 10 Mb/s virtual facility for voice. Each voice call is 64 Kb/s PCM, using 20 ms packetization rate and RFC 1483 LLC encapsulation of IP over ATM, using AAL5 for voice transport. So, every 20 ms, we send 160 PCM samples in IP packets over ATM, with 20 bytes of IP header, 8 bytes of UDP header, 8 bytes of LLC encapsulation header, and 8 bytes of AAL5 trailer, for a total of 204 bytes. Given that an ATM cell for AAL5 has a 48-byte capacity, we need to send 5 cells every 20 ms, or 53 x 5 x 8 = 2120 bits per 20 ms, or 106 Kb/s per voice circuit.

Using this calculation, the 10 Mb/s bandwidth on the virtual facility can handle 90 calls, without oversubscription worries.[1] The 4096 circuits connecting the two exchanges need to be replaced with approximately 434.176 Mb/s of virtual capability to enjoy the same call-drop probabilities.

---

1.   The same 90 calls on the PSTN correspond to 90 DS0s, or 5.76 Mb/s.

Using similar analysis, if the packetization rate is increased to 10 ms, each G.711 call will consume 127.2 Kb/s, and the 4096 TDM circuits need to be replaced with 522 Mb/s of bandwidth. Herein lies one of the early compromises in VoIP network engineering: packetization rate (i.e., delay) versus bandwidth consumption, because bandwidth is still not cheap.

The question then becomes, if we cannot gain capacity from statistical multiplexing of voice circuits, what is the benefit? Voice can be oversubscribed with lower priority, best-effort data applications, such as Internet access. Bandwidth consumption due to voice calls will always expand to use its nominal allocation, but statistical multiplexing gains for data can be substantial, especially for any time outside the BHBD for voice calls.

Even with this simple thinking, things can still get very complex. Fax calls, voiceband calls and mixes of various voice compression schemes can coexist in a subscriber area, and it is not exactly predictable which caller with which voice coding format will make the most calls during the busy hour. We cannot predict fax/modem calls unless we have prior data from the demographics or customer detail records (CDRs), if such information is available.

Finally, signaling for VoIP calls is most likely to traverse the same real links as the media streams, thus making it FAS (although it may traverse different virtual facilities on the link). We have seen in all the call flows that signaling exchanges involve many "arrows," which are loaded with information. This must be accounted for in the performance computations (calls per second) and the bandwidth requirement for the virtual signaling facilities. Signaling stops when a call reaches the "established" state, but up to that point, we could have upwards of 10 "arrows" traversing the links, and this bandwidth will amount to a significant quantity as the system capacity scales to serve large populations.

Appendix B

Abbreviations and Acronyms

3GPP	Third Generation Partnership Project		**CAS**	Channel-Associated Signaling
ACELP	Algebraic Codebook-Excited Linear Prediction		**CATV**	cable television
			CBCH	cell broadcast channel
ACK	Acknowledgment		**CCCH**	common control channel
ADM	add/drop multiplexer		**CCH**	control channel
AF	Assured Forwarding		**CCW**	counterclockwise
AH	Authentication Header		**CDMA**	Code Division Multiple Access
AIN	Advanced Intelligence Network		**CFA**	call forwarding-always
AS	autonomous system		**CFNR**	call forwarding-no response
AS	application server		**CFU**	call forwarding-unconditional
ASP	application server process		**CIC**	Circuit ID Code
AUR	Authentication Register		**CM**	cable modem
BCCH	broadcast control channel		**CMS**	call management server
BG	border gateway		**CMTS**	Cable Modem Termination System
BGP	Border Gateway Protocol		**CPE**	customer premises equipment
BICC	Bearer-Independent Call Control		**CR-LDP**	Constraint-Based LDP
BLSR	bidirectional line-switched rings		**CSA**	Carrier Service Area
BS	Bearer Services		**CW**	Call Waiting
BSS	Base Station System		**DCP**	Destination Point Code
BSSGP	BSS GPRS Protocol		**DCS**	Digital Cross-connect System
CAC	Call Admission Control		**DL**	data link

DLC	digital loop carrier
DLCI	Data Link Connection Identifier
DOCSIS	Data over Cable Service Interface Specification
DPC	Destination Point Code
DSCP	Differentiated Services Code Point
DSN	Delivery Status Notification
DTMF	dual-tone multiple frequency
DWDM	Dense Wavelength Division Multiplexing
EBP	Exterior Border Proxy
EF	Expedited Forwarding
EO	End Office
ESP	Encapsulation Security Payload
FAS	facility-associated signaling
FCAPS	Fault, Configuration, Accounting, Performance, and Security
FDDI	fiber-distributed data interface
FDM	Frequency Division Multiplexing
FDMA	Frequency Division Multiple Access
FEC	Forward Error Correction
FEC	Forwarding Equivalence Class
FF	Fixed Filter
FG	fax gateway
FOTS	Fiber Optic Transmission System
GGSN	Gateway GSM Support Node
GK	gatekeeper
GPRS	General Packet Radio Service
GTP	GPRS Tunneling Protocol
GTT	Global Title Translation
HFC	hybrid fiber coax
HLR	Home Location Register
IAD	integrated access device
IB	in-band
IE	Information Element
IFP	Internet Fax Protocol
IGP	Interior Gateway Protocol
IRQ	information request
IMA	Inverse Multiplexing over ATM
IRR	Information Response
IUA	ISDN User Adaptation

IVR	interactive voice response
IXC	Interexchange Carrier
LDP	Label Distribution Protocol
LEC	Local Exchange Carrier
LLC	Logical Link Control
LNP	Local Number Portability
LR	Label Request
LSA	Link State Advertisement
LSP	Label-Switched Path
LSPID	LSP Identifier
LTE	Line Terminating Equipment
M2UA	MTP2 User Adaptation
M3UA	MTP3 User Adaptation
MAC	Media Access Control
MAP	Mobile Application Port
MCU	multipoint control unit
MDN	Message Disposition Notification
MGC	Media Gateway Control (or Controller)
MGCP	Media Gateway Control Protocol
MMS	Multimedia Messaging Service
MN	matched nodes
MO	Mobile Originate
MOS	mean opinion scores
MPLS	Multiprotocol Label Switching
MS	Mobile Station
MS/TCS	Master-Slave/Determination and Terminal Capability Set
MSC	Mobile Switching Center
MSU	MTP3 signaling unit
MT	Mobile Terminate
MTA	multimedia terminal adapter
NAT	Network Address Translation
NE	network element
NNI	network-to-network interface
NSAP	Network Services Access Point
OC	optical carrier
OEO	Optical-Electrical-Optical
OLC	open logical channel
OOB	out-of-band
OSPF	Open Shortest Path First

PAMS	Perceptive Analysis Measurement System
PAT	Port Address Translation
PCM	pulse code modulation
PDCH	Packet Data Channel
PDD	post-dial delay
PDTCH	Packet Data Traffic Channel
PDU	Protocol Data Unit
PHB	per-hop behavior
PLMN	Public Land Mobile Network
POH	Path Overhead
POTS	Plain Old Telephone Service
PP	point-to-point
PR	Protection Ring
PSQM	Perceptive Speech Quality Measurement
PSTN	public-switched telephone network
PTE	Path Terminating Equipment
RAS	Reliability, Availability, and Survivability
RAS	Registration, Admission and Status (H.323-specific definition)
RCF	Registration Confirm
RFCH	Radio Frequency Channel
RIP	Request in Progress
RRQ	Registration Request
RSVP	Resource Reservation Protocol
RTP	Real-Time Transmission Protocol
RTT	round-trip time
SAAL	Signaling ATM Adaptation Layer
SACK	Selective Acknowledgment
SAM	subsequent address message
SC	service center
SCP	Service Control Point
SCTP	Stream Control Transport Protocol
SDCCH	Standalone Dedicated Control Channel
SDH	Synchronous Digital Hierarchy
SDP	Session Description Protocol
SE	Shared Explicit
SG	signaling gateway
SGSN	Serving GSM Support Node
SI	Service Indicator
SIO	Service Information Octet
SIP	Session Initiation Protocol
SIP-T	SIP telephony
SME	Short Message Entity
SMS	Short Message Service
SMSCB	Short Message Service Cell Broadcast
SPE	Synchronous Payload Envelope
SSCOP	Service-Specific Connection-Oriented Protocol
SSN	subsystem number
STP	Signaling Transfer Point
STS	Synchronous Transport Signal
SUA	SCCP User Adaptation
TA	transport address
TALI	Transport Adapter Layer Interface
TCB	Transmission Control Block
TCE	Terminal Capabilities Exchange
TCF	Training Check Field
TCH	traffic channel
TCP	Transmission Control Protocol
TDMA	Time Division Multiple Access
TLS	Transport Layer Security
TM	Terminal Multiplexer
TOS	type of service
TS	time-slot
TSN	Transmission Sequence Number
TTL	time-to-live
UAS	User Agent Service or Server
UDP	User Datagram Protocol
UDT	Unitdata
UDTS	Unitdata Service
ULP	Upper Layer Protocol
UMTS	Universal Mobile Telecommunications System
UNI	user-to-network interface
UPSR	unidirectional path-switched rings
UUIE	User-User Information Element
VLR	Visitor Location Register
VoIP	Voice over Internet Protocol

VOVPN	Voice over VPN
VPI/VCI	Virtual Path Identifier/Virtual Channel Identifier
VPN	virtual private network
VR	virtual ring
VT	Virtual Tributary
WDM	Wavelength Division Multiplexing
WF	Wildcard Filter
WR	Working Ring
XUDT	Extended Unitdata
XUDTS	Extended Unitdata Service

Index

K

KeepAlive, 112, 113, 115, 130, 131, 150

L

LA, *see* Latency
Latency, 172
LDP, 5, 108-115, 303
LEC, 31, 46
LLC, 5, 42, 43, 48, 51, 56, 315
LNP, 244
LocalConnectionOptions, 169, 173, 180
loopback (M:loopback), 169, 174, 193, 205
LR, 113-114
LSA, 102-104
LSP, 102-104, 107-120
LSPID, 114
LTE, 78, 83

M

M2UA, 26, 28, 272-280, 281, 299
M3UA, 26, 28, 272-280, 299
MAC, 5, 27, 28, 48, 50, 264, 271, 282
MAP, 54, 55
MCF, 292, 298
MDCX, 17, 165, 167, 168, 176, 180, 183, 187, 188
MDN, 294
Megaco, 3, 4, 9, 15, 16, 20, 23-25, 34, 38, 65, 123, 130, 161, 162, 166, 196, 199-220, 222, 234, 235, 238, 240, 242, 248, 251, 254, 255, 299, 303
Message Authentication Code (MAC), 264
MGC, 6, 16, 17, 25, 33-36, 65, 167, 178, 203, 204, 299
MGCP, 3-5, 15-20, 23, 25, 29, 161-188, 191-196, 199-207, 218, 219
MMS, 64
MN, 318
MO (Mobile Originate), 55, 63
Modify Termination, 25, 244

ModifyConnection, *see* MDCX
MOS, 35, 64, 67, 306
Move Termination, 25
MPLS, 5, 41-45, 67, 68, 95-120, 315
MS, 54-64
MS/TCS, 134, 135, 138, 139, 143, 152, 176, 181, 183
MSC, 54-57
MSU, 272
MT, 63
MTA, 46-52

N

NAT, 29, 158, 184
NE, 79, 83, 85-88
netwloop (M:netwloop), 174
Network byte order, 264
netwtest (M:netwtest), 174
NNI, 11, 21, 22, 95
NotificationRequest, *see* RQNT
NotifiedEntity, 169, 170, 175, 178, 179, 181, 185
Notify, 14, 17, 25, 112, 167, 168, 176, 178, 179, 189, 203, 205, 212-214, 238, 275, 280, 197
NSAP, 48
NSC, 292
NSF, 292, 297
NSS, 292, 297
NTFY, 17, 167-171, 176-179, 185, 187, 188, 189, 191, 275, 280

O

ObservedEvents, 170, 205, 212, 213, 214, 238, 240
OC, 34, 73, 74, 80, 82-86
Octets
    Received, 172, 211
    Sent, 172
OEO, 91
OLC, 143
OOB, 48, 49